David Lichtman

Practical
Vacuum Techniques

WILLIAM F. BRUNNER, JR.
and THOMAS H. BATZER
Lawrence Radiation Laboratory
Livermore, California

PREPARED UNDER THE AUSPICES OF THE
DIVISION OF TECHNICAL INFORMATION,
U.S. ATOMIC ENERGY COMMISSION

ROBERT E. KRIEGER PUBLISHING COMPANY
HUNTINGTON, NEW YORK   1974

ORIGINAL EDITION 1965
Reprint 1974

Printed and Published by
ROBERT E. KRIEGER PUBLISHING CO., INC.
BOX 542, HUNTINGTON, NEW YORK 11743

©Copyright assigned 1965 to
The General Manager of the United States
Atomic Energy Commission
by Reinhold Publishing Corporation
Reprinted by arrangement

Library of Congress Card Catalog Number 65-25375
ISBN Number 0-88275-146-8

Manufactured in the United States of America

Foreword

Several excellent high vacuum texts exist, mainly at the levels of the design engineer or physicist. These supply the necessary information which should result in adequate performance. However, the technician who assembles, installs, tests and operates the vacuum equipment has been neglected in text material concerning these practical techniques. If the technician is not knowledgeable, the desired performance will not be realized. This book is for the technicians. It contains sufficient theory of gases and the kinetics of flow to allow the engineer to communicate with the technician. It delineates the operating principles of gages, pumps, baffles, valves and leak detectors at the basic, fundamental level. The sections on maintenance and repair, and on symptomatic trouble-shooting are extremely pertinent. All the latest developments in vacuum techniques are described, enabling the ambitious technician to keep up in a rapidly expanding field. The authors have had wide experience in training and teaching technicians and have recognized the need for this book. They have responded with their best.

CHARLES L. GOULD
Alternating Gradient Synchrotron
Brookhaven National Laboratory
Upton, N.Y.

Preface

Vacuum technology is a field of constantly increasing importance. Many processes, both in science and industry, cannot be carried on in the open atmosphere and require the specialized environment of vacuum. In scientific research, the well-known particle accelerators such as the cyclotron and bevatron need vacuum to operate; the mass spectrometer and electron microscope are examples of other scientific tools requiring vacuum.

Vacuum applications in industry range from the manufacture of electron tubes to the canning of orange juice. The production of electronic components, the mass production of titanium, and the packaging of many foods are but a few of the industrial processes requiring vacuum.

One of the most demanding requirements on vacuum technology is in the U. S. Atomic Energy Commission's Sherwood Program, a program directed toward the achievement of a controlled thermonuclear reaction. This program, if successful, could provide almost unlimited energy for the world's use; its progress depends to a large extent on the progress of vacuum technology.

As the field of vacuum technology continues to grow in scope and importance, the vacuum technician will play an increasingly significant role. It is the vacuum technician who constructs the vacuum equipment, assembles the components into a system, checks the system for leaks, operates, and maintains the system. In order to do this job the vacuum technician must have a thorough knowledge of several basic areas of vacuum technology; it is the purpose of this book to aid in the acquisition of this knowledge.

Livermore, California
July, 1965

WILLIAM F. BRUNNER, JR.
THOMAS H. BATZER

Acknowledgments

Because the content of this book has been drawn largely from experience, acknowledging our sources of information would necessarily mean listing most of those persons in the vacuum business with whom we have come into contact. This acknowledgment is hereby given without the list, which would be tediously long and have many regretful omissions.

To those who gave their time in reviewing the manuscript we are most grateful. Their criticisms and suggestions were both helpful and enlightening.

Our greatest thanks go to John Hurd, of the Technical Information Division of the Lawrence Radiation Laboratory, whose editorial perseverance provided continuity and, we hope, clarity.

Contents

CHAPTER 1

The Behavior of Gases

The word "vacuum" is defined in the dictionary as an "empty space, a space devoid of matter." Philosophically speaking, it may be impossible to produce a condition that satisfies this definition, that is, a "perfect vacuum." A perfect vacuum is a condition analogous to the absolute zero of the temperature scale; it is a theoretical limit used only as a zero point from which the actual pressure can be measured. In a practical sense, a vacuum is defined as "a space filled with gas at a pressure less than atmospheric pressure." According to this definition, then, to have a vacuum in an enclosure simply means that the enclosure is filled with gases at some pressure less than atmospheric pressure.

Although the gas pressures that will concern us in this book are extremely low — at times less than one billionth of atmospheric pressure — the gases that are at these pressures still behave as gases, and consequently are described as such. For this reason, the first step in understanding vacuum is to understand how gases behave and how they are described.

CHARACTERISTICS OF A GAS

A sample of a given kind of gas is completely described when the values of four quantities that relate to it are known. These quantities are its pressure, volume, temperature, and the amount of gas in the sample.

Pressure

Pressure is defined as the force per unit area that a gas exerts on the walls of its container. In vacuum work, pressure is measured in *torr*. A torr* is 1/760th of atmospheric pressure; thus the atmosphere exerts a

---

*The unit *millimeter of mercury* (abbreviated *mm Hg*) is sometimes used in place of the torr. They are, for all practical purposes, equivalent units.

pressure of 760 torr, or 14.7 lbs. per square inch. Low pressures are sometimes measured in *microns:* a micron is 1/1000th of a torr.

Volume

Volume is simply a measure of the space a gas takes up. It is measured
in *liters:* a liter is slightly more than a quart.

Temperature

In vacuum work temperature is measured in either degrees centigrade
or degrees absolute, both of which have the same scale divisions. On the
centigrade scale, commonly used in scientific work, the zero point of the
scale (0° C) corresponds to the freezing point of water and 100° C corresponds to the boiling point of water. Thus there are 100 equal divisions
between the boiling and freezing points of water on the centigrade scale.
(For conversion formulas between Fahrenheit and centigrade temperatures,
see Appendix B.)

The zero point of the absolute scale corresponds to $-273°$ C on the
centigrade scale. This point is referred to as *absolute zero.* Absolute
temperatures are written "°K" after Lord Kelvin, who first suggested use
of the scale.

Amount of Gas

The amount or mass of gas in a given sample is measured in gram moles.
A gram mole contains roughly 600 thousand billion billion molecules.*
(Thus two gram moles contain 1200 thousand billion billion molecules,
and so on. This way of measuring the number of gas molecules is similar
to measuring eggs in dozens or time in decades; in each case a quantity
is measured in groups of a set number.) In this book gram moles will be
referred to simply as *moles.* It has been found that one mole of *any* gas, at
a temperature of 0° C and a pressure of 760 torr (atmospheric pressure)†
occupies a volume of 22.4 liters. From this relationship it is possible to
calculate the molecular density of any volume of gas if its temperature and
pressure are known. For example, 1 cubic centimeter of air at S.T.P. contains 2.7×10^{19} molecules; at a pressure of 1 torr and a temperature of
0° C, 1 cubic centimeter of air contains 3.54×10^{16} molecules.

---

*Six hundred thousand billion billion can be written more simply as 6×10^{23}, where the
exponent of the 10 (23) tells the number of zeroes to place after the 6. Thus, $3 \times 10^4 =$
30,000, and $5 \times 10^7 = 50,000,000$. See Appendix D for a discussion of scientific notation.

†0° C and atmospheric pressure are known as *standard temperature and pressure* and are
abbreviated "S.T.P."

THE GAS LAWS

There are certain relationships that hold among the four quantities pressure, volume, temperature and amount of gas; using these relationships, it is possible to find the value of any one quantity if we know the values of the other three.

There are four "laws" governing the behavior of gases that we shall consider: Boyle's law, Charles' law, the Avogadro law, and the ideal gas law.

Boyle's Law

Assume a given amount of gas in a cylinder (as shown in Fig. 1.1a) at a certain temperature and pressure as indicated on the gages. Pushing the piston down (Fig. 1.1b) reduces the volume of the gas in the cylinder.

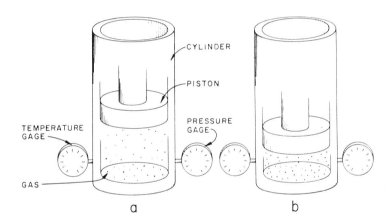

Fig. 1.1

What change is noted on the pressure gage? As the volume decreases, the pressure increases. If the temperature is held constant during the process, the increase in pressure is exactly proportional to the decrease in volume. This can be summarized in a simple equation: if the initial volume was V_1 and the initial pressure P_1, and the smaller volume V_2 and the higher pressure P_2, then

$$P_1 V_1 = P_2 V_2 \tag{1.1}$$

In other words, the product of the initial pressure and the initial volume equals the product of the final pressure and the final volume (providing the temperature is kept constant).

Example: If the initial volume of the cylinder were 3 liters and the initial pressure of the gas were 100 torr, what would the pressure be if the volume were reduced to 1 liter (at constant temperature)?

Solution:

Given: $P_1 = 100$ torr   Find $P_2 = ?$ torr

$V_1 = 3$ liters

$V_2 = 1$ liter

Solving Eq. (1.1) for P_2 gives

$$P_2 = \frac{P_1 V_1}{V_2}. \text{ Substituting, } \frac{(100)(3)}{(1)} = 300 \text{ torr (ans.)}$$

Charles' Law

Now assume that the cylinder in Fig. 1.1 has an immovable piston and that it contains a fixed amount of gas. Note the temperature and the pressure on the gages. Now heat the cylinder (and the gas within it) and again read the temperature and pressure gages. What change is seen in the pressure? There will be an increase in pressure; the increase in pressure is directly proportional to the increase in the *absolute* temperature if the volume is held constant. Summarizing these results in a simple equation where P_1 is the initial pressure, T_1 the initial temperature, P_2 the final pressure and T_2 the final temperature, then

$$\frac{P_1}{T_1} = \frac{P_2}{T_2} \tag{1.2}$$

Example: If the initial pressure were 100 torr, the initial temperature 100° C, and the final temperature 200° C, what would the final pressure be?

Solution:

Given: $P_1 = 100$ torr   Find $P_2 = ?$ torr

$T_1 = 100°$ C

$T_2 = 200°$ C

Since Charles' law is in terms of *absolute* temperature, degrees centigrade must be converted to degrees absolute. Since 0° C = 273° K, 100° C = 373° K, and 200° C = 473° K.

Solving Eq. (1.2) for P_2,

$$P_2 = \frac{P_1 T_2}{T_1}. \text{ Substituting values for } P_1, T_1, \text{ and } T_2,$$

$$P_2 = \frac{(100)(473)}{(373)} = 127 \text{ torr (ans.)}$$

The Avogadro Law

The Avogadro law states that *equal volumes of any gas at the same temperature and pressure contain the same number of molecules.* From this law an important relationship between the number of moles in a sample and the pressure the gas exerts can be obtained. Again assume that the cylinder in Fig. 1.1 has an immovable piston and that it contains n_1 moles of gas at a pressure P_1. What would happen if some of the gas was pumped out? Removing gas reduces the pressure (provided the temperature is not changed). In fact, if the removal left n_2 moles of gas in the container, they would exert a pressure P_2 in accordance with the equation

$$\frac{P_1}{n_1} = \frac{P_2}{n_2} \tag{1.3}$$

Example: A cylinder contains 3 moles of hydrogen at a pressure of 760 torr (atmospheric pressure). How many moles must be pumped out to reduce the pressure to 1 torr (at constant temperature)?

We have $P_1 = 760$ torr

$n_1 = 3$ moles

$P_2 = 1$ torr. Solving Eq. (1.3) for n_2, $n_2 = \dfrac{P_2 n_1}{P_1}$.

Substituting, $n_2 = \dfrac{(1)\,(3)}{(760)} = 0.004$ mole. This is the number of moles *remaining* in the cylinder; to find the number pumped out, subtract this from n_1: $n_1 - n_2 = 3.000 - 0.005 = 2.995$ moles. This is equivalent to 1.8×10^{24} molecules. It should be noted that there is still a large number (2.4×10^{21} molecules) remaining in the vessel after the pressure has been reduced to 1/760th of its original pressure.

Equation (1.3) is an extremely important relationship in vacuum work, for the temperature and volume in vacuum systems are nearly always constant; the pressure, therefore, is reduced by removal of gas.

The Ideal Gas Law

The ideal gas law is extremely useful in that it relates *all* four of the quantities needed to describe the state of a gas. The ideal gas law states that

$$PV = nRT \tag{1.4}$$

P is pressure (in torr); V is volume (in liters); n is amount (in moles); and T is temperature (in absolute degrees). R is a constant of proportionality (called the universal gas constant); its value is 62.4 torr·liter/mole·°K. It will be seen from this equation that if any three of the four gas variables

P, V, n, and T are known, the value of the fourth can be found by solving the equation (remember that R is a constant whose value is always known).

This law is known as the "ideal" gas law because it is exactly true for a fictitious "ideal" gas only; however, all gases behave more nearly like an ideal gas as their pressure is decreased.

Example: What pressure will 4 moles of gas at a temperature of 100° C and a volume of 2 liters exert?

Solution:

$n = 4$ moles   Find $P = ?$ torr

$T = 100°$ C

$V = 2$ liters

$R = 62.4$ torr liter/mole ° K

Since the ideal gas law is in terms of *absolute* temperature, it is necessary to convert 100° C to absolute degrees. Since 0° C = 273° K, 100° C = 373° K. Solving Eq. (1.4) for P,

$$P = \frac{nRT}{V}. \text{ Substituting, } P = \frac{(4)(62.4)(373)}{2} = 46{,}600 \text{ torr (ans.)}$$

$$(61.3 \text{ atmospheres})$$

KINETIC THEORY

After the gas laws were developed, attempts were made to explain the behavior of gases in terms of the behavior of the individual molecules that comprise the gas. The theory that resulted is known as the *kinetic theory*, and its results are in close agreement with the gas laws. The theory is based on the following assumptions:

(1) A gas is composed of a large number of tiny particles called molecules.

(2) The molecules are separated by distances which are large in comparison with their own dimensions.

(3) The molecules are in a constant state of random motion.

(4) They exert no force on each other or the walls of their container except when they collide.

No known gas behaves in exact accordance with these assumptions, but the theory based on them explains quite satisfactorily why real gases behave as they do.

The word *kinetic* refers to motion, and this explains why the word is used in connection with a theory that describes a gas as being composed of minute particles that are in constant motion. The molecules of a gas are free to wander throughout any space available to them. The temperature of a gas is a measure of the kinetic energy of the particles; the higher the temperature the greater the particle velocity, and the lower the temperature the lower the velocity.

The pressure on the walls of a vessel containing a gas is due to the impact of the gas molecules. An increase in temperature causes the molecules to move faster and hit harder and more often, creating a higher pressure. This is in accordance with Charles' law (an increase in temperature causes an increase in pressure).

If some of the gas is removed from a confining vessel (which has rigid walls and therefore constant volume), fewer molecules are left in the vessel to strike the walls, and accordingly the pressure is reduced. This is in accordance with Eq. (1.3) and also with the ideal gas law (decreasing n, the amount of gas in Eq. (1.4), decreases P if the other variables are held constant).

Further, decreasing the volume of a given amount of gas (at a constant temperature) results in a reduced area which the original number of molecules (having their original kinetic energy) strike. The force per unit area, or pressure, is increased. This is in accordance with Boyle's law (decreasing the volume increases the pressure).

MEAN FREE PATH

An important bit of information that can be derived from the kinetic theory is the *mean free path* of a molecule, or average distance a molecule can travel before colliding with another molecule. We have described a gas as a collection of molecules in constant motion, with the molecules colliding with each other and with the walls. Between collisions the molecules travel in straight lines; their courses through a vessel are thus zigzag lines. The average length of the path of a given molecule between collisions is called its mean free path. The mean free path can be calculated from the following equation derived from kinetic theory:

$$\lambda = \frac{1}{\sqrt{2}\pi D^2 N} \tag{1.5}$$

where the Greek letter λ (lambda) is the mean free path in centimeters, D is the diameter of the gas molecule in centimeters, and N is the number of gas molecules per cubic centimeter. Notice that the value of the mean free path is inversely proportional to the number of molecules per unit volume. Since pressure is proportional to the number of molecules per unit volume, the mean free path is also inversely proportional to the pressure. This information will be of importance in the design of vacuum equipment.

A close approximation of the mean free path of air molecules at $20°$ C which will be adequate for most purposes is given by the following equation:

$$\lambda = \frac{0.005}{P} \qquad (1.6)$$

where λ is the mean free path (in cm) and P is the pressure (in torr).

DALTON'S LAW OF PARTIAL PRESSURES

Dalton's law states that *in a mixture of gases in which the gases do not react chemically each gas exerts its own pressure independently, as if no other gas were present.* In other words, the pressure a gas exerts is not affected by the presence of other gases in the same vessel.

Take, for example, a vessel filled with oxygen at a pressure of 20 torr. Add to the vessel an amount of helium that would exert a pressure of 30 torr if it were alone in the vessel. The *total* pressure exerted by the oxygen-helium mixture is the sum of the pressure each exerts; these individual pressures are called *partial pressures*, since they contribute to the total pressure. The pressure exerted by the oxygen is 20 torr, and the pressure exerted by the helium is 30 torr. The total pressure exerted on the vessel will be 20 torr + 30 torr = 50 torr. In equation form,

$$P_{\text{total}} = P_{\text{oxygen}} + P_{\text{helium}}$$

For a mixture of a number of gases, the total pressure is the sum of the partial pressures of the constituent gases. In equation form,

$$P_{\text{total}} = P_1 + P_2 + P_3 + \ldots P_n \qquad (1.7)$$

where P_1, P_2, P_3, etc. are the partial pressures exerted by the individual gases. This equation is the mathematical statement of Dalton's law.

Example: Put 2×10^{-6} mole of helium and 3×10^{-6} mole of oxygen in a 3-liter container at $20°$ C. What pressure will the mixture exert on the container? (See Appendix D for a discussion of negative exponents.)

Solution: compute the pressure each gas would exert were it alone in the vessel. Then add the two partial pressures to obtain the total pressure.

Given: 2×10^{-6} mole helium

3×10^{-6} mole oxygen

$T = 20°$ C $= 293°$ K.

The pressure the oxygen would exert if it were alone in the vessel is given by the ideal gas law

$$P_{\text{oxygen}} = \frac{nRT}{V} = \frac{(3 \times 10^{-6})(62.4)(293)}{3} = 1.83 \times 10^{-2} \text{ torr}$$

Similarly, were the helium alone in the vessel it would exert a pressure of

$$P_{\text{helium}} = \frac{nRT}{V} = \frac{(2 \times 10^{-6})(62.4)(293)}{3} = 1.22 \times 10^{-2} \text{ torr}$$

$$P_{\text{total}} = P_{\text{oxygen}} + P_{\text{helium}} = 1.83 \times 10^{-2} + 1.22 \times 10^{-2}$$
$$= 3 \times 10^{-2} \text{ torr (ans.)}$$

CHANGE OF PHASE

Matter can exist in three states: solid, liquid, and gas. Solids have a definite shape and volume. They also have definite boundaries that separate them from neighboring solids, liquids, and gases. Liquids have a definite volume, but they have no definite shape, assuming the shape of their container. Liquids, as well as solids, have definite boundaries that separate them from neighboring matter. With gases the situation is much different; gases have no definite boundaries and mix readily with other gases. They have no definite shape and their volume changes radically with changes in temperature and pressure.

It is possible to change the state of substances by changing the temperature, pressure, or both. This change in the physical state of a substance is called a change of *phase*. Water is an example of a substance that can be made to change from the solid phase (ice) to the liquid phase (water) to the gas phase (steam, or water *vapor*) at atmospheric pressure simply by changing its temperature.

EVAPORATION, CONDENSATION, EQUILIBRIUM AND VAPOR PRESSURE

Consider a substance (solid or liquid) in a closed vessel. Molecules of the substance will spontaneously leave its surface and go into the gas phase. This gas phase of a substance normally a solid or a liquid at room temperature and atmospheric pressure is called a *vapor*. The process is known as *evaporation*, and its rate is determined by the temperature of the substance. Some of the evaporated molecules will, in the course of their random motion, hit the surface again and stick to it. This process is known as *condensation*, and its rate is determined by the concentration of the gas-phase molecules (and hence by the pressure of the evaporated gas). Eventually the number of molecules leaving the surface is equal to the number returning to it (that is, the rate of evaporation is equal to the rate of condensation). This condition is known as *dynamic equilibrium* (see Fig. 1.2), and the partial pressure of the vapor at which it occurs is known as the *vapor pressure* of the substance.

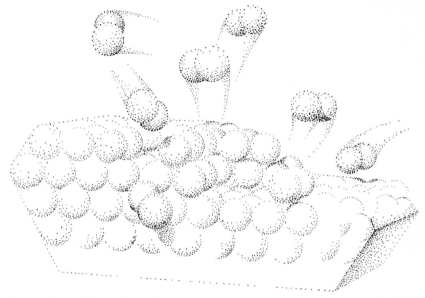

Fig. 1.2. A condition of dynamic equilibrium exists when the rate of evaporation equals the rate of condensation. (From "General Chemistry," Linus Pauling, 2nd Ed., W. H. Freeman and Co., San Francisco, 1953.)

Again take water as an example: the vapor pressure of water at 10° C is 9 torr. If a beaker filled with water is placed in a closed vessel and the temperature of both the water and the vessel is held at 10° C, the pressure due to the water vapor alone (that is, the partial pressure of the water vapor) would rise to 9 torr. This does not mean that the water stops evaporating when that pressure is reached, but simply that at 9 torr the rate at which the liquid is changing to the vapor phase (evaporation rate) is equal to the rate at which the vapor is changing to the liquid phase (the condensation rate).

A change in temperature causes a change in evaporation rate accompanied by a change in condensation rate until a new equilibrium pressure is reached. At 20° C the vapor pressure of water is 17.5 torr, and at 30° C it is 31.8 torr. (See Fig. 1.3 for a graph showing the relation between temperature and vapor pressure.) It should be kept in mind that the closed vessel does not have to be evacuated for this to occur; the partial pressure due to the water vapor will rise to this level, providing there are no chemical reactions.

If one were to pump on the vessel containing the water-filled beaker, the water that is in the gas phase would be removed at a fixed rate (depending

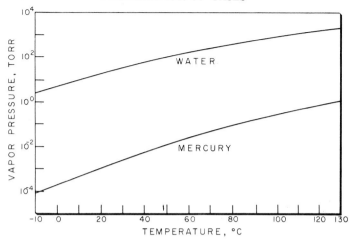

Fig. 1.3. Change of vapor pressure of water and mercury with temperature.

on its temperature), but equilibrium would never be reached, for most of the molecules that had evaporated would be evacuated before they could condense; eventually all the water would change to the gas phase and be pumped away. It should be pointed out that during the evacuation the water is continually evaporating at a rate dependent on its temperature; it does not wait for the pressure in the vessel to fall below its vapor pressure.

GAS FLOW

A vacuum is produced by removing gas from a vessel by means of a pump; and since it is seldom possible to attach a pump directly to the vessel, there is usually a connecting passage between pump and vessel. The gas, then, flows from the vessel through the connecting passage to the pump, where it is either held or ejected to the atmosphere, depending on the type of pump.

The *rate* at which gas flows is an important aspect of the behavior of gases in vacuum systems. It determines the time required to reach the operating pressure; it may also determine how much gas in the way of in-leakage (gas leaking into the system from the outside) and outgassing (gas produced somewhere *within* the system) can be tolerated without the pressure in the vessel rising above the desired operating pressure.

The rate at which gas flows through a vacuum system can be expressed in two ways: as a volumetric flow rate and as a mass flow rate.

Volumetric flow rate is given the designation S and is the *volume* of gas flowing past a given point in a system per unit time. The volumetric flow rate measured at the pump inlet is called the pump speed S_p.

Mass flow rate is given the designation Q and is the *amount* (that is, it is proportional to the number of moles and hence to the mass) of gas flowing past a given point in the system per unit time.

Volumetric flow rate and mass flow rate are related by the equation

$$Q = SP \tag{1.8}$$

where Q is the mass flow rate measured in torr·liter/sec and S is the volumetric flow rate in liter/sec measured at P, the pressure in torr.

Under conditions of equilibrium, that is, when the amount of gas entering the system is equal to the amount of gas leaving, Q is a constant at every point in the system. That is, the amount of gas flowing past a given point in the system is the same as at any other point.

The rate at which gas flows through the vacuum system depends on the pump speed, the geometrical shape and dimensions of the passages, and the type of flow. The shape and dimensions of the connecting passage must allow a gas flow compatible with the speed of the pump during the type of flow that is anticipated.

Gas flow in vacuum systems can be divided into three distinct types or "regimes": turbulent, viscous, and molecular. At high pressures and flow rates the flow is usually turbulent; as the pressure is reduced it merges into viscous flow; and finally, at rather low pressures, it is molecular.

Turbulent flow (see Fig. 1.4) is characterized by its complexity and lack of order; the gas swirls and eddies, and individual particles of the gas may have velocities and directions which are quite different from the average

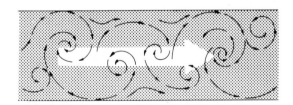

Fig. 1.4. Turbulent flow. Small arrows represent velocities of individual molecules; large arrow represents velocity of aggregate.

velocity and direction of the aggregate. Except for special cases (very large vacuum systems, for instance) the duration of turbulent flow is short compared with viscous and molecular flow and therefore it will not be considered further here.

Viscous flow is much simpler than turbulent flow. It is smooth and orderly; every particle passing a point follows the same path as the preceding particles that passed that point (see Fig. 1.5). Flow lines are straight lines or gradual curves (in turbulent flow this is not the case). The mean free path of the molecules is small compared to the dimensions of the tube during this type of flow, so that collisions between molecules will occur

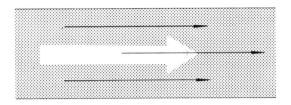

Fig. 1.5. Viscous flow.

more frequently than collisions of molecules with tube walls. As a consequence, intermolecular collisions are predominant in determining the characteristics of flow, and flow rates will be affected by the viscosity of the gas.

Molecular flow is characterized by molecular collisions with the tube walls rather than with other gas molecules. As the pressure in the system is reduced, the mean free path of the gas molecules increases. The dependence of flow rate on viscosity begins to decrease because collisions between molecules are becoming less frequent. At pressures sufficiently low for the mean free path to be several times greater than the diameter

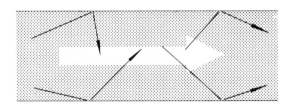

Fig. 1.6. Molecular flow.

of the containing vessel or tube, molecules migrate through a system freely and independently of each other (see Fig. 1.6). This is called free-molecule flow or simply *molecular flow*, and the gas flow rates will be affected mainly by collisions of molecules with the tube walls.

Equations for Determining Gas Flow Rate*

During *viscous flow*, the mass flow rate through a straight tube of circular cross section can be determined by Poiseuille's equation:

$$Q = \frac{\pi D^4 \bar{P}}{128 \eta L}(P_1 - P_2) \tag{1.9}$$

where D is the diameter of the tube, L is the length of the tube, η (the Greek letter eta) is the viscosity of the gas, and $\bar{P}$ is the average of P_1 and P_2, the pressures at opposite ends of the tube.

For dry air at 20° C the equation becomes

$$Q = \frac{3000\ D^4 \bar{P}}{L}(P_1 - P_2) \tag{1.10}$$

where Q is the mass flow rate in torr·liter/sec, D is the tube diameter in inches, L is the tube length in inches, and P is the pressure in torr.

During *molecular flow* the mass flow rate through a long straight tube is given by Knudsen:

$$Q = \frac{\pi D^3}{12L} v_a(P_1 - P_2) \tag{1.11}$$

where D is the diameter of the tube, L is its length, v_a is the average velocity of the molecule, and P_1 and P_2 are the pressures at opposite ends of the tube.

For dry air at 20° C and with D and L in inches and P in torr, the equation becomes

$$Q = \frac{80\ D^3}{L}(P_1 - P_2) \tag{1.12}$$

The change in flow type from viscous to molecular is not abrupt, but a gradual merging of one flow type into another. Therefore, during this transition period when both viscous and molecular flow occur together, the mass flow rate will be determined from the sum of the viscous and molecular flow rates. This is, during the transition period:

$$Q = \left[\frac{3000\ D^4 \bar{P}}{L}(P_1 - P_2) \right] + \left[\frac{80\ D^3}{L}(P_1 - P_2) \right] \tag{1.13}$$

*The gas flow equations given are shortened forms which will be adequate for the type of calculations required here. More accurate equations can be obtained from Dushman's "Vacuum Technique" (J. M. Lafferty, Ed.; John Wiley & Sons, Inc., New York, 1962) or Guthrie and Wakerling's "Vacuum Equipment and Techniques" (McGraw-Hill Book Company, Inc., New York, 1949).

Resistance

A connecting passage impedes the flow of gas through it; thus the passage can be said to have a *resistance* to gas flow. This resistance, Z, is defined as the drop in pressure across the connecting passage per unit mass flow rate:

$$Z = \frac{P_1 - P_2}{Q} \tag{1.14}$$

where P_1 is the pressure at the beginning of the passage and P_2 is the pressure at the other end. The units of Z are sec/liter.

Conductance

Conversely, a line can be said to have a gas flow *conductance*, that is, the ability to transmit gas. Conductance is the reciprocal of resistance:

$$C = \frac{1}{Z} = \frac{Q}{P_1 - P_2} \tag{1.15}$$

The capacity of a vacuum line for gas flow is customarily expressed in terms of conductance. Conductance has units of liter/sec.

If one knows the conductance and the pressure drop across the passage or line, it is possible to determine the mass flow rate:

$$Q = C(P_1 - P_2) \tag{1.16}$$

Although conductance and volumetric flow rate are expressed in the same units (liter/sec) they are not synonymous; the conductance of a line is a geometric property of the line — a property that fixes the line's capacity for handling gas.

Molecular and Viscous Conductance

From Eq. (1.15) and the equations for viscous and molecular flow rates, equations for determining the conductance of vacuum passages during these flow regimes can be obtained:

$$C_{\text{viscous}} = \frac{Q_{\text{viscous}}}{P_1 - P_2} = \frac{\dfrac{3000\ D^4\bar{P}}{L}(P_1 - P_2)}{(P_1 - P_2)} = \frac{3000\ D^4\bar{P}}{L} \tag{1.17}$$

and

$$C_{\text{molecular}} = \frac{Q_{\text{molecular}}}{P_1 - P_2} = \frac{\dfrac{80\ D^3}{L}(P_1 - P_2)}{(P_1 - P_2)} = \frac{80\ D^3}{L} \tag{1.18}$$

where

$C_{viscous}$ and $C_{molecular}$ are in liter/sec

Q is in torr·liter/sec

$\bar{P}$, P_1, and P_2 are in torr, and

L and D are in inches.

For a given line diameter there will be a pressure above which only viscous conductance is important and a pressure below which only molecular conductance is important. Limits can be determined from the conductance equations by assuming molecular conductance to be unimportant when it is 15% or less of viscous, and viscous conductance to be unimportant when it is 15% or less of molecular conductance. That is, only viscous conductance need be considered when $C_{molecular} = 0.15\ C_{viscous}$. Substituting the expressions for $C_{molecular}$ and $C_{viscous}$, one obtains

$$\frac{80\ D^3}{L} = 0.15 \times \frac{3000\ D^4 \bar{P}}{L}$$

or

$$\bar{P}D = 0.18 \text{ (approx)} \tag{1.19}$$

Therefore, if the $\bar{P}D$ product is 0.18 or more, only the viscous equation is used. Conversely, if $C_v = 0.15\ C_m$, then

$$\frac{3000\ D^4 \bar{P}}{L} = 0.15 \times \frac{80\ D^3}{L}$$

and

$$\bar{P}D = 0.004 \tag{1.20}$$

This indicates that with a $\bar{P}D$ of 0.004 or less, only the molecular equation is needed.

When the $\bar{P}D$ product lies between 0.004 and 0.18, both equations must be used. Since both types of flow are occurring in the same pipe at the same time, the conductances are in parallel and the total conductance will be the sum of the viscous conductance and the molecular conductance:

$$C_{total} = C_{viscous} + C_{molecular}$$

For example, consider a line 2 inches in diameter. The flow is viscous if the PD product is 0.18 or more. Therefore, if $\bar{P}D = 0.18$ and $D = 2$, then

$$\bar{P} = \frac{0.18}{2} \quad \text{or} \quad 0.09 \text{ torr } (9 \times 10^{-2} \text{ torr})$$

When the average pressure in a 2-inch-diameter line is above 9×10^{-2} torr, only viscous flow need be considered. On the other hand, the flow is entirely molecular if the $\bar{P}D$ product is less than 0.004. Therefore

$$\bar{P}D = 0.004$$

$$\bar{P} = \frac{0.004}{2} \quad \text{or} \quad 0.002 \text{ torr } (2 \times 10^{-3} \text{ torr})$$

For an average pressure of 2×10^{-3} torr or less, in a 2-inch-diameter line, only molecular flow is important.

For an average pressure between 2×10^{-3} torr and 9×10^{-2} torr, both molecular flow and viscous flow must be considered.

Conductances in Parallel

When a passage is made up of conductances in parallel, (see Fig. 1.7) the total conductance C_t of the passage is the sum of the individual conductances:

$$C_t = C_1 + C_2 + C_3 + C_4 + \ldots + C_n \tag{1.21}$$

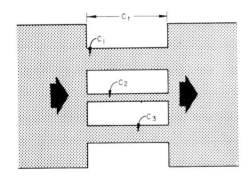

Fig. 1.7. Conductances in parallel

Example: In Fig. 1.7, if $C_1 = 8$ liter/sec, $C_2 = 2$ liter/sec, and $C_3 = 5$ liter/sec, then

$$C_t = C_1 + C_2 + C_3 = 15 \text{ liter/sec.}$$

Conductances in Series

When a passage is made up of conductances in series (see Fig. 1.8) the total conductance is given by:

$$1/C_t = 1/C_1 + 1/C_2 + 1/C_3 + \ldots + 1/C_n \tag{1.22}$$

Example: In Fig. 1.8, if $C_1 = 8$ liter/sec, $C_2 = 2$ liter/sec, and $C_3 = 5$ liter/sec, then

$$\frac{1}{C_t} = \frac{1}{C_1} + \frac{1}{C_2} + \frac{1}{C_3} = \frac{1}{2} + \frac{1}{5} + \frac{1}{8} = \frac{20 + 8 + 5}{40}$$

$$C_t = \frac{40}{33} = 1\frac{7}{33} \text{ liter/sec}$$

(approx 1/10 of the parallel conductance).

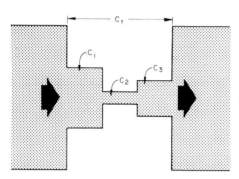

Fig. 1.8. Conductances in series.

Fundamental Equation of the Vacuum System

The volumetric flow rate at a given point in the vacuum system may be called the pumping speed.* At the entrance to a passage, for example, one may have a pumping speed of $S_1 = Q/P_1$, where Q is the mass flow rate and P_1 is the pressure at the entrance. At the exit, the pumping speed may be $S_2 = Q/P_2$. (As previously noted, Q is a constant throughout the system.) From Eq. (1.16) we know that, for this passage,

$$Q = (P_1 - P_2)C$$

Substituting $P_1 = Q/S_1$ and $P_2 = Q/S_2$, one obtains

$$Q = \left(\frac{Q}{S_1} - \frac{Q}{S_2}\right)C = \left(\frac{1}{S_1} - \frac{1}{S_2}\right)QC.$$

Dividing both sides of the equation by QC, one obtains

$$\frac{1}{C} = \frac{1}{S_1} - \frac{1}{S_2}$$

or

$$\frac{1}{S_1} = \frac{1}{S_2} + \frac{1}{C} \tag{1.23}$$

*This is not the same as *pump speed* S_p, which is the volumetric flow rate measured at the pump inlet.

This is the fundamental equation of the vacuum system. Using this equation, the pumping speed S_1 can be determined at any point in a system by knowing the speed S_2 at some other point and the conductance of the system between the points. For example, a pump with speed S_p pumping onto a vessel through a passage with a total conductance C_t will produce a pumping speed S_t at the vessel given by

$$\frac{1}{S_t} = \frac{1}{S_p} + \frac{1}{C_t}$$ (1.24)

Example: A pump with $S_p = 10$ liter/sec is connected to a vessel by tubing whose conductance is also 10 liter/sec. What pumping speed will be available at the vessel?

$$\frac{1}{S_t} = \frac{1}{S_p} + \frac{1}{C_t} = \frac{1}{10} + \frac{1}{10} = \frac{2}{10} = \frac{1}{5} \qquad S_t = \frac{5}{1} = 5 \text{ liter/sec.}$$

(Note that a conductance $C_t = S_p$ still throttles the pump to 50% of its rated speed.)

Entrance Conductance

It has been pointed out that when the conditions of molecular flow exist, there is no bulk movement of gas. Instead, there is a random movement of particles (molecules) in straight paths between collisions with the walls of the vacuum system. Therefore, for gas to move into a passage from a vessel in which the conditions of molecular flow exist, the gas molecules must hit the entrance to the passage in their random movement before they can leave the vessel. The entrance to the passage can therefore be said to have a "conductance" for gas molecules which is dependent on the area of the opening. For dry air at room temperature the quantity $75A$ (where A is the area of the entrance in square inches) gives a close approximation of the molecular conductance of a circular entrance, in liters per second. This entrance conductance will be in series with the conductance of the passage, therefore the total conductance of entrance and passage will be given by

$$\frac{1}{C_t} = \frac{1}{C_e} + \frac{1}{C_p}$$ (1.25)

where

C_t = total conductance of entrance and passage

C_e = conductance of the entrance

C_p = conductance of the passage

The conductance of an entrance has a large effect on short passages, that is, passages where L is less than $20D$. Where L is greater than $20D$, the effect of the entrance on the total conductance is small enough to be neglected.

The molecular conductance of a bend or elbow in the vacuum line is calculated by using the equation for a straight pipe, using the centerline distance along the bend for the length L.

The molecular conductance of a rectangular passage is calculated from

$$C = \frac{400A^2}{BL} \tag{1.26}$$

where A is the cross-sectional area of the passage in square inches, B is the perimeter of the passage cross section in inches, and L is the passage length in inches.

The molecular conductance of the annular passage between two concentric tubes has the same equation, but in this case B is the sum of the vacuum-side perimeters of the two tubes.

The molecular conductance of the entrance to an annular passage is also $75A$, where A is the area of the annular entrance in square inches (in.^{2}).

The molecular conductance of an orifice of area A in.^{2} in a passage of cross sectional area A_p in.^{2} is given by

$$\frac{75A_p}{A_p - A} \times A = C = \frac{75A}{1 - (A/A_p)}.$$

More conductance equations, for various geometries, can be found in Dushman's "Vacuum Technique" and Guthrie and Wakerling's "Vacuum Equipment and Techniques."

THE EFFECTS OF EVACUATING A VESSEL

The effect of vacuum on both equipment and techniques can be illustrated by following the evacuation of a vacuum vessel. Assume that the vessel is moderately sized (about 30 liters) and leak-free, and that there is a pump attached to it. Evacuation will begin at atmospheric pressure and proceed down to 1×10^{-6} torr.

From 760 to 1 Torr

The initial portion of the pumpdown gives rise to a rather startling effect if the relative humidity of the air is high. The water vapor in the vessel will condense (due to the cooling effect of the sudden drop in pressure) into a gray fog which swirls around with a turbulence that is characteristic of gas flow at this relatively high pressure and flow rate.

When the pressure in the vessel has been reduced from 760 torr to about 1 torr, the most obvious change that will have taken place is the pressure differential between the inside of the vessel and the atmosphere outside. This differential is about 14.7 pounds per square inch, so the walls of the vessel must be strong enough to safely withstand this pressure. An observation window of 6-inch diameter, for instance, must be strong enough to withstand a force of 415 pounds without deflecting enough to cause a leak.

In the pressure range from 760 torr to 1 torr, another more subtle change is taking place; this is a slow change in the composition of the gas remaining in the vessel. While the major component of the gases in the vessel is air, there are usually certain oils, grease, water, etc., on the walls of the vessel. As seen in the section on vapor pressure, these materials exist in a gas phase as well as in a solid (or liquid) phase, and as the air is pumped out of the vessel, the gas phase of these materials will be pumped out also. Eventually almost all the air will have been pumped out; the grease and water will continue to evaporate, and their partial pressures will constitute a much larger proportion of the total pressure. Thus there is a radical change in the relative concentration of gases removed. At first mostly air was removed, with a small amount of impurity vapors. As lower and lower pressures are reached, it is mostly the gas phase of the impurities and little air that is removed.

From 1 to 10^{-4} Torr

Below a pressure of 1 torr, the ability of the gases remaining in the vessel to conduct heat begins to decrease quite rapidly. Between 1 torr and 1×10^{-4} torr the thermal conductivity (a measure of the ability of a substance to conduct heat) of the gas in the vessel goes from a value that is very close to its value at atmospheric pressure to nearly zero. This insulative characteristic of a vacuum is well demonstrated by vacuum bottles used to keep beverages hot or cold and by the Dewar flasks used to store liquid nitrogen. This drop in thermal conductivity is one of the more significant changes in gases at low pressure; it is so uniform that instruments have been developed which indicate a change in pressure in this range by measuring the change in thermal conductivity of the gases remaining in the vessel. While this effect is useful in some cases (the vacuum furnace, for instance), it carries with it some disadvantages, too. If the process in the vessel involves friction of any kind, the heat generated by the friction may not be easily dissipated, and overheating may result.

A change in the electrical characteristics of the gas also begins to show up at pressures below 1 torr. The voltage necessary to start a discharge across the two electrodes of the tube pictured in Fig. 1.9 decreases as the

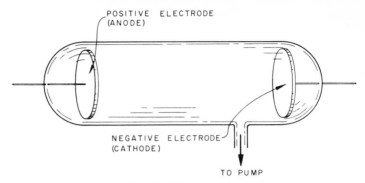

Fig. 1.9. Discharge tube.

pressure decreases and reaches a minimum around 1 torr. At this point the voltage required begins to increase again quite rapidly as the pressure drops further. At a pressure between 5×10^{-2} torr and 1×10^{-3} torr (depending on the dimensions of the tube and the voltage across the electrodes) discharge of this type will cease. By observing the nature and intensity of the discharge in a tube of fixed dimensions, it is possible to get a close approximation of the pressure. The pressure at which the discharge ceases is especially repeatable.

From 10^{-4} Torr to 10^{-6} Torr

As the pressure goes below 10^{-4} torr and the molecular density is reduced still further, the increase in the mean free path of the gas molecules becomes quite important. From Eq. (1.5) we see that at 1×10^{-4} torr the mean free path will be approximately 50 cm. Fifty centimeters is a distance which could easily be equal to or greater than the dimensions of a vacuum vessel. This means that at pressures of 10^{-4} torr and below, gas molecules may be colliding as much with the walls of the vacuum vessel as with each other and that the movement of a gas molecule from one part of the system to another is no longer a true flow but more of a random bouncing from wall to wall. Thus a molecule's progress through a tube will be a matter of probability.

As the pressure approaches 10^{-6} torr a change occurs in sliding friction. The thin layer of adsorbed gas that exists on the surface of mechanical parts in the atmosphere is reduced in a vacuum, resulting in an increase in sliding friction.

PUMPDOWN TIME

It is helpful to know the time it takes to pump a vessel from atmospheric pressure down to some lower pressure. The equation for pumpdown time is

$$t = 2.3 \frac{V}{S_p} \log \frac{P_1}{P_2} \tag{1.27}$$

where t is the time it takes to pump a vessel of volume V from a pressure P_1 to a pressure P_2 with a pump whose net speed is S_p. Consistent units must be used for these symbols, such as V in liters, S in liters/sec, and t in seconds. Here P_1 and P_2 can be in any appropriate units because their ratio is a dimensionless number whose logarithm is used in the equation. (If logarithms are new to you, see Appendix D.) Since the net pump speed S_p decreases with a drop in pressure during viscous flow, the pump-down calculations are usually made in steps. Also, the pump speed S_p to be used in the equation is the average speed over that step. The calculations are simplified if the low pressure P_2 in each step is made a factor of ten below the high pressure P_1. For example, for the first step, atmospheric pressure (P_1) is taken as 1000 torr and P_2 is 100 torr; the logarithm of P_1/P_2 is thus the log of 10, which is 1. In the second step, P_1 is 100 torr, P_2 is 10 torr, and the logarithm is still 1, and so on.

The use of the pumpdown equation should be limited to conditions where the pressure is no less than 0.001 torr, and preferably not below 0.01 torr. At 0.01 torr and below, much of the gases being pumped are being desorbed (evaporation of impurities from walls of system) from the walls of the system. Consequently, pumpdown time in this region depends as much on the condition of the walls of the system as on the net speed of the pumps, and the equation becomes meaningless.

Actually, this situation is also true to a lesser extent at higher pressures. In practice it has been found necessary to assume a fictitiously large volume to account for the gases being desorbed and for loss of mechanical pump efficiency. This is done by multiplying the volume, V, by a factor K, which becomes larger as the pressure drops. Thus the pumpdown equation becomes

$$t = K2.3 \frac{V}{S_p} \log \frac{P_1}{P_2}. \tag{1.28}$$

A table listing satisfactory values for K is given below and examples illustrating these principles are given in Chapter 4. The table lists values of K which have given satisfactory values for average conditions. Increments are the same as before, for simplification.

Pressure (torr)	Factor (K)
1000 to 100	1
100 to 10	1.25
10 to 1	1.5
1 to 0.1	2
0.1 to 0.01	4

CHAPTER 2

The Components of a Vacuum System

A vacuum is achieved by exhausting most of the gas from a container; the remaining gas in the container is of low density and consequently at low pressure. The container to be exhausted is referred to as a *vacuum vessel*, and the gas is removed by means of a pump. (As will be seen later, the gas need not always be completely removed from the vessel, but only removed from the gas phase.) A pump and vessel, together with the necessary "plumbing" and vacuum-measuring equipment, are referred to as a *vacuum system*.

There are so many different uses to which vacuum is put that it is difficult to generalize about types of systems. They can, however, be classified to some degree. For example, a system may be either static or dynamic. In a static system the pumps are isolated from the vessel after it is evacuated; the process requiring vacuum is conducted under static conditions. In a dynamic system, the pumps continue to work on the vessel during the process after the operational pressure is reached. Dynamic systems vary greatly in size, from small portable units to the extremely large permanent installations used in particle accelerators and space chambers.

Vacuum systems can be classified according to the pressure range in which they operate: rough, low, high, very high, and ultrahigh vacuum. The type, size, and number of the components used vary with these classifications.

The components of a typical dynamic high-vacuum system are listed and shown in Fig. 2.1. The vacuum vessel A, outfitted with a high-vacuum gage L and vacuum-release valve N, is connected to two pumps, a vapor pump B and a mechanical pump C. The mechanical pump is used in the initial or "roughing" phase of the pump-down. During this phase the

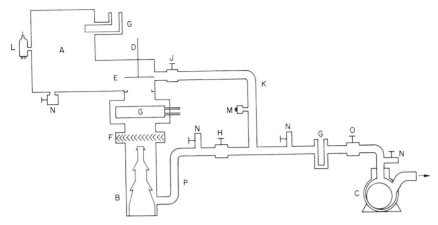

Fig. 2.1. Schematic diagram of a typical high-vacuum system. The components are: A. Vacuum vessel; B. Diffusion pump; C. Mechanical pump; D. High-vacuum isolation valve; E. High-vacuum manifold; F. Baffle; G. Traps; H. Backing valve; J. Roughing valve; K. Roughing line; L. High-vacuum gage; M. Forevacuum gage; N. Vacuum-release valves; O. Mechanical-pump valve; P. Foreline.

roughing valve J is open, while the high-vacuum isolation valve D and the backing valve H are closed, isolating the vapor pump B. Thus the flow of gas during roughing is from the vessel, through the roughing line K, and out the exhaust of the mechanical pump. When the pressure as indicated by the gage M is sufficiently low, the roughing valve J is closed and the high-vacuum isolation valve D and the backing valve H are opened, putting the vapor pump into the "circuit." The flow of gas is now from the vessel, through the high-vacuum manifold E, the vapor pump, the foreline P, the mechanical pump, and out the mechanical-pump exhaust. The mechanical pump is now being used as a "backing pump," pumping on the exhaust of the vapor pump, which cannot exhaust its gases to atmosphere. The mechanical pump valve O is an optional feature, used mostly in checking the condition of the mechanical pump.

There is usually a baffle, F, near the inlet of the vapor pump to condense vapor that has escaped from the pump and return it to the pump boiler. There are also one or more traps, G, either in the vessel or near the inlet to the vapor pump.* These are devices that adsorb some of the gases and vapors entering the system from the vapor pump or emanating from the process in the vacuum vessel.

Several of the components warrant further description; these are: vacuum pumps, baffles, traps, valves, connecting lines, ports, lead-ins, and seals.

*As will be seen below, traps are often placed at several places in the vacuum system.

VACUUM PUMPS

There are two basic approaches to reducing the pressure in a vacuum vessel: the first involves physically removing gas molecules from the vessel and exhausting them from the system. Vapor and mechanical pumps utilize this approach. The second approach is to remove gas molecules from the gas phase, but retain them in the system. There are a number of devices that use this: surfaces within the system that adsorb or condense the gas, chemicals that react with the gas to remove it from the gas phase, and devices that ionize the gas molecules, giving them electric charges so they can be removed from the gas phase by means of electric fields.

Operating Limits

No matter which method a pump uses to remove gas, the performance of every pump can be described by specific characteristics, called *operating limits*, i.e.,

(a) Base pressure (lowest pressure the pump will produce).

(b) Maximum permissible inlet pressure (highest pressure at which the pump can operate).

(c) Maximum tolerable discharge pressure (highest pressure against which the pump can exhaust; does not apply to sorption or ion-getter pumps).

(d) Speed throughout its operating range (from maximum inlet pressure to base pressure).

Pump manufacturers supply instructions with a pump which define the operating limits; catalogs issued by the manufacturers will also give this information. It is essential to take these operating limits into account when choosing a pump for a specific job.

Mechanical Pumps

The Rotary Pump. The pumping mechanism of all rotary pumps consists of a solid cylinder (the rotor) which rotates within a cylindrical housing of larger diameter (the stator). As it rotates, the rotor sweeps the gas in the volume between it and the stator from inlet port to exhaust port. Gravity flow of oil from a reservoir through various oil feed lines floods the inner surfaces of the pump, providing a gas seal, as well as lubricating and cooling the pump. The seal provided by the oil film is adequate because the pump parts are accurately machined to very close clearances.

The various makes of pumps differ mainly in the method of sweeping the volume between rotor and stator. Figures 2.2, 2.4, and 2.5 illustrate three of the methods used. Figure 2.2 shows the double-vane type. In this case

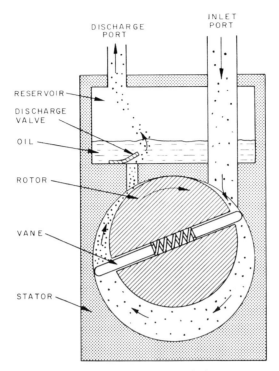

Fig. 2.2. Double-vane mechanical pump.

the rotor has a diametrical slot which accommodates two free-sliding vanes, held apart by springs that press them uniformly on the surface of the stator. The rotor is mounted concentrically on the pump shaft. The shaft is eccentrically located in the stator. When the rotor turns, the vanes sweep the crescent-shaped volume between rotor and stator, moving the gas contained in this volume from inlet to exhaust. Figure 2.3 shows this operation in greater detail.

An oil film between the vanes and the stator prevents gas from leaking back to the inlet side of the pump, provided the surface of the stator is not scored or gouged. The main seal against leakage in Fig. 2.2 is at the point where the stator and rotor are closest together. The clearance here may be as little as 0.0001 inch in some pumps. To prevent gas from leaking back across the pump heads, a close fit between the rotor and heads, plus an adequate flow of oil from the reservoir, is needed.

Figure 2.4 shows a single-vane pump. The vane is not located in the rotor, but is mounted in the stator between inlet and exhaust ports. It is spring-loaded against the rotor surface. The rotor is eccentrically mounted

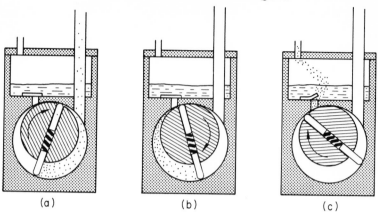

Fig. 2.3. Double-vane mechanical pump in action. (a) The two sliding vanes are moving with the turning rotor. The volume between the inlet and the lower vane is increasing; this causes gas to move into this area from the inlet. (b) The gas has been isolated from the vacuum system and is being pushed toward the discharge valve. (c) The gas has been compressed to slightly above atmospheric pressure. The dicharge valve has opened, and the gas is being ejected out of the pump through the oil in the reservoir.

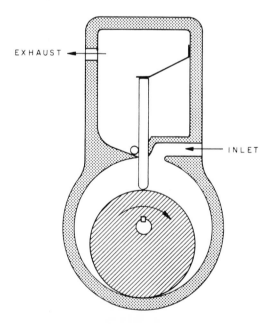

Fig. 2.4. Single-vane mechanical pump.

on the pump shaft, and the shaft is centrally located in the stator. In this pump, the rotor itself sweeps the crescent-shaped volume as it turns, and the vane provides the stationary seal.

The pump shown in Fig. 2.5 is different from either of the two other pumps. The rotor is eccentrically mounted on the pump shaft, and the shaft is centrally located in the stator. During operation the rotor turns with the shaft, which causes the piston to sweep the volume between it and the stator. The piston does not turn in this case. The vane-like extension on the piston, called the slide, moves up and down in an oscillating seal called the slide pin. Most of the larger rotary pumps are of this design.

No matter which of the above designs is used, a single-stage rotary pump will achieve pressures of about 10^{-2} torr. To get below this (without resorting to a vapor pump) a two-stage rotary pump is necessary. A two-stage, or compound, pump consists of two pumping chambers (one rotor-stator combination is a pumping chamber) connected in series. The exhaust of the first stage is coupled to the inlet of the second stage. The pressure difference across the first stage is reduced by the second stage, which allows the compound pump to reach pressures of about 1×10^{-3} torr.

The single-stage pump is made in two different styles, simplex and duplex. The simplex has only one pumping chamber. The duplex has two,

INLET

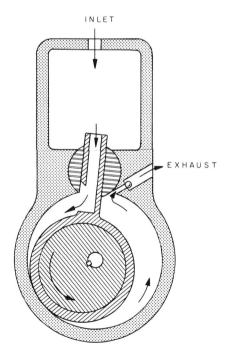

EXHAUST

Fig. 2.5. Rotary-piston mechanical pump.

but instead of being connected in series like the two-stage or compound pump, the pumping chambers are connected in parallel. The inlets of both chambers are manifolded together, as are the exhausts. With a given-sized pumping chamber, the duplex will pump almost twice as fast as the simplex, and at higher pressures, almost twice as fast as the compound pump. The latter, however, will pump at pressures lower than the limit of the simplex or duplex.

Rotary pumps are manufactured with rated gas capacities from 0.2 liter/sec to over 300 liters/sec at S.T.P. The rating of a simplex pump is determined by the displacement of the pump (the displacement is the difference in volume between stator and rotor) multiplied by the number of revolutions per unit time. In a duplex pump the displacement of both chambers is counted. In a compound pump only the displacement of the first stage is counted; the second stage pumps on the first stage only.

The rating of a pump holds true only at inlet pressures near atmospheric. As the pressure drops, the density of the gas being pumped is lower, so that the amount of gas moved per sweep is less. This means less gas moved per unit of time. Further, due to the clearance volume on the discharge of the pump which allows re-expansion of gas at discharge pressure into the displacement volume of the pump, the speed will decrease as the base pressure is approached. A curve showing how the pumping speed of a typical rotary pump changes with pressure is shown in Fig. 2.6.

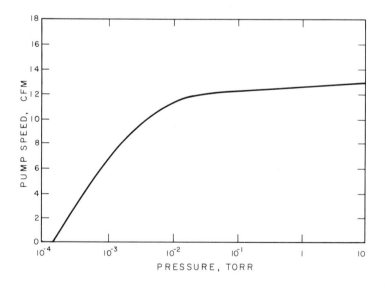

Fig. 2.6. Pump speed vs pressure for a typical rotary pump.

Difficulties with Rotary Pumps. Under normal operating conditions and with moderate caution and care, the rotary pump will give little trouble. The difficulties which do arise usually stem from three general sources:

Solid Particles Entering the Inlet of the Pump. Because the rotary pump is solidly built and massive, it is sometimes considered indestructible. Actually, because of its close clearances, it is easily damaged by solid particles entering the pump inlet and scoring or gouging the sealing surfaces. Unfortunately, any damage is quite likely to be permanent. The scores and abrasions caused by small particles will allow gas to bypass the oil-film seal; large particles may cause a cracked stator or shear a shaft or key. Screens are sometimes used at the inlet to stop particles, but they become clogged in time. Also they must be removed and cleaned periodically, or the speed of the pump will be reduced. Dirt traps are effective and have very little effect on the speed of the pump. The best measure in any case is to prevent loose particles from entering the pump inlet by keeping the system itself free of them.

Gas Leaking into the Pump. On any rotary pump the rotor is driven by a shaft which must pass through the pump housing at least once. There are two main methods of maintaining a gas-tight seal at this point: (1) By means of a packing seal, which maintains a gas-tight contact between the rotating shaft and the pump housing; this seal, used on small pumps, fails only from wear, unless the portion of the shaft it is sealing has been scored, allowing atmospheric air to bypass it. (2) By means of an oil-bleed seal, which allows a small amount of oil to leak into the pump chamber instead of air. The oil-bleed seal is used on large pumps. While seal failure here may be the result of a scored shaft, it is usually due to an improper amount of oil flowing to the seal, since there is always a certain amount of air dissolved in the oil, the base pressure of the pump will be raised if too much oil is allowed to leak into the pump chamber through the seal. On the other hand, if not enough oil is supplied, air will enter directly, and the seal will be inadequate. A "happy medium" of oil flow between these two extremes is necessary for optimum pump operation.

Contamination of the Oil. The oil in a rotary pump circulates continuously. From the reservoir it flows into oilways, to be directed onto the various pump surfaces. The oil from these surfaces is swept along and ejected, with the gas, from the pumping chamber back into the reservoir. The rotary pump has a valve on the discharge side which is held in a closed position by a spring. To be ejected, the gas from the inlet must be compressed until it is at a pressure equal to atmospheric, plus the pressure of the spring holding the discharge valve closed. During this compression period, vapors present in the gas being pumped may condense and the liquid condensate mix with oil. This causes two problems: first, the condensed vapor will be carried back to the low-pressure side of the pump by the oil, where it re-evaporates. This re-evaporated vapor must then be pumped out, and this results in a drop in pump efficiency and an increase in the base pressure. Second, the condensate may break the oil down chemically, forming a sludge which interferes with oil flow. This sludge causes inadequate sealing, cooling, and lubrication, and, in extreme cases, pump "seizure."

Many pump manufacturers now use the principle of *gas ballast* to cope with the problem of contamination. Essentially, gas ballast involves admitting a controlled amount of dry gas (usually air) at the compression stage of the pumping cycle. This gas mixes with the gases being pumped. As a result, there is a reduction in the compression necessary to exhaust the gases and, consequently, a decrease in the amount of vapor that condenses. Of course, if the vapor itself breaks down the oil, without condensing, the gas ballast will be less effective. In such a case it is sometimes possible to select a pump oil that resists the action of that particular vapor.

The use of gas ballast increases the amount of oil carried out the exhaust. Therefore the oil level may drop faster when it is used.

Care of the Rotary Pump. The life of a rotary pump can be extended, and the system on which it is used protected, by observing the precautions listed below:

(1) When the rotary pump is stopped, its inlet should be vented to the atmosphere. If it is not, oil may be drawn into the pump chamber from the reservoir and cause flooding. A large pump has enough oil in its reservoir to overflow the pump chamber and run into the lines between pump and vessel. If a pump is started with a flooded pump chamber, the pump, or possibly the drive motor or drive belts, may be damaged. (A flooded chamber can be cleared by pulling the pump through several revolutions by hand.)

Since the rotary pump is not a reliable vacuum seal when it is stopped, a shutoff valve should be installed on the inlet side of the pump. Also, some means should be provided between this valve and the pump for releasing the vacuum. The same arrangement can be used to check the base pressure of the mechanical pump — a procedure which is of considerable help in diagnosing the ailments of a vacuum system.

(2) A pump driven by a three-phase motor and being started for the first time, or a pump that has been moved to a new location, should be checked for correct direction of rotation immediately upon starting. Cleaning a system which has been flooded with oil by a pump turning in a reverse direction is a time-consuming and obnoxious task; a thoroughly flooded system must be completely dismantled to get rid of the oil.

(3) The inlet of a large rotary pump should be bypassed to air when the pump is started. During this operation, the mechanical-pump valve should be closed and the vacuum-release valve open; the pump is then started and allowed to gain momentum. At this time, the valve that controls the oil supply is opened, the vacuum-release valve is closed, and the pumpdown sequence can begin. Some manufacturers provide a valve for this purpose as part of the pump.

(4) Some mechanical pumps have a water-cooled jacket. On many such pumps the water flow is interlocked with the electrical power, and the water must be turned on before the pump will run. In any case, water flow should be provided before the pump is started. If a water-cooled pump is stopped and left at atmospheric pressure for some time, the water should be shut off, because condensation from the atmosphere will take place on the cooled interior walls of the pump. In severe climates, tap water becomes very cold in winter and will cause the oil to thicken, impairing the action of the pump. A pump should run warm to the touch, which may require throttling the tap water in cold weather.

(5) In most cases there should be a flexible section of line inserted between a mechanical pump and the rest of the vacuum system. Even the smallest pumps, when fastened solidly to the rest of the vacuum system, will cause annoying vibration. The vibration induced in the vacuum lines creates strains which can lead to leaks. Sylphon bellows, rubber or plastic tubing, and corrugated metal tubing are examples of vibration-damping media commonly used. With any of these materials it should be remembered that there will be a pressure of 14.7 pounds per square inch on the outside surfaces, and the possibility of collapse should be considered.

(6) While the mechanical pump is in operation and especially during roughing, oil is carried out the exhaust. Being well-atomized, this oil vapor floats everywhere. Breathing the vapor continuously is a decided health hazard. The vapor will also leave a sticky film on all surfaces near the pump. A duct to carry the vapors outside is recommended when there are pumps operating within the laboratory or shop. This duct should not have a vertical run directly from the pump exhaust; the temperature of the pump exhaust is approximately 130° F, and the temperature of the duct is room temperature (70° F). The lower temperature of the duct will cause vapor which has passed through the pump to condense. If the duct rises vertically from the pump, this condensate will drain back into the pump reservoir and recombine with the oil. Any vertical run should be from a settling tank that can be drained periodically.

Troubleshooting the Rotary Pump. When the rotary pump does give trouble, it will show up as a low pump speed or high base pressure, or both. If the speed is slow over the entire pressure range from 760 torr down, the problem is usually mechanical. If the slow speed is in the pressure range of 200 microns down, the trouble is usually the state of the oil. If the base pressure is above 500 microns, the trouble is likely to be a mechanical failure, and if the base pressure is less than 200 microns, the trouble is most often the state of the oil.

Slow pumping and a high base pressure usually occur together. When either situation seems indicated, the first step is to make sure the fault lies with the pump and not with the system. (This is a simple and short procedure if there is a mechanical-pump valve on the system.) If the pump is not performing properly it may be due to one or a combination of the following:

(1) Slipping belts can cause slower pump rotation and therefore a slow pumping speed. In this case the base pressure is not necessarily affected. To check, remove the belt guard and inspect the belt. If the belt is loose or defective, either move the motor mount for proper belt tension or change belts.

(2) The oil level should be checked. If it is below the discharge valve, the valve will not be a gas-tight seal. To check, look at the sight gage; it is usually marked to show the proper level.

(3) The discharge valve sometimes sticks open. If it is open, close the mechanical-pump valve and open the vacuum-release valve so that a heavy burst of air is allowed to flow through the pump. This may sweep a lodged particle loose or jar the discharge valve so that it will close.

(4) The main shutoff valve to the oil lines may be completely or partly closed. To check a solenoid-operated valve, switch it off and on several times. A sharp click should be heard each time the switch is turned on. If the click is not heard or if it is intermittent, the valve should be reworked. The hand-operated valve should be checked also, to make sure it is opening.

(5) A clogged oil line can be checked by removing the oil coupling closest to the pump while the power to the pump is off. When the power to the pump is turned on, oil should flow freely from the line. Clogged oilways in the pump casting are difficult to check. If the oilways are clogged, a major overhaul is usually necessary, although a thorough flushing with a light-weight oil or kerosene may help.

(6) The oil-seal metering valves may be out of adjustment. As a first check, mark the setting of each valve, then open them an additional turn or two. If no difference is apparent, reset the valves to their original setting. If an improvement is seen, slowly begin closing all valves together approximately one-eighth turn at a time, until an optimum point is reached. Some improvement may be obtained after this by changing the valve

settings individually a little at a time. There will be a long time lag between the change in valve setting and a change in pressure; at least three to five minutes should be allowed for each change to take effect.

(7) The discharge valve may be damaged. There is usually some form of inspection plate covering the discharge valve; a manufacturer's operational instruction sheet will show its location. The valves should be inspected for broken springs, corroded seats and jamming — anything that would prevent the valve from seating.

If the above procedures do not uncover the difficulty, a major pump overhaul may be necessary. This step is not advisable for anyone not having a service facility staffed with trained personnel and equipped with the fixtures needed for reassembly of the pump. Most pump manufacturers maintain some sort of pump service facility at moderate cost; it is a good idea to check into this before the need arises.

Mechanical Booster Pumps. Another type of mechanical pump is the mechanical booster pump, designed to provide higher speed in the pressure region between 1 micron and 500 microns. In this pressure region the oil-sealed rotary pump is losing efficiency and the vapor pump is just beginning to gain efficiency.

A cross section of a typical mechanical booster pump is shown in Fig. 2.7. The two double-lobe impellers are mounted on parallel shafts and rotate in opposite directions. They are geared together so that the correct relative positions of the impellers with reference to each other can be maintained. The impellers do not touch each other or the pump housing. No sealing fluid is used; the back-leakage is small compared to the total speed of the pump in its useful range.

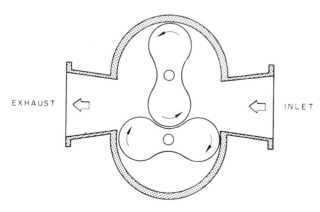

EXHAUST   INLET

Fig. 2.7. Mechanical booster pump (Roots type).

During operation gas from the inlet side is trapped between an impeller and the pump housing. No compression takes place while the gas is moved from inlet to discharge port. When the leading lobe of the impeller passes the discharge port, gas from the discharge area (which is at higher pressure) enters, but is swept out again by the trailing lobe.

Since mechanical booster pumps have a useful compression ratio of about 10 to 1, they must be backed by an oil-sealed rotary pump in order to reach their best operating pressure range. This can easily be seen if one considers that a booster pump with a compression ratio of 10 to 1 could only achieve a pressure of 76 torr operating from atmospheric pressure (1/10th of 760 torr = 76 torr). If it discharges to the inlet of the mechanical rotary pump, the base pressure of the mechanical booster pump will, of course, be much less. Most mechanical booster pumps will produce a pressure of 0.1 torr or less; some are reported to produce less than 1×10^{-3} torr.

Advantages of this pump are high pumping speed in the region where the oil-sealed rotary pumps and vapor pumps are not fully efficient, and clean, relatively oil-free operation.

Small clearances and high rotational speed make it advisable to use screens on the inlet to keep small particles from entering the pump. For the same reasons (small clearances and high speed), these pumps are susceptible to overheating and seizure.

The mechanical booster pump is very effective in reducing the time required to rough out a large or "gassy" system to the operating pressure of a vapor pump. The size of the oil-sealed rotary pump required to back a vapor pump can be reduced by placing a mechanical booster pump between the vapor pump and the oil-sealed rotary pump.

Vapor Pumps

Vapor pumps, as their name implies, pump by means of a stream of vapor. They have no moving parts, pumping being accomplished by a high-velocity, high-density beam of vapor that is directed away from the pump inlet and toward the pump outlet. Gas molecules are given directed velocity by this vapor stream and are thus removed from the system. Two types of vapor pumps will be discussed: the diffusion pump and the ejector pump.

Diffusion Pumps. The diffusion pump is a vapor pump having a boiler pressure of the order of a few torr and capable of pumping gas with full efficiency at intake pressures not exceeding about 20 microns and discharge pressures (forepressures) not exceeding about 500 microns. The diffusion pump cannot operate independently; a separate pump is required to reduce the vessel pressure to or below the diffusion pump's maximum intake pressure before it will operate. Also, while operating, a separate pump is required to maintain the discharge pressure below the maximum tolerable. The mechanical pump is the type normally used to provide these functions.

In a typical high-vacuum system, the diffusion pump is placed between the mechanical pump and the vessel to be evacuated. The mechanical pump reduces the vessel pressure below the maximum intake pressure of the diffusion pump. At this point the diffusion pump is put into operation. The discharge pressure of the diffusion pump will then begin to rise, but will be held below the maximum tolerable level by the mechanical pump.

The diffusion pump is used when the required operating pressure is below the range of the ejector pump and the mechanical pump. The expected gas load at this pressure will determine the required size. There are diffusion pumps with speeds as low as a few liters/sec and some as high as thousands of liters/sec. Inlet diameters range from 1 inch to 48 inches.

The lowest pressure a diffusion pump will produce (base pressure) depends on the kind of fluid used (oil or mercury) as well as on the pump.

Construction. A diagram of a typical diffusion pump is shown in Fig. 2.8. The casing A has its upper two-thirds water-cooled to slightly below ambient (room) temperature. This provides a condensing surface for the vapor of the working fluid H which is vaporized in the boiler B by a ring heater E. Alternate methods for vaporizing the fluid are the immersion heater (placed directly in the liquid) and the cartridge heater, which is inserted in a well extending into the boiler area from below. The vapor rises up the chimney C and out the nozzles D. The nozzles direct the flow of vapor outward and downward to the cooled casing wall. Figure 2.9 shows a three-stage diffusion pump. The number of stages varies, but there are generally three or four.

The standard construction material for diffusion pumps is metal, usually mild steel, stainless steel, or aluminum, although many small pumps are made entirely of glass, or have glass casings with a metal chimney.

Operation. The operation of the diffusion pump shown in Fig. 2.8 is as follows: the inlet G of the pump is first attached to the vessel to be evacuated and a mechanical pump is attached to the forearm or outlet F. The pressure in the entire system is then reduced by the mechanical pump to about 50 microns. At this point the diffusion-pump heater E is turned on, heating the fluid in the boiler B. The heated fluid evaporates and produces a rise in pressure in the boiler. This rise in pressure forces the vapor up the chimney C, where it streams out of the nozzles D into the surrounding area of lower pressure. The nozzles deflect the vapor as a jet downward and outward to the cooled casing walls where the vapor condenses. Gas molecules from the vessel enter the pump throat and diffuse through the less dense fringe at the edge of the vapor beam. When a gas molecule has penetrated into the high-density core of the beam, the probability of its

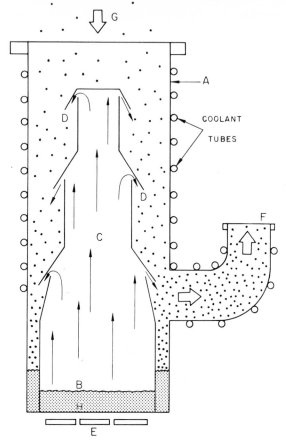

Fig. 2.8. Diffusion pump.

being knocked back toward the inlet is less than the probability of its being carried along with the vapor beam toward the outlet. Thus the predominant direction of molecular travel is away from the inlet and toward the outlet.

In a multistage pump the gas molecules are directed toward the next nozzle, where the action is repeated. Several succeeding stages will compress the low-pressure gas at the inlet to a higher pressure at the outlet, where it is removed to atmosphere by the mechanical pump.

It is apparent from the action of the diffusion pump just described that the gas molecules are being swept from an area of low pressure to an area of higher pressure by the vapor beam. This will continue only as long as the region of higher pressure or "forepressure" does not exceed a critical limit. If this critical pressure is exceeded, the high pressure will rupture the

Fig. 2.9. Cutaway view of a diffusion pump (with cold cap) (National Research Corporation).

"curtain" between the high-pressure area and low-pressure area formed by the vapor beam, and the pump will cease to function. Consequently, it is necessary for a diffusion pump to be "backed" by a mechanical pump capable of maintaining the forepressure below the critical limit. In practice it is customary to select a backing pump that has two or three times the minimum capacity required. This insures that the diffusion pump will not be put out of action due to large "gas bursts" in the system, and will also make allowance for some deterioration of mechanical-pump efficiency during its service. A factor which has considerable effect on the pressure level at which this critical point occurs is the heat input to the boiler of the diffusion pump. If the wattage applied to the boiler is below that recommended by the pump manufacturer, the vapor beam will be slower and less dense than it should be. Also, the critical point will occur at a pressure lower than that for which the pump is rated. A wattage input higher than that recommended, even though it raises the critical pressure, has a distinct disadvantage. The vapor beam, although faster and denser than normal, will aggravate a condition referred to as "backstreaming." Backstreaming is the direct flight of pump-fluid molecules out of the pump inlet and into the vessel. This causes a decrease in net pumping speed, since the pump must now pump out the molecules of pumping fluid which have backstreamed, in addition to pumping the gas originating in the system.

Figure 2.10 gives a typical pumping speed-versus-pressure curve for a diffusion pump.

Pump Fluids. Diffusion pumps use oil or mercury as pump fluid. Although the general configurations of mercury pumps and oil pumps are similar,

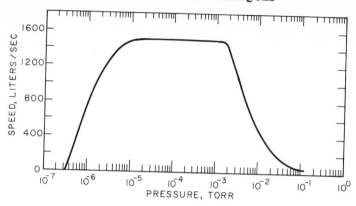

Fig. 2.10. Pump speed vs pressure for a typical diffusion pump.

it is *not* practical to substitute oil in a mercury pump, or vice versa. The choice of pump fluid depends upon the specific application of the pumping system.

Organic vapor-pump fluids (classified collectively as "oils") are available with vapor pressures from 10^{-4} torr to below 10^{-7} torr at room temperature. Oil pumps can thus produce pressures of the order of 10^{-7} torr without the use of refrigerated traps. Also, the temperature of a baffle need be only a few degrees below room temperature.

The organic fluids used in oil diffusion pumps are complex chemical compounds, and as such, are subject to some decomposition even under normal use (this decomposition is accelerated if the normal operating temperature is exceeded or if the oil is exposed to air while hot). In general, decomposition increases the vapor pressure of the pump fluid. Silicone-base oils have been developed that greatly resist this decomposition. They can be exposed to air at operating temperature without disastrous results.

Even under normal operating conditions the gases resulting from the decomposition of organic pump fluids contribute, to some extent, to the pressure in the vessel. Because these decomposition gases have a wide range of vapor pressures, some can be condensed at room temperature, but others may have high vapor pressures even at liquid-nitrogen temperatures.

Mercury is an elemental fluid and will not decompose, regardless of how hot it becomes; thus a mercury pump can be designed to work with a very high forepressure tolerance. Mercury has a rather high vapor pressure (about 1 micron at room temperature) and is relatively easy to trap out of a high-vacuum system with a liquid-nitrogen-cooled trap. Mercury as a pump fluid is useful when hydrocarbon contamination would adversely affect the process. Oil seriously affects the operation of the mercury pump; a trap should be placed in the foreline to prevent the migration of mechanical-pump oil into the mercury boiler.

Precautions must be taken to protect the equipment operator and the working area from mercury vapors, which are highly toxic. Mercury may migrate through the forelines and into the atmosphere; therefore it is necessary that the mechanical pump not be exhausted indoors. It is essential that anyone working with mercury diffusion pumps become familiar with the hazards of mercury vapors.

Difficulties with Diffusion Pumps. Although a diffusion pump has no moving parts, and, therefore, is not subject to mechanical breakdown, there are times when it may refuse to function properly. When a diffusion pump is not operating correctly, there are usually four major causes:

(1) *Exposure of the Hot Pump Fluid to the Atmosphere.* Accidentally letting the pump up to air (i.e., atmospheric pressure) while the pump is hot is by far the most frequent occurrence leading to pump malfunction. The results of this exposure are somewhat different for mercury than for oil. The pumping properties of mercury are not affected by such exposures, although the loss of mercury to the system may cause the pump to malfunction. In the case of oils, severe cracking (breaking down of the oil molecules) and oxidation may occur, depending on the type of oil. (Some silicone fluids are not affected.) Such cracking and oxidation lead to abnormally high base pressures. Also, cracked products will deposit on the jet structure and block the openings. Therefore, after such an exposure the pump and system must be thoroughly cleaned, and the pump charged with new fluid. A safety measure to prevent such an occurrence is to interlock the valve-operating mechanisms so that the diffusion pump cannot be inadvertently let up to air. This is accomplished easily on large systems where all the valves are remotely operated. On small systems, where the valves are manually operated, about the only effective safety device is the mental alertness of the operator.

(2) *Interruption of Coolant Flow.* Diffusion pumps may be cooled by water, air, or mechanical refrigeration systems. Overheating due to interruption of coolant flow decomposes the oil in oil diffusion pumps and causes excessive backstreaming and fluid migration in both oil and mercury diffusion pumps. A standard safety measure is to interlock the coolant flow with the power input. Then an interruption of coolant flow will cut off the power to the pump heater. When the diffusion pump is not operating and is exposed to the atmosphere, the flow of coolant should be stopped, as the cooled pump walls will condense moisture from the air. This condensate will then drain into the pump fluid, causing a large gas load on startup. It is convenient to have an indicator which gives a visual check

of coolant flow. If the indicator is calibrated, it can be used to balance the coolant flow with the heat input for maximum pump performance.

(3) *Interruption of Electrical Power to the Vacuum System.* Interruption of electrical power to the diffusion pump will not cause any great harm to the pump itself; the pump will simply stop and will start again when power is restored. The major difficulty arises from the fact that, in the event of a power failure, the mechanical pump will also cease to function. The mechanical pump does not form a reliable vacuum seal when stopped, and air will enter the diffusion pump through the mechanical pump, causing the same condition as (1). Another difficulty is that the diffusion pump backstreams excessively during the shutdown and start-up necessitated by a power interruption. This leads to the same condition as in (4) below. Both difficulties can be prevented by installing in the foreline a valve that will close automatically whenever power to the system is interrupted (quite frequently the mechanical-pump valve is this type, thus serving two purposes). At the same time as the valve in the foreline is closed, the high-vacuum valve should also be closed, because an unbacked diffusion pump will soon begin to backstream excessively into the vessel.

(4) *Excessively High Forepressure.* If the forepressure (pressure at the outlet of the diffusion pump) exceeds the tolerable limit of the pump, the action of the pump is stopped and the vessel is usually drenched with pump fluid. If the rise in forepressure does not exceed the tolerable limit, the pump suffers considerable loss of speed and an increase in backstreaming. Both situations can be avoided by cutting off the power to the pump heater when the forepressure rises above a predetermined level. This cutoff is usually accomplished by an electrical signal from the forevacuum gage. Several commercial gages are available with such a feature.

Diagnosis of Diffusion Pump Trouble. When the diffusion pump does not operate correctly, it usually exhibits one or more of the following symptoms:

(1) It does not pump at all. This can be caused by:

    (a) not enough oil in the pump,

    (b) no heat to the pump boiler, or

    (c) forepressure above the tolerable limit of the pump.

(2) It has low speed or low gas-handling capacity. This is generally the reult of:

    (a) low heat input to the boiler,

    (b) pressure too high in the foreline, but not above the tolerable limit,

    (c) a leak within the pump itself, or

    (d) displaced or incorrectly assembled jets.

(3) It has an abnormally high base pressure. This is most likely to result from:

(a) not enough pump wall cooling,

(b) heat input too high, or

(c) high vapor-pressure contaminants in the working fluid.

Ejector Pumps. An ejector pump is a vapor pump having a boiler pressure of more than a few torr capable of pumping gas with full efficiency at intake pressures of more than about 20 microns and discharge pressures (forepressures) exceeding about 500 microns.

The ejector pump (illustrated in Fig. 2.11) pumps by drawing gas into a low-pressure area created by the expansion of a beam of vapor. Pump-fluid vapor is forced through a small nozzle and expands rapidly, forming

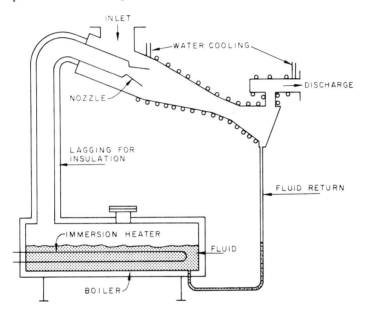

Fig. 2.11. Ejector pump.

a low-pressure area into which system gas is drawn. As with the diffusion pump, there are usually several stages; the process is repeated at each stage.

While the ejector pump and the diffusion pump are similar in that they pump by means of a jet of vapor, they are different in the way thay "catch" the gas molecules. In the diffusion pump, only those molecules that *diffuse* into the pump, in the course of their random motion, are acted on by the vapor, while in the ejector pump, gas is actually *drawn* into the low-pressure area created by expanding vapor. In the diffusion pump the gas entering the pump moves in molecular flow; in the ejector pump it enters in viscous or turbulent flow. Thus the ejector pump is most useful in pressure ranges in which the predominant flow regime is viscous and the diffusion pump in the molecular-flow pressure range. The ejector pump is typically placed between the diffusion pump and the mechanical pump. It provides another stage of pumping and allows the system to handle a larger quantity of gas. The amount of gas anticipated and the required pressure will determine the size necessary. The speeds range from a few liters/sec to thousands of liters/sec; the inlet diameter from a few inches to 30 inches. Pump fluids used are oil (special types), mercury, or water.

Getter Pumping

Getter pumping is one of the pumping methods that does not actually remove gas from the system but puts it "out of action" (i.e., takes it out of the gas phase) by trapping it *within* the vacuum system. It does this by forming chemical compounds with the gas molecules. Some metals, such as molybdenum, zirconium, and titanium, will combine readily with many gases. When these metals are vaporized in a system they combine chemically with the gases in that system. The chemical compounds that are formed are stable and have a much lower vapor pressure than the gas alone. Thus the gas, while not removed from the system, is put into a form in which it contributes very little to the total pressure. This process, called gettering, is an effective pumping action. One of its most common uses is to obtain a final reduction of pressure in electron tubes.

Ion-Getter Pumping

The ion-getter pump combines two pumping methods: gettering (explained in the preceding section) and ionization, which involves giving gas molecules a positive electric charge so that they are attracted to and buried in a surface. There are two types of ion-getter pumps: a "cold-cathode" and a "hot-cathode" pump.

The cold-cathode pump consists of an enclosure which contains a number of anode structures mounted between cathode plates (see Fig. 2.12). A permanent magnet outside the enclosure supplies a magnetic field which is perpendicular to the cathodes. Electrons emitted by the cathodes and attracted to the anode are forced by the magnetic field to move in a helical path, rather than in a straight, or slightly curved line. This greatly extended path length increases the probability that electrons will collide with gas molecules before they strike the anode. The positive ions formed by the collisions are attracted to and strike the cathode. This is "ion pumping." The impact buries the ions in the cathode and knocks cathode-metal atoms from the cathode plates. This process is known as *sputtering*. The sputtered metal deposits on various surfaces in the enclosure. Because the cathode is made from a chemically active metal (usually titanium) it forms stable

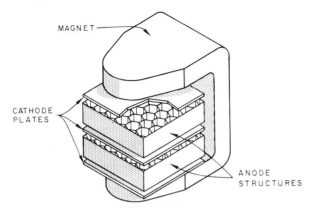

MAGNET

CATHODE
PLATES

ANODE
STRUCTURES

Fig. 2.12. Cold-cathode ion-getter pump.

compounds with the chemically active gases in the pump and removes them from the gaseous state (getter pumping). Inert gases such as argon and helium which will not form compounds with the active metal are pumped by being ionized and attracted to the cathode with sufficient energy to bury them.

The hot-cathode type of ion-getter pump also uses active metal, generally titanium, to form stable compounds with active gases. In this case the active metal is deposited on the pump surfaces by thermal evaporation. Electrons are emitted from a hot-filament cathode and are drawn to a grid structure maintained at a positive voltage. En route they collide with gas molecules to form the positive ions. The ions are driven into the pump walls and covered with evaporated metal.

Since the ion-getter pump uses no pump fluid, the system is not exposed to pump-fluid vapors. This also means that traps (which "trap" pump-fluid vapors) are unnecessary.

Ion-getter pumps are obtainable with speeds from 1 liter/sec to thousands of liters/sec. The smaller pumps are often used as permanent appendages on large electron tubes such as klystrons. The larger pumps (20 liters/sec and up) are constructed by incorporating many cathode-anode assemblies or "cells" into one pump.

The ion-getter pumps are not practical above a pressure of 20 microns. They are most effective below 1×10^{-5} torr and are particularly useful when the presence of pump fluids is objectionable.

Adsorption Pumping

Some materials (charcoal, for instance) have a great capacity for adsorbing* gas and may be used as "pumps" in a vacuum system. The adsorbing

*Adsorption is the adhesion of gas molecules to the surface of a material.

material is activated by pumping on it as it is heated until most of the gases already adsorbed are released. The material is then cooled under vacuum. It is then ready to adsorb gases in a vacuum vessel. Cooling the adsorber further with liquid nitrogen increases the amount of gas that can be adsorbed.

In the same category with charcoal are the zeolites, often called the "molecular sieves." This material has the ability to take in gases and hold them until they are driven out by heat.

Adsorption pumping may be used alone or in conjunction with an ion-getter or other pump.

BAFFLES

All vapor pumps backstream during operation. This backstreaming exposes the vessel and everything in it to contamination by pump fluid. It also represents a continuous loss of pump fluid from the boiler that would ultimately stop the operation of the pump if it were allowed to continue. Backstreaming can be kept under control with a baffle.

A baffle (see Fig. 2.13) is a system of cooled surfaces placed near the inlet of a pump to condense backstreaming vapor and *return it to the pump.* *

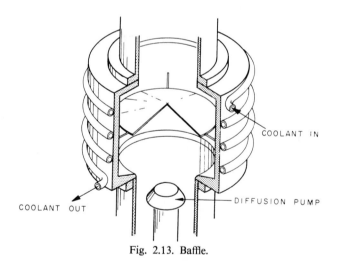

Fig. 2.13. Baffle.

The fluid usually returns by a simple gravity drain. The returning fluid must not be allowed to drip on hot nozzle parts, as it would re-evaporate. Re-evaporation would add to the backstreaming and also rob heat from

*This point is emphasized to make clear the difference between a baffle, which returns fluid to the pump, and a trap, which does not.

the nozzle parts, which would interfere with the pump's effectiveness. In cases where the baffle does drain on the pump nozzles, a wire can be attached from the baffle to the pump wall, providing a path for the liquid to flow to the pump wall, down it, and back to the boiler.

The temperature of the surface of the baffle should be above the freezing point of the condensed pump fluid. If the fluid were to freeze, the loss of pump fluid might be as severe as with no baffle at all. The cooled surfaces of the baffle are arranged to intercept all optical (line-of-sight) paths between the top, or first, jet and the vacuum vessel with a minimum loss of baffle conductance.

Baffles are also placed in the outlet of the diffusion pump to reduce loss of pump fluid.

TRAPS

A trap is a device used to reduce the partial pressure of gases and vapors in a vacuum system. Trapping surfaces are placed appropriately in vacuum systems and act as pumps for those gaseous molecules which, when they strike the trap surface, are held there. Two main types of trap are used, the refrigerated trap and the adsorption trap.

Refrigerated Traps

The refrigerated trap is an array of cooled surfaces that is placed in the vessel or in the passage between the baffle and the vessel. When placed in the vessel it is called a "cold thimble" and when placed in a vacuum line, an "inline trap."

Cold Thimble. The refrigerated cold thimble is a container of refrigerant that is suspended in a vacuum vessel (see Fig. 2.14a). The surface exposed to the vacuum will be at very nearly the same temperature as the boiling refrigerant. The cold surfaces will condense molecules in the vapor phase and efficiently trap those vapors which have a vapor pressure negligibly small at the temperature of the refrigerant.

The construction material for a cold thimble is usually stainless steel or glass. The filling neck of the thimble is the support, and a material of low thermal conductivity must be used to avoid boiling the refrigerant off too rapidly.

Liquid nitrogen is the refrigerant used most extensively. Where a significant portion of the gas to be removed is condensible at boiling liquid-nitrogen temperature, a cold thimble will add greatly to the speed of the system. For water vapor, the most common condensible, the speed is 95 liters/sec per square inch of exposed surface, neglecting the effect of the conductance path to the cold surface. Its use is inconvenient, however,

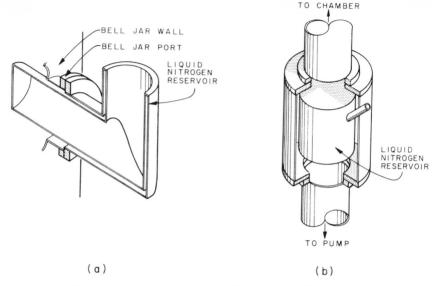

Fig. 2.14. Refrigerated traps. (a) Cold thimble. (b) Inline trap.

because the condensate must be held on the surface of the trap until the operation is completed; then, when the vessel is brought up to atmospheric pressure, the trap must be taken out, cleaned, and replaced.

Inline Traps. *High-Vacuum (Inline) Traps.* Although the vapor-pump inlet baffle will condense the vapors that backstream from the pump, the condensate will have a high vapor pressure, since, as stated above, the baffle temperature cannot be very cold or the pump fluid freezes. The inline trap (see Fig. 2.14b) greatly reduces the partial pressure of the vapor by recondensing it and reducing its temperature before it reaches the vessel. The function of the inline trap is to hold to a negligible value the amount of vapor which reaches the vessel from the pump. To this end, many inline traps are provided with "anticreep" barriers which prevent pump fluids from creeping past the trap along the warm outer walls.

As the gases from the vessel must go through the inline trap, its conductance should be compatible with the pump speed.

The trap housing is usually made of stainless steel (glass in small systems). The cold surfaces are frequently copper (for maintaining a low thermal gradient). The trap may have a reservoir within the vacuum equipped with fins, or it may have fins cooled by a tube through which the refrigerant is circulated. The surface of these fins is arranged so that a molecule from any possible direction must hit a cold surface at least once to pass through the trap.

Forevacuum Traps. It is possible for oil from the mechanical pump to migrate into the forevacuum lines unless preventive measures are taken. During pumpdown of the vessel the gas flow in the lines is viscous, and oil molecules will not usually move more than a few mean free paths into the line. However, as the pressure is reduced and molecular flow conditions are established, the vapors of oil exposed on the inlet side of the mechanical pump can travel to the forearm of the diffusion pump. The mechanical-pump oil condenses at the diffusion-pump exhaust baffle and drains into the diffusion-pump boiler. This will affect the operation of the diffusion pump adversely, as mechanical-pump oil decomposes readily at diffusion pump-boiler temperature, and has a much higher vapor pressure at this temperature than do diffusion-pump fluids. Mercury diffusion pumps are especially sensitive to oil contamination. The forevacuum trap prevents this situation from occurring.

The forevacuum trap also provides protection to the mechanical pump. Vapors from the system are condensed on the trap before they can combine with the mechanical-pump oil. This extends the service time of the mechanical pump and improves its condition during this time.

Construction details are similar to those of the high-vacuum inline trap, except that anticreep barriers are rarely used.

Sorption Traps

The sorption trap contains a sorbent material such as artificial zeolite, activated alumina, or activated charcoal. While it may be used at room temperature, a further reduction in partial pressure of adsorbable gas can be accomplished by cooling it to liquid-nitrogen temperature. When used as an appendage on the vessel (similar in function to the cold thimble) it is usually called a sorption pump. When placed in the vacuum line, it is called an inline trap.

Before use, the trap must be baked in place at high temperature ($300-450°$ C) for 8 to 24 hours while being pumped on by the diffusion pump in order to activate the sorbent material. Saturation of the trap is indicated by a rise in the base pressure in the vessel. The trap can be reconditioned after saturation by repeating the initial bakeout procedure.

The trap housing is usually made of stainless steel (or glass in small systems). The walls are lined with sorbent material held in place with a stainless steel screen. A blocking plate is suspended in the center of the trap housing by heavy supports of high thermal conductivity to prevent a large thermal gradient in the sorbent material.

An anticreep barrier can be provided by appropriate placement of the sorbent material.

VACUUM GAGES

Vacuum gages can be either absolute or indirect. An absolute gage is one whose calibration can be determined from its geometry and which reads accurately for all gases. Indirect gages measure characteristics of gases that are related to pressure, the most common being thermal conductivity and ionization. Indirect gages must be calibrated with an absolute gage before they can measure pressure quantitatively. Also, since pressure-related characteristics depend on the kind of gas being measured, a true indication of pressure can be had only if the composition of the gas in the vessel is known. Most gages of this type are calibrated for nitrogen at 20° C.

An important problem for the vacuum technician is the selection of the proper pressure gage in a given situation. The correct choice depends on a knowledge of the working principles of the gage, the range of pressures it can measure, and its accuracy in that range. The ranges of some gages are given in Fig. 2.15. Several types of mechanical, thermal-conductivity, and ionization gages will be discussed here.

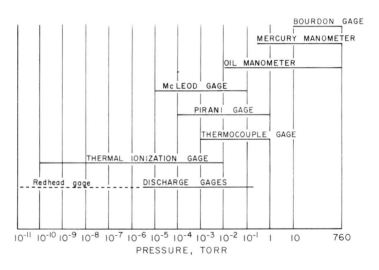

Fig. 2.15. Vacuum-gage ranges.

Mechanical Gages

Bourdon Gage. The Bourdon gage consists of a tube, with an elliptical cross section, formed in an arc; the tube is rigidly fixed at one end and closed at the other end. When the pressure in the tube increases, the radius of the arc increases; that is, the tube tries to straighten out. When the pressure decreases, the radius decreases. Thus, the free end of the tube moves in response to a change in pressure. A system of levers and gears attached to the free end operates a pointer which moves over a calibrated scale.

The standard form of this gage is relatively inaccurate. However, it is useful in the rough-vacuum range from 760 torr to about 10 torr, before more sensitive gages are needed.

Liquid-level Gages. *The Mercury Barometer.* All liquid-level gages embody the principle of the mercury barometer, invented by Torricelli in 1643. It consists of a glass tube, closed at one end, which is filled with mercury and then inverted in a dish of mercury (see Fig. 2.16). The level of the mercury in the tube will fall until the pressure due to the height of the

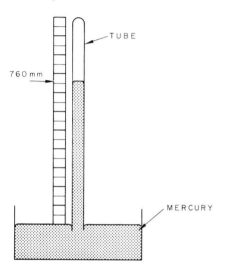

Fig. 2.16. Mercury barometer.

column in the tube is equal to the pressure (usually atmospheric) on the surface of the mercury in the dish. The pressure on the surface of the mercury in the dish can be read directly from the height of the column in the tube in "millimeters of mercury." Atmospheric pressure is 760 millimeters of mercury.

U-tube Gage. The U-tube gage consists of a glass U-tube (see Fig. 2.17) partially filled with a liquid, usually mercury. When both arms are exposed to the same pressure, the two columns of mercury will be of equal height. If the pressure on either arm is changed, a difference in column height will result, and the difference in pressure can be read directly in millimeters of mercury.

In operation, one arm of the U-tube is connected to the pressure to be measured, while the pressure above the other arm is held at some fixed

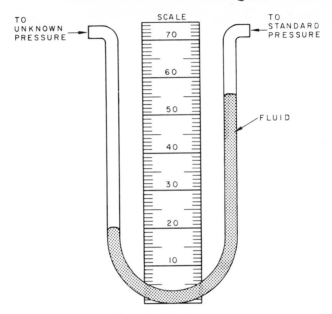

Fig. 2.17. U-tube gage.

reference value. Usually the pressure above the reference arm is held very low compared to the pressure to be measured. In this way the reference pressure can be considered as zero pressure, and the unknown pressure can be directly read in millimeters of mercury.

The accuracy of the gage is determined by how closely the difference in height of the two arms can be measured. The sensitivity of the gage depends on the density of the fluid used.

McLeod Gage. The McLeod gage uses the principle of Boyle's law to amplify and measure pressures that are too small to be measured with a U-tube gage. To do this, a sample of gas from the system is isolated and reduced in volume by a known amount. By Boyle's law, this reduction in volume causes a proportional increase in the pressure of the gas. The increased pressure will now produce a readable difference in column height. For example, if a volume of 200 cm³ of gas at an unknown pressure is reduced in volume to 0.2 cm³, the pressure will increase one thousand times (provided the temperature is kept constant). If this increased pressure gives a manometer reading of 10 torr, the unknown pressure of the sample in its original state must have been 1/1000th of 10 torr, or 0.01 torr.

One form of the McLeod gage is shown in Fig. 2.18a. The bulb V is the region in which the gas sample from the vacuum system is isolated. This bulb communicates with the vacuum system through the tube C. An auxil-

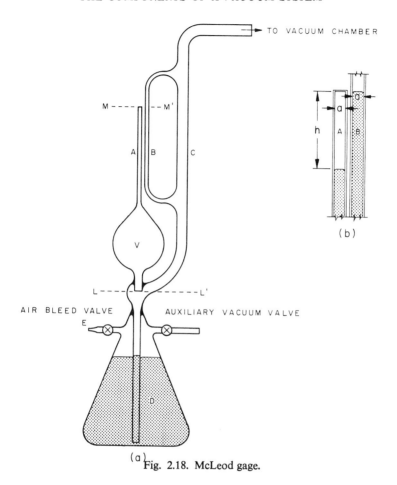

Fig. 2.18. McLeod gage.

iary vacuum supplied to the mercury reservoir *D* provides the means for raising and lowering the mercury level in the gage during a pressure measurement. The capillaries *A* and *B*, in which the manometer readings are taken, have equal cross-sectional areas, *a*.

In order to measure the pressure in a vacuum system (or, more precisely, the pressure in bulb *V*, which communicates with the vacuum system), air is admitted to *D* through *E* to raise the mercury in the tube *C*. As the surface of the mercury reaches the level *LL'*, the volume in *V* is isolated from the remainder of the system and is subsequently compressed into capillary *A* as the mercury continues to rise. The mercury is raised to a height *MM'* in capillary *B*, which is level with the top of capillary *A*. (Figure 2.18b shows this in detail.) The mercury level in capillary *A* will be a distance, h, below the level in capillary B. This distance, h, in mm Hg, measures the pressure of the compressed sample of gas in capillary A. The volume of this trapped sample will be equal to the product of the cross-sectional area, a, and the height, h. The original volume, V, of gas at the original pressure P has thus been reduced to a volume ah at a pressure of h mm Hg, so that, by Boyle's law,

$$PV = h(ah) = ah^2, \quad \text{or}$$

$$P = ah^2/V.$$

The values of V and a are constant for each individual gage, and are determined by measurements taken at the time the gage is made. With both V and a constant, the pressure P is proportional to h^2.

Extreme care must be taken not to admit gas into the vacuum while a sample is being read. A sudden pressure rise may force the mercury into the capillary with sufficient force to shatter it, endangering the operator. In any event, a plastic shield should be placed over the capillary.

Some McLeod gages can be used to measure pressures down to 10^{-5} torr, if the mercury and the glass are kept scrupulously clean. However, because of the compression by which it operates, only the pressure of those gases that do not condense with such an increase in pressure can be measured, since the volume of the condensed liquid is negligibly small compared to its volume as a gas.

The McLeod gage is a bulky and fragile instrument, and, since it cannot be read continuously, it is seldom used on a vacuum system. Its major use is in the calibration of other forms of vacuum gages. When used in this way, it is important to take into account the fact that it does not measure pressures of condensable gases.

Thermal Conductivity Gages

Below 1 torr a change in the pressure of a gas will cause a change in its thermal conductivity (the ability of a gas to conduct heat). Thus a heated object suspended in a vessel at a pressure below 1 torr will lose heat by gas conduction at a rate determined by the vessel pressure. If the suspended object is heated by a fixed power source, then its temperature will be determined by thermal losses and therefore will depend on the vessel pressure. This is the principle on which the thermal-conductivity gage is based.

The "heated object" is usually a wire filament suspended in a metal or glass tube that can be attached to the vessel whose pressure is to be measured. The constant power input is provided by a power supply unit that also contains the meter on which the wire temperature is registered. The meter can usually be read directly in units of pressure.

Thermal-conductivity gages measure the total pressure in a system; that is, they will measure the pressure of vapors as well as the pressure of permanent gases. They will read continuously and remotely. The circuitry required is not complex; it is relatively simple to provide a control signal from it to other circuits. The gage tube elements are not usually harmed by operation at atmospheric pressure for short periods, although the calibration will change if the wire surface becomes coated with charred oil or any similar substance.

Because the characteristics of all gases differ, the response of a thermal-conductivity gage will vary for each. Therefore, to be accurate, the gage must be calibrated for the gas to be measured with a primary or absolute gage such as a McLeod gage. Unless specified otherwise, commercial thermal-conductivity gages are calibrated at the factory with nitrogen.

The two types of thermal-conductivity gages, the Pirani gage and the thermocouple gage, differ mainly in the way the wire temperature is measured.

Pirani Gage. The Pirani gage utilizes the change in electrical resistance of a wire with temperature. The filament's resistance is measured with a Wheatstone bridge network which also supplies the power to heat the

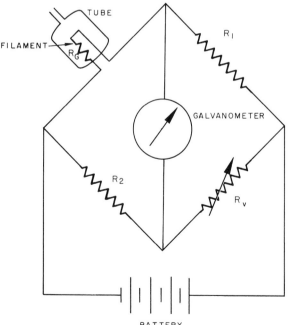

Fig. 2.19. Pirani gage.

filament. A simple form of the circuit is shown in Fig. 2.19. The wire filament of the gage (R_G) forms one arm of the bridge. Two of the arms (R_1 and R_2) have a fixed resistance close to that of the filament. The resistance of the fourth arm (R_v) is variable, which allows the bridge to be balanced. (The bridge is balanced when the galvanometer reads zero current.) Balancing of the bridge is done with the gage tube at a very low pressure (a pressure lower than the gage limit). Any increase in pressure causes the wire temperature, and also its resistance, to change. This change unbalances the bridge, causing a current through the galvanometer and registering a pressure reading on the dial. The operating range of most Pirani gages is from 2 torr to 1×10^{-3} torr.

Thermocouple Gage. In the thermocouple gage (Fig. 2.20), the filament temperature is measured by a thermocouple junction mounted in close thermal contact with the wire surface. The output wattage of the thermo-

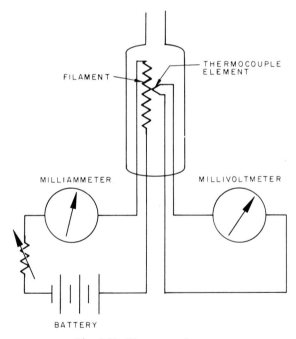

Fig. 2.20. Thermocouple gage.

couple junction changes with a change in wire temperature, thus driving a meter that is scaled in pressure units. The heater current is kept constant, and the thermal voltage developed by the junction produces a current in the thermocouple circuit that is read by a milliammeter. The cold junction is at the temperature of the gage tube. The range of this gage lies between 1 torr and 1×10^{-3} torr.

Ionization Gages

When fast-moving electrons pass through a gas they can knock some outer electrons off the gas molecules. The remaining part of the molecule then has a positive charge and is called an ion; the process is called ionization by bombardment. For a constant current of electrons at a given velocity, the rate at which positive ions are formed will be proportional to the concentration of gas molecules. This provides a means for measuring the gas pressure, since molecular concentration is proportional to pressure — assuming the temperature of the gas remains constant. The ionization efficiency varies with the kind of gas, so any gage that uses the rate of ionization to measure gas pressure must be calibrated for the gas with which it is to be used. In general, all ionization gages indicate pressure in this way. The difference between the various types is mainly in the way electrons are provided and in the way ion formation is measured. (See Figs. 2.21 to 2.24.)

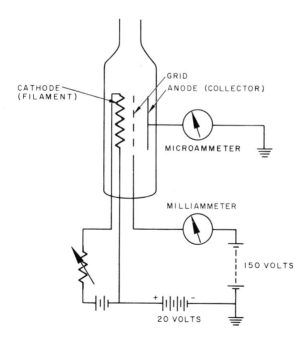

Fig. 2.21. Thermionic ionization gage.

Thermionic Ionization Gage. Sometimes called a hot-cathode ionization gage, this gage uses the geometry of a simple triode vacuum tube (cathode, grid, and anode), as shown in Fig. 2.21. The cathode is a filament heated to electron-emission temperature by about 10 volts at 3 to 4 amperes. Voltage on the grid is maintained at a fixed value of some 100 or 200 volts positive with respect to the cathode. The electrons emitted from the filament are drawn toward the grid by this voltage. Most of the electrons will not strike the grid on the first pass, but will oscillate around it several times before being collected. This results in a high concentration of electrons between grid and anode, so efficient use of electrons is provided in this

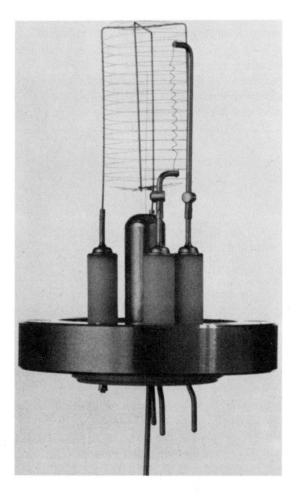

Fig. 2.22. Varian nude ionization gage.

space. Positive ions are attracted to and collected by the anode (in the ionization gage this is not truly an anode but a *collector*). The ion collector is maintained at a fixed value of from 20 to 30 volts negative with respect to the cathode. A microammeter placed in this collector circuit will measure the current produced by the collected ions, and therefore the pressure. The meter is usually graduated in units of pressure. There are several disadvantages in this type of gage, most of which relate to the hot cathode.

The life of the filament is moderately short, and with careless handling it becomes extremely short. Some filaments burn out if exposed to the atmosphere while hot. Operating for extended periods above 1×10^{-3} torr will also reduce the life considerably. The filament is eroded rapidly by the presence of water vapor. Some gages incorporate a nonburnout type of filament reputed to have a considerably longer life than standard filaments. Most filaments operating at high vacuum will last for many months.

The circuitry of the ionization gage is moderately complex, since a power supply for a thermionic ionization gage must provide a variable source of voltage for the filament, fixed voltages for grid and collector, a means of regulating and reading emission current, and a means of reading positive-ion current. This complexity naturally leads to some maintenance difficulty. In spite of these limitations, the thermionic ionization gage is the most widely used instrument for measuring low pressures. With conventional gage construction, as described above, maximum pressure limit is 1×10^{-2} torr; the lower limit is 1×10^{-7} torr. This lower limit is due to its design. An inverted gage geometry has moved this lower limit down to 1×10^{-10} torr.

Fig. 2.23. Consolidated Vacuum Corporation ionization gage.

In this gage the filament is mounted outside the grid; the collector is a wire mounted inside the grid.

Cold-Cathode Ionization Gage. This gage (also called a Philips gage, Penning gage, or "pig") is based on the glow discharge which occurs in gas at low pressures in the presence of a magnetic field. The geometry of the gage is quite simple. It consists of two cathode plates parallel to each other, with a ring-shaped anode in the space between them, as shown in Fig. 2.24. A direct-current voltage of about 2000 volts is supplied between cathodes and anode, and a magnetic field of approximately 400 gauss is normal to

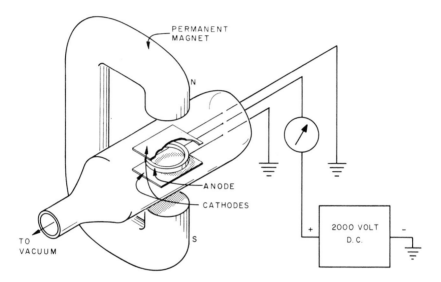

Fig. 2.24 Cold-cathode ionization gage.

the cathode surfaces. Electrons which originate in one or the other of the cathodes do not go directly to the anode because of the magnetic field; instead, they travel back and forth in helical paths between cathodes many times before striking the anode. The increased path length provides a high probability of ionization per electron, even at low gas pressures, where a glow discharge does not normally occur. The positive ions formed are attracted to the cathodes. The total discharge current, which is the sum of the positive-ion current to the cathodes and the electron current from the cathodes, is used to measure the pressure.

This gage will not measure pressures as low as the hot-cathode type; the lower limit is about 1×10^{-5} torr. Its upper limit, however, is much higher — about 300 microns. Pressure measurements are not as accurate as with the hot-cathode gage. The calibration curve relating discharge current to pressure has breaks in it which are unpredictable and not fully understood. The gage has a high pumping speed (it is a form of ion pump) leading to a pressure differential between the gage tube and the system proper. Difficulty is sometimes encountered in starting the gage at low pressures. The operating potential (2000 volts) of this gage is quite high; proper precautions should be observed by the user. There are many advantageous features of the Philips ionization gage, however. It will not burn out if it is operated at atmospheric pressure (although it will become exceedingly "dirty" if operated for extended periods at pressures above one micron). It is relatively easy to clean, resistant to damage by physical shock, and relatively inexpensive. The control circuit is quite simple, and the construction of the gage tube itself is elementary.

VACUUM MEASUREMENTS

Some general considerations should be taken into account in connection with vacuum measurements. For instance, the position of a gage in a vacuum system is quite important. A comparison can be made between this situation and that of the location of a thermometer in a heated room. If the thermometer is close to the source of heat, the indicated temperature will be high, and vice versa. If an indication of the average temperature is sought, some thought as to the location of the thermometer is necessary. So it is with the pressure gage. If the gage is close to the pump, under certain conditions (a dynamic vacuum system, for instance) the pressure indication will be low; if it is remote, the indication will be high. Again, some thought must be given to the best location of the gage to give a reading of the pressure in the area of interest. The conductance of the tube connecting the gage to the system also has a definite effect. If the conductance of this tube is low, for example, and the gage has pumping capabilities of its own, the pressure in the gage will be lower than that in the system. If a gage has a tendency to outgas excessively, the pressure in the gage will be higher than that in the system.

VALVES

All vacuum systems require valves. Valves control the rate and direction of flow and isolate components. Many different types are used, and most vacuum systems contain more than one. Frequently a particular type of valve is used to perform quite different functions in the same system.

When dynamic vacuum systems were being developed, the valves used were generally modifications of standard fluid-control valves. Nowadays, there are many vacuum equipment manufacturers with a complete line of valves designed specifically for vacuum service.

Before describing vacuum valves, it will be helpful to list the parts of a valve (see Fig. 2.25):

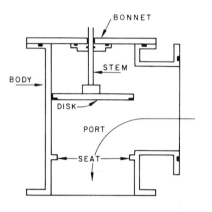

Fig. 2.25. Valve nomenclature — a fabricated angle valve.

The *body* is the "housing" of the valve.

The *port* is the opening within the valve body through which the gases flow in going from inlet to outlet.

The *seat* is the section of the valve surrounding the port against which the seal is made.

The *disk* is the part of the valve that is pressed against the seat and stops the flow.

The *stem* is the mechanism by which the disk is opened and closed.

The *bonnet* provides the seal and support for the stem.

A vacuum valve must be leak-tight across the seat, along the stem seal, and across the bonnet seal. It must safely withstand an external pressure of 14.7 psi. The sealing material used must be compatible with the total pressure and temperature expected in the region in which the valve is to be used.

Valve Types

Gate Valve. In the gate valve (sometimes called the slide valve), the disk moves back into a lateral extension of the body in a plane perpendicular to the direction of gas flow (see Fig. 2.26). The valve has a very short flow path and therefore a high conductance. For this reason it is used extensively as an isolation valve on the inlet side of the diffusion pump. In some gate valves the stem moves the disk by rotary motion, in others by reciprocating (back-and-forth) motion. Most stem seals are elastomers, although a bellows-sealed rotary motion has been used. A hand-operated gate valve is shown in Fig. 2.27.

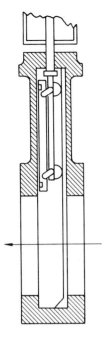

Fig. 2.26. Gate valve. The "gate" disk moves down to make the seal.

Fig. 2.27. A hand-operated gate valve (Consolidated Vacuum Corp.)

Some gate valves have a bonnet and can be disassembled by withdrawing the disk and stem without removing the valve from the line; others have no bonnet but are split along the centerline and must be removed from the line to be disassembled. In either case the seat is normally an *elastomer*.

Sizes (port opening diameters) range from less than 1 inch to over 30 inches. Gate valves capable of being baked at 450° C have been made; these valves employ metal seals.

Angle Valve. The inlet and outlet of the angle valve are usually perpendicular to each other (see Fig. 2.28; Fig. 2.25 shows a fabricated angle valve). The port is on a parallel plane with one or the other. The stem

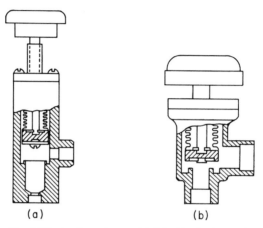

(a)   (b)

Fig. 2.28. Angle valves. (a) Machined from bar stock. (b) Cast.

carries the disk perpendicular to the port. Sizes up to about 2 inches are machined from solid stock or are castings or forgings. Larger sizes (from 3 inches to over 30 inches) are fabricated from rolled plate, either mild steel, stainless steel, or aluminum. Most angle valves have a bonnet gasketed to the body with metal or elastomer seals. The stem seal on small valves is most often a metal bellows, but O rings are also used. Larger valves, because of their greater stem travel, seldom use metal bellows as stem seals.

These valves can usually be disassembled (for cleaning or repair) without removing them from the line.

Poppet Valve. (See Fig. 2.29.) In the vacuum version of the poppet valve, the inlet and outlet are parallel and at opposite ends of the body. The port is usually at the inlet. When the valve is opened the stem lifts the disk into an enlarged portion of the body. The enlargement of the body

TO VESSEL

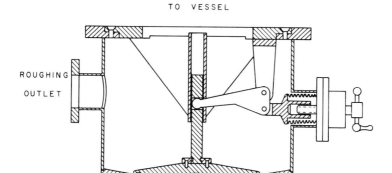

ROUGHING
OUTLET

TO DIFFUSION PUMP

Fig. 2.29. Poppet valve.

provides conductance.. The disk thus forms an obstruction in the line-of-sight path through the valve and may act as a baffle. These valves as used in vacuum service are almost exclusively high-vacuum isolation valves and are referred to as baffle valves.

Stem seals are usually bellows, and the bonnet and disk seals are usually elastomer.

Ball Valve. The ball valve (see Fig. 2.30) differs from the usual vacuum valve in that it does not have a disk. The heart of the valve is a ball; a hole through the ball forms the port. The ball rotates in specially shaped

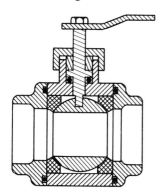

Fig. 2.30. Ball valve (shown in open position).

plastic seat seals. When the valve is in the open position the hole in the ball is lined up with inlet and outlet, allowing free flow. Turning the ball throttles flow, until at 90° the flow is stopped. The ball is turned by the stem, which is seated in a slot cut out in the ball. The stem is usually sealed by O rings. The ball valve is usually made of stainless steel, mild steel, aluminum, or brass.

It should be pointed out that the ball valve is simply turned to open, and turned to close. If it does not seal in the closed position, additional pressure cannot be applied to improve the seal. It will not seal if grit or chips score the surface of the ball.

Needle Valve. Needle valves (see Fig. 2.31) are generally quite small, seldom over ¼ inch. Most frequently the seal between the needle and port is metal-to-metal. They are used mainly to control the flow rate closely.

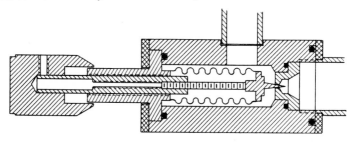

Fig. 2.31. Needle valve.

Stem seals are predominantly metal bellows, but O rings are also used. Needle valves are made of stainless steel or brass.

CONNECTING LINES

Vacuum lines can be made of metal, glass, plastic, or rubber; the choice of material is based on the type of vacuum system under consideration and the location of the line in the system.

The high-vacuum lines in an ultrahigh vacuum system, for instance, should have smooth internal surfaces to facilitate cleaning. Also, in some cases these lines must withstand bakeout* temperatures of over 400° C. The vapor pressure of the line material should be small compared to the total system pressure at bakeout temperatures; for instance, the vapor pressure of the zinc in brass at 400° C is 0.2 micron, which is much too high. Glass pipe is acceptable, but satisfactory glass-to-metal seals that withstand bakeout are often difficult to achieve. Glass tubing is acceptable and can be joined by standard glass-working techniques. Connecting lines made of metal tubing are best joined by welding, but where it is necessary high

*Bakeout is, literally, baking parts of the system at temperatures from 300–400° C to facilitate degassing (the pumping out of adsorbed gas).

melting-point solders with low vapor pressure are acceptable. The use of demountable joints is avoided wherever possible. When their use is unavoidable, flanges designed to provide very high compressive forces are used with metal gaskets. A sketch of such a joint is shown in Fig. 2.32.

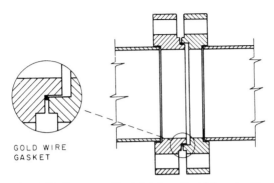

GOLD WIRE
GASKET

Fig. 2.32. Demountable joint for ultrahigh vacuum.

Almost without exception the metal used for lines in ultrahigh vacuum systems is a 300-series stainless steel. The gaskets are usually copper, copper-nickel, gold, or aluminum.

A wider choice of materials and joining methods is allowed for the connecting lines in a high-vacuum system that is not to be baked. Joining techniques are relatively unlimited, except where the presence of some

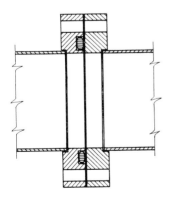

Fig. 2.33. Demountable joint for high vacuum.

joining materials may be detrimental to the pressure or the process to be conducted. Figure 2.33 shows a sketch of a typical demountable joint for metal tubing. This joint uses machined flanges with rubber O rings.

PORTS, LEAD-INS, AND MOTION SEALS

Conducting a process within a vacuum requires access through the wall of the vacuum vessel. Ports are required to set the process up, to change it, or to watch it. Electricity, coolant, and a means of mechanical motion frequently have to be introduced into the vessel. Whenever the wall of the vacuum system is penetrated to provide these requirements, a vacuum seal is necessary. The method of making this seal depends on the access required and the type of vacuum system on which it is to be installed.

Ports

Ports vary in size; some are large enough to look through, and others big enough to walk through. For high-vacuum service the method of sealing is usually by elastomer gaskets having a round, square, or rectangular cross section. For ports less than 36 inches in circumference (or perimeter), standard molded O rings can be used. For those larger than this, a similar type of ring is made up from a length of extruded elastomer equal to the circumference or perimeter of the port, with the ends vulcanized or cemented together. A groove machined into the cover plate or the flange of the port provides a method for holding the gasket in place. Where it is impossible to provide a groove to hold the gasket, a ring-shaped gasket molded in an L-shaped cross section is available for port diameters up to 24 inches. This type of gasket is also available in extruded lengths. A method of holding gaskets in place without using grooves is to secure metal strips around the port opening on the surface of the flange or port. The thickness of the strips should be about 70% of the gasket thickness, to provide adequate compression. The strip need be only wide enough to prevent the gasket from being drawn into the vacuum.

For ultrahigh vacuum service the copper and copper-nickel pinch gasket, gold and aluminum wire seals, aluminum foil, and welded flanges are used. A relatively new material, "Viton," which has a low vapor pressure, can withstand temperatures up to 250° C without disassociation; it resembles rubber in other physical characteristics, and was developed for use in less demanding situations. (It is advisable not to exceed 150° C to prevent set and sticking.) "Viton" is a fluorocarbon elastomer and can be obtained in molded O rings, sheet stock, or extruded shapes. Joint design is similar to that for standard rubber gaskets. The amount of gasket exposed to the vacuum is kept as small as possible.

Viewing ports can be made up as glass-to-metal seals, with the metal portion of the seal then welded or brazed to the system wall or to a metal gasket flange. Some success has been achieved by using flat "Pyrex" or quartz disks and a copper- or gold-wire gasket. It is, of course, possible to use a fluorocarbon O ring in the same general manner as on the ports for high-vacuum service.

Electric Lead-ins

Electric leads require insulation as well as a vacuum-tight seal. Therefore, two seals must be made: one between the conductor and the insulator, and one between the insulator and the vacuum wall. For high-vacuum service a seal in both places is most often made with gaskets, usually O rings. Several insulating materials can be used, such as "Lucite," "Micarta," or a ceramic. Selection is based on the properties of the material as they affect the vacuum. Ceramic insulators, while difficult to fabricate, have the best vacuum characteristics. Insulated seals have been made by molding a plastic, such as one of the epoxies, over a conductor. If an O-ring flange is included in the mold, a complete insulated seal assembly is possible.

For ultrahigh vacuum service the insulator of an electric lead-in is almost always glass, quartz, or ceramic. The seal between the conductor and the insulator in the case of glass or quartz is made by glass-working techniques. The ceramics must be metallized, then brazed to the conductor. Between insulator and vacuum wall the same techniques are sometimes used. However, electric leads may have to be changed frequently, so the usual approach is to seal the insulator to a metal gasket flange instead. Several companies manufacture electric lead-ins of this type for ultrahigh-vacuum service.

Coolant Lead-ins

When only moderately low coolant temperatures are anticipated (not below $-30°$ C), coolant lines can be brazed or welded into an O-ring flange for high vacuum, or a metal gasket flange for ultrahigh vacuum. When very low coolant temperatures are to be used, the flange is designed to offer a minimum heat leak to the coolant lines.

Motion Seals

When it is necessary to manipulate a mechanism in a vacuum, it is sometimes possible to place the means of manipulation within the vacuum; for example, small solenoids or electric motors may be installed in the vessel. It is also possible to use a magnetic coupling through a thin nonmagnetic vacuum wall. In each case there are definite limitations and disadvantages — outgassing or overheating in the former, limited torque in the latter. Usually it is necessary to generate the motive power outside the vacuum and transmit it through the vacuum wall via a vacuum-tight seal.

Wilson Seals. For high-vacuum service, two adequate methods for sealing between a vacuum wall and a moving shaft are the Wilson seal and the

chevron seal. In the former, shown in Fig. 2.34, the seal is made by a
rubber disk having a hole in its center. The hole is made smaller than the
shaft diameter; one or two disks may be used. One disk is actually sufficient

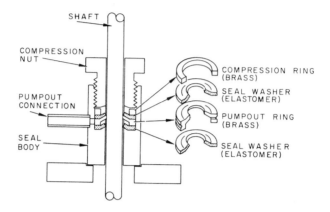

Fig. 2.34. Wilson seal.

to make the seal; the second provides a pump-out space between the disks,
which can be used to detect or reduce leakage through the seal. Satisfactory
results with the Wilson seal require that the shaft have a smooth surface,
that the hole in the gasket disk have smooth well-defined edges, and that
the gaskets and shaft be sufficiently lubricated. The combination of atmospheric pressure and the elastic strength of the rubber provide the only
sealing force on the shaft. Compression by the nut serves only to effect
a seal between the gasket and the body; it has no effect on the gasket-to-

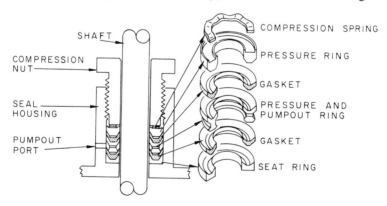

Fig. 2.35. Chevron seal.

shaft seal. Too much compression on the nut merely deforms the rubber gasket excessively, with the possibility of seal failure.

Chevron Seals. The chevron seal, shown in Fig. 2.35, is similar to the Wilson seal. The major difference is in the gasket. Where the Wilson-seal gasket is a ring with a rectangular cross section, the chevron-seal gasket is a ring with a V cross section, with the point of the V placed towards the vacuum. As the nut is tightened, metal rings spread the sides of the V to press the gasket edges tightly against both the body of the seal and the shaft. In contrast to the Wilson seal, tightening the chevron seal does affect the shaft seal. Gaskets are usually made of rubber or "Teflon."

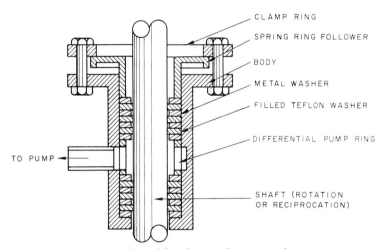

Fig. 2.36. Seal for high-speed rotary motion.

Either the Wilson or the chevron seal will provide a seal on a shaft rotating at moderate speed (up to about 100 rpm). They will also seal a reciprocating shaft. However, the shaft will carry a film of air into the vacuum each time it enters, unless two seals spaced a stroke length apart are used with an auxiliary vacuum chamber between them.

Many special shaft seals have been developed using the O-ring asketg, but they are too numerous to describe. All vary according to the ingenuity of the designer. The sealing pressure is provided by the dimensions of the retaining groove, as in a hydraulic cylinder, or by an adjustable compressive force, as provided by a compression nut.

High-speed Seals. A seal capable of higher rotational speed (about 2000 rpm) that is satisfactory for many ultrahigh vacuum applications is shown in Fig. 2.36. This seal is made by alternating filled-"Teflon" washers

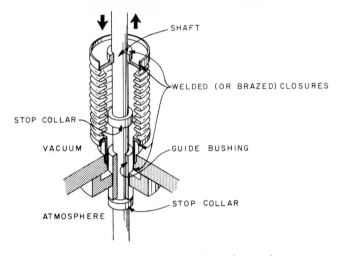

Fig. 2.37. Bellows seal for reciprocating motion.

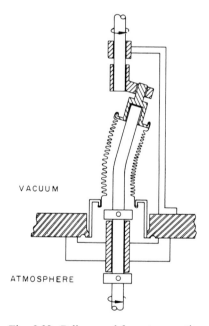

Fig. 2.38. Bellows seal for rotary motion.

and metal spacers in a body similar to the Wilson and chevron seal bodies. The "Teflon" washer fits snugly on the shaft and in the body recess. The metal spacers have clearance around the shaft. Spring washers are used between the compression nut and the gasket assembly to maintain a continuous sealing pressure. This type of seal can be used in ultrahigh vacuum service for sealing rotating shafts. Two such seals should be used with an auxiliary vacuum between them.

Metal Bellows. Metal bellows are used in several ways to seal moving shafts. Reciprocating motion is easily accomplished, as shown in Fig. 2.37.

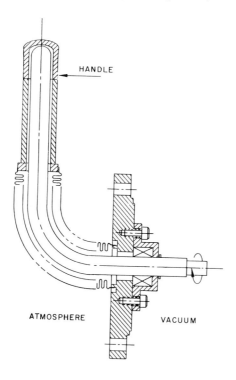

Fig. 2.39. Bellows seal for hand-operated rotary motion.

The limit of travel is set by the stress characteristics of the bellows. Rotating motion can be sealed by bellows, as shown in Figs. 2.38 and 2.39.

CHAPTER 3

Techniques and Procedures

In the preceding chapter the components of a typical high-vacuum system were introduced and described. How these components are assembled into a vacuum system, tested, and how the system is operated will be the subject of this chapter.

PERFORMANCE CHARACTERISTICS OF A VACUUM SYSTEM

The three main performance characteristics of a vacuum system are: (1) the pumping speed of the system at the working pressure (the working pressure is the pressure in the system during the process and, therefore, is higher than the base pressure); (2) the base (lowest) pressure that can be obtained in the vessel; and (3) the time it takes to reach the base pressure.

Pumping Speed

Pumping speed at the working pressure is of major importance. In most processes there is a maximum pressure above which the process may be adversely affected. It is obvious that the pumping system must have a speed at the working pressure greater than the maximum gas load expected from the process. The pumping speed of the system must also be sufficient to reach the operating pressure in the specified time.

Base Pressure

The base pressure, or lowest possible pressure attainable in the vessel, is an indication of the total leakage into the system. The total leakage includes real leakage (due to holes) and virtual leakage (due to contaminant vapors, adsorbed gas, or air trapped in the system during assembly). The equilibrium between the net speed of the pumping system and these gas sources establishes the base pressure. Assuming the vessel to be clean and tight, the base pressure is a good indication of the condition and quality of the pumping system.

Time to Achieve Base Pressure.

If the vessel is gas-tight but not completely clean, it may reach the base pressure but take a long time to do so. If there are any sources of contaminant vapors trapped in such places as the crevices of improperly designed weld joints, or in the bottom of blind drilled and tapped holes with screws in them, the time to reach base pressure will be prolonged. Until the vapors from such sources have been exhausted, the vessel will not reach base pressure. An excess amount of adsorbed gas (such as might be held on heavily sandblasted walls) will frequently extend pumpdown time also. Thus the time to achieve base pressure is an indication of the quality and cleanliness of the vessel, assuming the pumping system is in a condition to reach the base pressure.

PROCESSES USING VACUUM

The components used in the system should be selected with the process in mind. The size of the vessel must be sufficient to accommodate the process. The pumps must be able to handle the gas load expected at the operating pressure. The type of pump used is dependent on the process (some types of pump may be less compatible with a given process than others).

A selection of materials to be used in construction of the system also depends on the process. If plastics are to be processed, then the presence of a moderate amount of them in the system is probably not objectionable. If extreme measures are used to exclude organic* vapors from the vessel, then construction materials should be inorganic.

Some of the more common processes in which high-vacuum systems are used are discussed below.

Drying and Freezing by Vacuum

Vacuum drying and freezing processes evolve quantities of vapors. The required working pressure is usually about one micron. The volume of the system will be of less concern than the surface area of the material to be processed, since the surface area and its vapor pressure determine the volume of gas evolved, and therefore the gas load. Refrigerated traps are very effective, because they increase the speed of the system by condensing much of the vapor before it reaches the pumps. Mechanical

---

*Here, "organic" refers to plastics, rubbers, oils, etc., which are carbon-containing compounds.

booster pumps or vapor booster pumps (ejector pumps) are often used, backed by a rotary pump equipped with gas ballast.

Particle Accelerators

Particle accelerator vessels are usually quite large. The operating pressure necessary is about 10^{-6} torr. The gas load is mainly the degassing rate of the vessel surfaces, although the device for injecting particles to be accelerated generates a considerable gas load. Organic vapors are especially objectional (due to large size of organic molecules), since they interfere with the beam of the particles. The pumping system must be carefully baffled and trapped to reduce the amount of backstreaming from the pump. Materials are selected to be compatible with the electrical characteristics of the system.

Vacuum Furnaces

Furnaces for the heat treating, brazing, or degassing of metals require a working pressure of 10^{-4} torr or less; the thermal conductivity of gases at this pressure is at the practical minimum so that lower pressures are usually not required. The gas load is predominantly due to the degassing of the material in process and may be difficult to predict; pumping systems are therefore designed to have high speeds at the working pressure. Heating may be accomplished by means of resistance elements or by induction heating. The vessel, although it is usually protected from the hot zone by radiation shields, must be able to withstand a necessarily high temperature. The seals and lead-ins are frequently water cooled. The vessel size varies greatly, depending on the process, from less than 100 liters to thousands of liters.

Electron-Beam Welding, Melting, and Machining

The working pressure for these processes must be less than 10^{-4} torr unless the electron gun is differentially pumped. At higher pressures the electron beam initiates a glow discharge in the gas which, of course, disrupts the process.

Melting operations require high-speed pumping systems to carry away the gas bursts encountered.

Welding and machining operations do not normally generate as large a gas load as melting. Motion seals are required in the vessel and manipulative devices to position the part to be welded are also needed.

Evaporative Coating Units

The size of the evaporator vessel is dependent on the function of the unit, i.e., what is to be coated and how many at one time. Industrial processes such as the metallizing of plastics generally require large vessels. Because of the volatile components in the plastics, pumps must have high speeds at the maximum operating pressure of 10^{-4} torr. High-speed pumps will also reduce the cycling time, which reduces operating costs. Many lead-ins will be needed to bring in electrical power and mechanical motion.

Smaller coating units for pilot-plant production or development operations will have smaller vessels, usually bell jars from 12 to 24 inches in diameter. The working pressure in the vessel should be lower than 10^{-5} torr. High-speed pumps are not mandatory but are recommended. A large number of lead-ins for power and mechanical motion will be needed.

Evaporative coaters for thin-film circuitry or optical devices require lower pressures to assure films of good quality. Working pressures of 10^{-8} torr and lower are desirable. Metal gaskets are used as seals and ultrahigh vacuum techniques are followed where possible. Pumps are well trapped to keep partial pressures of pump fluid vapors as low as possible.

Space Research

The evaluation of materials to be used in the low pressures of space can usually be accomplished at working pressures between 10^{-5} and 10^{-8} torr. Observation of the phenomena associated with space conditions may, however, require the lowest attainable base pressure (less than 10^{-10} torr). The size of the vessel varies widely. Vessels of about 100 liters volume are used in evaluation of materials, but some have been built large enough to house entire space vehicles. Vessels may be equipped with a heat source to simulate solar radiation and with refrigerated walls to simulate the extremely low temperatures encountered in space. They are usually equipped with mechanical and electrical lead-ins.

Plasma Research

In plasma research it is desirable to reduce to an absolute minimum the contaminant gases; thus system cleanliness and lowest possible base pressure are paramount. Some large experimental plasma research facilities have base pressures in the 10^{-10}-torr range. It is also desirable to have large pumping speeds at these pressures.

TYPICAL HIGH-VACUUM SYSTEM (THE BELL-JAR EVAPORATOR)

Many of the processes described above can be, and, in fact, are accomplished in a bell-jar type of system (see Fig. 3.1). The bell-jar is the vacuum vessel; it is usually cylindrical with the upper end domed or covered by a flange. It can be raised to permit easy access to the inside and when lowered seals against the base plate. The base plate provides a stable

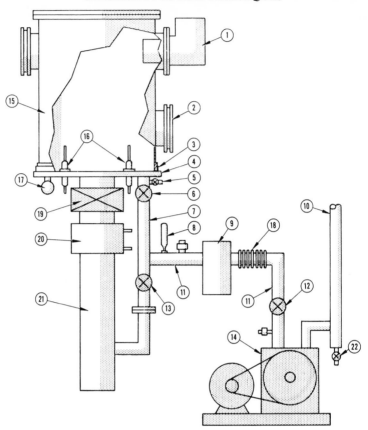

Fig. 3.1. Typical bell-jar system capable of producing high vacuum.
1. Liquid-nitrogen trap (cold thimble); 2. Port; 3. Gasket; 4. Base plate;
5. Vacuum-release valve; 6. Roughing valve; 7. Roughing line; 8. Forevacuum gage; 9. Foreline trap; 10. Exhaust duct; 11. Foreline; 12.
Mechanical pump valve; 13. Backing valve; 14. Mechanical pump; 15.
Bell jar; 16. Electrical lead-ins; 17. High-vacuum gage; 18. Vibration
damper 19. High-vacuum isolation valve; 20. Baffle; 21. Diffusion
pump; 22. Draincock.

mounting surface for lead-ins and motion seals. The pumping system is
suspended from the underside of the base plate. The base plate is supported
by a frame enclosed by sheet metal to protect the operator. The frame is
generally made large enough to provide mounting for gage power supplies
and accessory apparatus.

The arrangement described above is quite versatile, as evidenced by the
number that are kept in stock by vacuum equipment manufacturers. As
its use is so widespread, this type of system will be used as an example to

describe the techniques and procedures of constructing, assembling, testing, and operating a vacuum system. The methods and procedures outlined here will apply equally well to other types of systems.

The example described is a bell-jar system such as that used for small-scale evaporative coating. The system will have the following characteristics:

(a) The base pressure shall be 10^{-7} torr.

(b) The maximum permissible working pressure shall be 10^{-5} torr.

(c) The pumping speed (at working pressure) shall be 5 liters/sec per liter of bell-jar volume.

(d) The bell jar shall have a volume of 100 liters (24 inches high with a diameter of 18 inches).

(e) The time to achieve base pressure from atmospheric pressure (pump-down time) shall not exceed 30 minutes.

These requirements are reasonable for a small-scale evaporator; how they are met will be shown in the following sections. It should be kept in mind that while the techniques and procedures given in the following sections are for the vacuum system described above, they are general enough to be useful for *any* high-vacuum system. In the following sections the bell jar and the parts attached to it will be described, selection will be made of suitable units for the pumping system, and procedures for assembly, testing, and operating the system will be given.

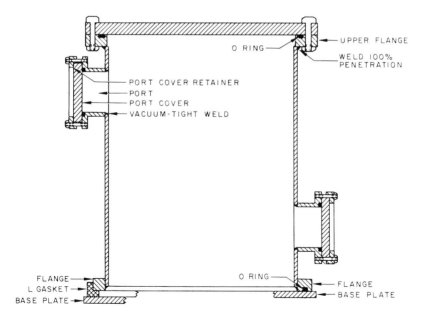

Fig. 3.2. Typical metal bell jar. An L-gasket seal between the bell-jar flange and the base plate is shown at the lower left; at the lower right an O-ring seal is illustrated.

The Bell Jar

Bell jars are available in glass, stainless steel, and aluminum. Glass is often used but is, of course, breakable. Stainless steel is an excellent mate-

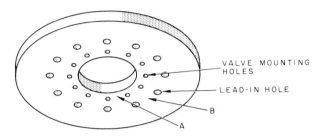

Fig. 3.3. Base plate. The small holes are for mounting the high-vacuum isolation valve; the larger holes are for lead-ins.

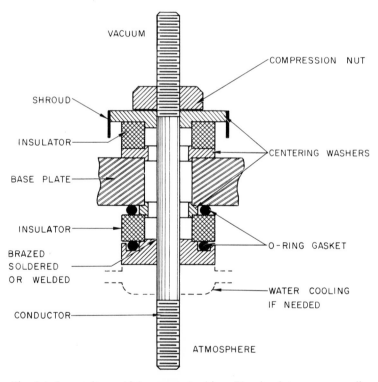

Fig. 3.4. Low-voltage, high-current lead-in. The insulators are usually glazed ceramic, the conductor is copper, and the compression nut is stainless steel or mild steel. Centering washers are made of stainless steel or aluminum and are slotted to provide for pumpout.

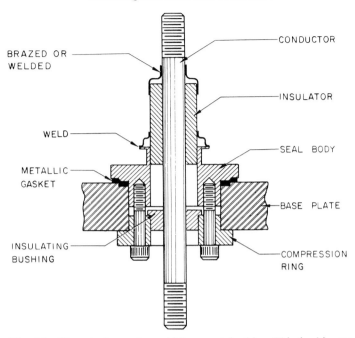

Fig. 3.5. Alternate low-voltage, high-current lead-in. This lead-in can be sealed with a metal gasket if desired. Several companies manufacture the ceramic-to-metal seal that forms the basis of this lead-in. The seals are stocked in a range of sizes. The insulating bushing provides rigidity, so that the seal is not broken when the leads from the electrical supply are attached. The bushing must be drilled through for probe gas to enter for leak checking.

rial, though expensive and difficult to fabricate. Aluminum is satisfactory in most cases and is less expensive. Figure 3.2 shows a typical bell jar with its components.

A typical base plate is shown in Fig. 3.3. The base plate is usually made of mild steel, stainless steel, or aluminum. When mild steel is used, it is generally nickel-plated to prevent corrosion and to permit easy cleaning. Stainless steel is the most convenient material; however, it is difficult to fabricate and therefore expensive. Aluminum is often used, though it is quite soft and will not stand rough handling very well. The entire top of the base plate should have an extremely smooth finish (at least 32 micro-inches) so that it will be easy to clean. A smooth finish on all internal vacuum surfaces is desirable, as it offers a smaller surface area for adsorbed gas and consequently a shorter degassing time. The sealing surfaces at A and B in Fig. 3.3 should be at least 63 microinches. A representative sample of base-plate lead-ins for general service would be:

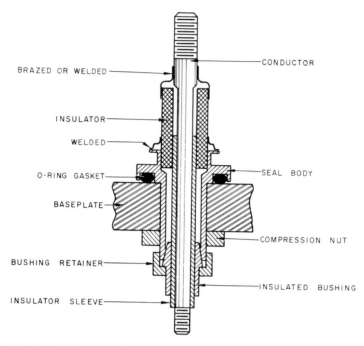

BRAZED OR WELDED

CONDUCTOR

INSULATOR

WELDED

O-RING GASKET

SEAL BODY

BASEPLATE

COMPRESSION NUT

BUSHING RETAINER

INSULATED BUSHING

INSULATOR SLEEVE

Fig. 3.6. High-voltage, low-current lead-in. The construction of this lead-in is generally the same as that of the high-current lead-ins except that the insulators offer a larger leakage path and thus allow greater voltage differences before breakdown. A shield should be provided on the vacuum side to keep the insulator from receiving a conductive coating during the process.

(a) Low-voltage, high-current lead-ins (see Figs. 3.4 and 3.5). These are used in evaporation or furnaces.

(b) High-voltage, low-current lead-ins (see Fig. 3.6). These are used for glow-discharge cleaning or electron-bombardment heating.

(c) Two rotary-motion or reciprocating seals (see Fig. 3.7).

(d) One high-vacuum-gage lead-in (see Fig. 3.8).

(e) One multiconductor lead-in for 110-volt supply to heaters or for thermocouple leads for monitoring temperature (see Fig. 3.9).

(f) One coolant lead-in (supply and return can be put through one lead-in) (see Fig. 3.10).

(g) One air vent (see Fig. 3.11).

The Pumping System

The pumping system must be considered as a unit, since an improper choice of any one component can decrease the effectiveness of the entire

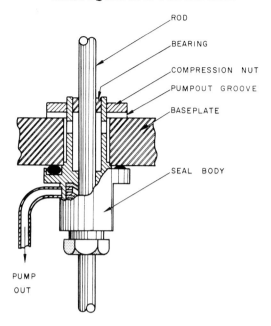

Fig. 3.7. Motion seal.

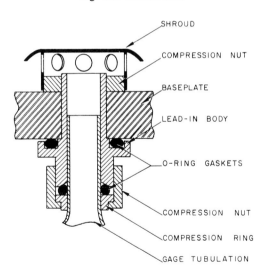

Fig. 3.8. Gage lead-in. It is usually most convenient to mount the vacuum gage on the base plate. Mounted in the bell jar, the gage is more liable to be broken, and its cable would have to be raised and lowered to keep particles from falling into it.

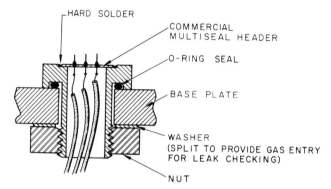

Fig. 3.9. Multiconductor lead-in. Such lead-ins are used for thermocouple leads or to heat surfaces to be coated.

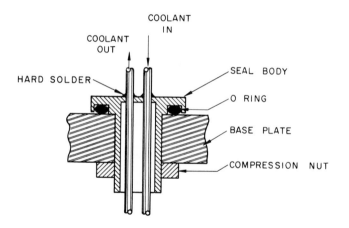

Fig. 3.10. Coolant lead-in.

system. Components requiring special attention are the diffusion pump, the high-vacuum isolation valve, the baffle, and the mechanical pump. Less critical components are the forevacuum line and valve and the roughing line and valve. Some simple calculations which indicate how these components are "sized" will be included in the discussion of each. Proper sizing of the components is necessary in order to achieve the required system pumping speed.

The Diffusion Pump. The rated pumping speed of the diffusion pump will not be available at the bell jar because of the impedance of the high-vacuum isolation valve and the baffle. According to the specifications set up

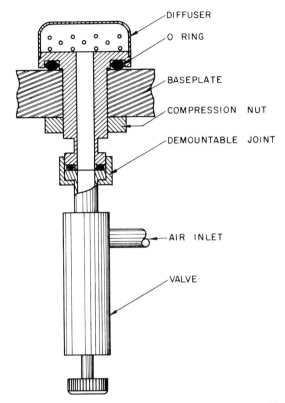

Fig. 3.11. Vacuum-release valve. Air should be bled in slowly; a diffuser is placed on the inlet to prevent damage from air blasts.

for the example, the process requires a pumping speed of 5 liters/sec per liter of bell jar volume. Since even the most efficient design of high-vacuum valve and baffle will reduce the speed of a diffusion pump to ½ or ⅓ of its rated speed, the pump selected should have 2 or 3 times the speed required at the bell jar. The bell jar in the example has a volume of 100 liters; thus a pumping speed of 500 liters/sec is needed at the bell jar, which requires a pump with a rated speed of 1500 liters/sec.

A pump that satisfies this requirement could have the following operating characteristics:

Speed at working pressure (10^{-5} torr) = 1500 liters/sec

Maximum tolerable forepressure = 0.3 torr

A pump with these characteristics would have a "nominal" throat diameter of 6 inches (actually 7 inches).

High-vacuum Isolation Valve. Vacuum systems are often cycled from atmospheric pressure to vacuum and back to atmospheric pressure many times during a day's operation. Since the fluid in the diffusion pump should not be exposed to atmospheric pressure while it is hot, the pump must either be cooled before the system is vented to atmosphere, or it must be isolated from the part of the system that is vented. Isolating the diffusion pump with a high-vacuum valve is usually preferred, as it results in a shorter cycling time. This valve, even when completely open, will unavoidably present some impedance to gas flow. However, the advantages gained by inclusion of the valve in the system usually outweigh the disadvantage of flow reduction.

To present minimum impedance to gas flow, the high-vacuum valve selected should have a flow path as large in diameter and as short in length as practicable. The sliding-gate valve has these characteristics. Several types of this valve are manufactured commercially in sizes corresponding to diffusion pump throat sizes.

A gate valve operated by an elastomer-sealed, rotating shaft is preferred to one with an elastomer-sealed, reciprocating shaft. The reciprocating shaft, unless differentially pumped for a length equal to its stroke, will carry in adsorbed gas on the shaft, thus causing a pressure rise in the system. However, in many vacuum systems, this is of minor importance.

To calculate the conductance of a nominal 6-inch gate valve, the method outlined by Levenson, Milleron, and Davis[1] will be used. For the purposes of the calculation, the dimensions of the valve are assumed to be those of a cylinder 7 inches in diameter by 8 inches long. The formula in reference 1 gives the conductance of a valve as $C_v = P(75A)$, where C_v is the conductance of the valve, P is a probability factor that depends on the geometry of the valve passage, and A is the area of the valve opening in square inches. For this valve, P is approximately 0.5. The conductance, then, is:

$$C_v = 0.5 \times 75 \times \frac{D^2\pi}{4} = 0.5 \times 75 \times 49 \times \frac{\pi}{4} = 1500 \text{ liters/sec.}$$

The Baffle. The purpose of a baffle, as stated in Chapter 2, is to minimize the amount of backstreaming pump fluid reaching the bell jar. This is accomplished by placing a cool surface in the line-of-sight path between the bell jar and the region from which the backstreaming vapors originate. The design of this surface has been the subject of a great deal of thought. The reason for this is that the more effective a baffle is in stopping vapor molecules from going toward the bell jar, the more restrictive is the passage for gas molecules going from the vessel to the pump. Consequently, many different arrangements have been tried. Four of the more frequently used designs are shown in Fig. 3.12.

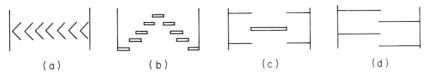

Fig. 3.12. Baffle designs.

The temperature of the baffle should be 10–100° F below room temperature. It should not be low enough to cause the pump fluid to congeal and remain on the baffle. Cooling is usually accomplished by circulating water, although some installations use mechanical refrigeration at temperatures down to about −35° F. The latter will provide better temperature control, but is usually more expensive and may involve some maintenance problems.

The condensed pump fluid will return to the pump by gravity flow. The returning fluid should not be allowed to drip on the nozzles of the pump; these nozzles are hot and cause fluid to re-evaporate and backstream. Also, the dripping fluid interferes with the operation of the nozzles, reducing diffusion pump performance. It is possible to correct a poorly designed drain by attaching wires to the portions of the baffle where the fluid collects. The wires are led to the wall of the pump, thus providing a path down which the fluid will flow.

Although many different baffle designs are available from vacuum equipment manufacturers, the requirements of a particular system or the preferences of a system designer often make it necessary to design a "special" baffle. If no manufacturer makes one like it, the baffle must be custom made.

A method for calculating the required dimensions of a given baffle design is given by Levenson *et al.* in the paper previously mentioned (refer-

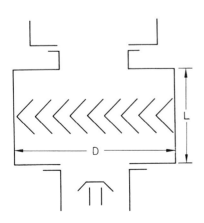

Fig. 3.13 Chevron baffle.

ence 1). This method will be used to calculate the dimensions of the chevron baffle shown in Fig. 3.13. First it is necessary to determine the required baffle conductance. Using Eq. (1.23),

$$\frac{1}{S_{vessel}} = \frac{1}{S_{pump}} + \frac{1}{C_{total}}$$

Since

$$\frac{1}{C_{total}} = \frac{1}{C_{valve}} + \frac{1}{C_{baffle}}$$

then

$$\frac{1}{S_{vessel}} = \frac{1}{S_{pump}} + \frac{1}{C_{valve}} + \frac{1}{C_{baffle}}$$

Solving for $\dfrac{1}{C_{baffle}}$,

$$\frac{1}{C_{baffle}} = \frac{1}{S_{vessel}} - \frac{1}{S_{pump}} - \frac{1}{C_{valve}}$$

The speed of the diffusion pump (S_{pump}) is 1500 liters/sec; 500 liters/sec is needed at the vessel (S_{vessel}). The conductance of the valve (C_{valve}) was found to be 1500 liters/sec. Substituting,

$$\frac{1}{C_{baffle}} = \frac{1}{500} - \frac{1}{1500} - \frac{1}{1500} = \frac{1}{1500} \text{ (approx)}$$

or

$$C_{baffle} = 1500 \text{ liters/sec.}$$

Thus, to obtain 500 liters/sec at the bell jar with a pump of speed 1500 liters/sec and a valve with conductance 1500 liters/sec, it is necessary that the baffle have a conductance of 1500 liters/sec. To find the dimension D (see Fig. 3.13) that will give this conductance, the formula $C_{baffle} = P(75A)$ from reference 1 will be used. In this case, the probability factor P has the value $\frac{1}{5}$, for a 45° chevron. Substituting into the formula,

$$1500 = \frac{1}{5} \times 75 \times \frac{\pi D^2}{4}$$

$$D^2 = \frac{1500 \times 5 \times 4}{75\pi} = 127. \quad D = 11.3 \text{ inches}$$

The impedance between both of the 7-inch-diameter openings and the chevron is small compared to that of the chevron itself. For calculations of this degree of accuracy, these impedances can be neglected. The ratio of baffle body length L to chevron length is arbitrary; L is usually taken to be three times the chevron length.

Valve-baffle Combination. It is possible to combine the high-vacuum valve and baffle into one housing by using a baffle in which the center plate becomes the disk of a poppet-type valve, as shown in Fig. 2.29.

To determine the required conductance of the valve-baffle combination for the example, Eq. (1.23) is used again:

$$\frac{1}{S_{\text{vessel}}} = \frac{1}{C_{\text{valve-baffle}}} + \frac{1}{S_{\text{pump}}}$$

which can be put

$$\frac{1}{C_{\text{valve-baffle}}} = \frac{1}{S_{\text{vessel}}} - \frac{1}{S_{\text{pump}}}$$

Substituting numerical values,

$$\frac{1}{C_{\text{valve-baffle}}} = \frac{1}{500} - \frac{1}{1500} = \frac{2}{1500}.$$

Thus

$$C_{\text{valve-baffle}} = 750 \text{ liters/sec.}$$

This is the conductance needed for the "sample" system. The diameter of the baffle opening is 7 inches, and the probability factor P for this valve-baffle geometry is 0.28. The conductance is given by

$$C_{\text{valve-baffle}} = P(75A) = 0.28(75)(38.5) = 808.5 \text{ liters/sec.}$$

Since this valve exceeds the required conductance of 750 liters/sec, the combined valve-baffle is acceptable.

Mechanical Pump. The mechanical pump will perform two functions: it will be used to rough the vessel down to the starting pressure of the diffusion pump and to back the diffusion pump once it is operating. Both functions must be considered in choosing the proper pump. However, adequate backing speed is the more important of the two. An inadequate roughing pump merely increases the time required to complete the roughing cycle. With inadequate backing, however, the gas-handling capacity of the diffusion pump suffers, and backstreaming is excessive. Accordingly, a mechanical pump is selected that will provide adequate backing. If its capacity is too low to provide roughing in the time required, a pump larger than the minimum necessary for backing can be used. In case of a very large vessel, two pumps may be used; a high-capacity pump for the roughing period, and a smaller, more economical pump for backing.

Sizing the Mechanical Pump. Selection of the proper size of mechanical pump depends on three factors: the process, unexpected gas bursts, and crossover conditions. First, the size of pump needed to accommodate the process will be determined.

The mechanical pump must be able to handle the maximum anticipated throughput while keeping the forearm pressure below the maximum tolerable forepressure. For the system under consideration, the desired pumping speed at the vessel is 500 liters/sec at a pressure of 10^{-5} torr. The throughput Q at the vessel is therefore $500 \times 10^{-5} = 5 \times 10^{-3}$ torr-liter/sec ($Q = SP$). The speed the mechanical pump must provide at the forearm to maintain the forepressure is given by

$$S_f = \frac{Q}{P_f}$$

where S_f is the pumping speed at the forearm, Q is the throughput, and P_f is the maximum tolerable forepressure. Since $Q = 5 \times 10^{-3}$ torr-liter/sec (Q is a constant throughout the system) and P_f for the diffusion pump is 0.3 torr (see p. 85), then

$$S_f = \frac{5 \times 10^{-3}}{.3 \times 10^{-1}} = 1.67 \times 10^{-2} \text{ liter/sec.}$$

To calculate the mechanical pump speed needed to achieve this pumping speed at the forearm, Eq. (1.23) will be used:

$$\frac{1}{S_f} = \frac{1}{S_{mp}} + \frac{1}{C_L}$$

where S_{mp} is the speed of the mechanical pump and C_L is the foreline conductance. Solving for $\frac{1}{S_{mp}}$,

$$\frac{1}{S_{mp}} = \frac{1}{S_f} - \frac{1}{C_L}.$$

The foreline conductance C_L can be calculated from the equation

$$C_L = \frac{Q}{(P_1 - P_2)}$$

where $P_1 - P_2$ is the pressure drop between the diffusion pump and the mechanical pump. This drop is usually limited to about 20% of the forearm pressure, or $0.20 \times 0.3 = 6 \times 10^{-2}$ torr. Substituting this value into the conductance equation, together with the throughput Q of 5×10^{-3} torr-liter/sec, one obtains

$$C_L = \frac{5 \times 10^{-3}}{6 \times 10^{-2}} = 8.3 \times 10^{-2} \text{ liter/sec.}$$

Substituting this value for C_L and the value $S_f = 1.6 \times 10^{-2}$ liter/sec into the system equation, one obtains

$$\frac{1}{S_{mp}} = \frac{1}{1.67 \times 10^{-2}} - \frac{1}{8.3 \times 10^{-2}} = 0.6 \times 10^2 - 0.12 \times 10^2 = 0.48 \times 10^2$$

$$S_{mp} = \frac{1}{0.48 \times 10^2} = 2 \times 10^{-2} \text{ liter/sec.}$$

Obviously, then, the demand on the mechanical pump during a normal process is small. However, gas bursts (sudden unexpected releases of gas during certain processes) may place heavier demands on both the diffusion and mechanical pumps. Most processes are adversely affected at pressures above 10^{-3} torr. Taking this condition to be the worst possible that could occur during a process, the mechanical pump speed required to maintain the forearm pressure below the maximum tolerable forepressure will be calculated. The diffusion pump is capable of a pumping speed at the vessel of 500 liters/sec at a pressure of 10^{-3} torr as well as at a pressure of 10^{-5} torr (see Fig. 2.10). The throughput at this pressure is $500 \times 10^{-3} = 0.5$ torr-liter/sec. Using the same approach as before,

$$S_f = \frac{0.5}{3 \times 10^{-1}} = 1.6 \text{ liters/sec.} \quad C_L = \frac{0.5}{6 \times 10^{-2}} = 8 \text{ liters/sec}$$

$$\frac{1}{S_{mp}} = \frac{1}{S_f} - \frac{1}{C_L} = \frac{1}{1.6} - \frac{1}{8} = 0.625 - 0.125 = 0.5$$

$$S_{mp} = \frac{1}{0.5} = 2 \text{ liters/sec} \quad (4.25 \text{ cfm}).$$

Another situation creating high gas loads exists for a cycled system. During crossover (when the vessel is first opened to the diffusion pump after roughing) the diffusion pump may be exposed to a quite high inlet pressure. If crossover is at 0.1 torr, for example, the throughput could be about 6 torr-liters/sec for short periods. The mechanical pump speed needed in this case to keep the forearm pressure below its maximum tolerable value is

$$S_f = \frac{6}{0.3} = 20 \text{ liters/sec}; \quad C_L = \frac{6}{6 \times 10^{-2}} = 100 \text{ liters/sec}$$

$$\frac{1}{S_{mp}} = \frac{1}{S_f} - \frac{1}{C_L} = \frac{1}{20} - \frac{1}{100} = \frac{4}{100};$$

$$S_{mp} = 25 \text{ liters/sec} \quad (50 \text{ cfm}).$$

The necessity for a pump this large may be reduced by roughing to a pressure less than 0.1 torr before crossover, thus reducing the throughput. At 5×10^{-2} torr crossover pressure, for instance, the throughput would be closer to 3 torr-liter/sec, which would indicate a 25-cfm mechanical pump and a C_L of 50 liters/sec. A lower crossover pressure also reduces the backstreaming past the baffle at crossover. The baffle is most effective during molecular flow conditions. At 10^{-1} torr, viscous flow will exist in most baffles; this allows diffusion-pump vapor to backstream into the vessel without necessarily colliding with a cold surface.

Based on the preceding calculations and assuming a maximum cross-over pressure of 5×10^{-2} torr, the mechanical pump size will be fixed at 14 liters/sec (30 cfm). This will allow for a 15% deterioration in mechanical pump performance during use.

Once a mechanical pump capable of providing adequate backing has been decided upon, a check should be made of its ability to rough out the vessel to diffusion-pump operating pressure in a reasonable time. The method for calculating pumpdown time was given in Chapter 1 and will be applied here. The pumpdown equation is

$$t = K2.3 \frac{V}{S} \log\frac{P_1}{P_2}$$

where t is the time in seconds, K is a factor that depends on the pressure range in question, V is the volume of the system, and S is the pumping speed. Crossover is assumed to be at 0.01 torr; consequently the pumpdown will be from 1000 torr to 0.01 torr (actually the initial pressure will not be above 760 torr; 1000 torr is chosen to simplify the calculation). The pumping speed S is dependent on the pressure; its value for any one pressure range can be read from Fig. 3.14. Table 3.1 gives these pumping speeds for the pressure ranges. Also shown in Table 3.1 are values of 2.3 V/S (V is 100 liters), K, and t for each pressure range. Adding up t for all the ranges, one obtains 250.7 seconds, or 4.2 minutes. Since the actual

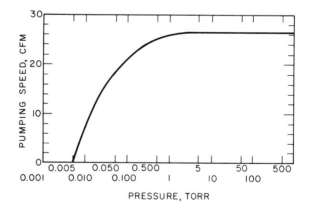

Fig. 3.14. Pumping speed vs pressure for 30-cfm mechanical pump. Note that the speed remains essentially unchanged from 10 to 1000 torr.

pumpdown would be from 760 torr (atmospheric pressure) rather than 1000 torr, the time would be somewhat less, but still approximately 4 minutes. As will be shown later, the roughing-line impedance will increase this time somewhat.

TABLE 3.1. PUMPDOWN TIME DATA.

Pressure ranges (torr)	S (liters/sec)	K	$2.3\,V/S$	t (sec)
1000–100	13	1	18	18
100–10	13	1.25	18	22.5
10–1	12.7	1.5	18.5	27.8
1–0.1	10.8	2	21.2	42.4
0.1–0.01	6.6	4	35	140

Forevacuum Plumbing. Forevacuum plumbing includes the roughing and backing lines; the roughing, backing and mechanical pump valves; and the gages and quick-disconnect outlets. A typical forevacuum line arrangement is shown in Fig. 3.15.

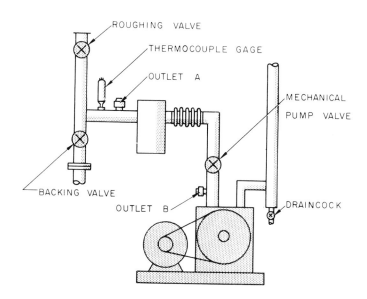

Fig. 3.15. Typical forevacuum line arrangement.

The roughing and backing lines are joined close to the diffusion pump, and thus only one common line is needed to connect the mechanical pump to the system. A thermocouple gage placed at this junction will indicate pressure during either roughing or backing. The quick-disconnect outlet B provides a means to let the mechanical pump up to atmospheric pressure.

Lines. The conductances of the lines and valves should be compatible with the speed of the mechanical pump (30 cfm). Obviously, line length depends on how close to the unit the mechanical pump can be located. When possible, the mechanical pump should be located outside the shop or laboratory. This eliminates the problems associated with pump noise and harmful exhaust vapors.

With the line length set, adequate conductance is obtained by choosing the proper line diameter. The major portion of the line will be used for both backing and roughing; therefore, both conditions must be taken into account.

During backing, the flow will initially be viscous. Therefore conductance will depend on the average pressure in the line and on line dimensions, as defined by the equation for viscous conductance (Eq. (1.17))

$$C = \frac{3000 \, \bar{P} D^4}{L}$$

The average pressure $\bar{P}$ is equal to $(P_1 + P_2)/2$, where P_1 and P_2 are the pressure at the forearm of the diffusion pump and the pressure at the mechanical pump, respectively. The values of P_1 and P_2 depend on the characteristics of the pumps used. Under the maximum-throughput conditions (3 torr-liters/sec as noted in the mechanical-pump sizing calculations) P_1 would be 0.3 torr and P_2 0.24 torr (allowing the maximum pressure drop of 20% in the line). Therefore, $\bar{P}$ is 0.27 torr. The minimum required line conductance was previously calculated as 50 liters/sec (see p. 91). Assuming the foreline to be 10 feet long,

$$C = \frac{3000 \, \bar{P} D^4}{L} \quad \text{or} \quad D^4 = \frac{CL}{3000 \, \bar{P}}$$

$$D^4 = \frac{50 \times 120}{3000 \times 0.27} = 7.40$$

$D = 1.65$ in. ($1\frac{3}{4}$-in.-o.d. tubing with $\frac{1}{16}$-in. wall thickness).

When the line is used for roughing, its conductance must be such that the resultant speed of the mechanical pump and line will be sufficient for the required roughing time. From the preceding calculations, it is noted that the last stage of the pumpdown time is the longest (see Table 3.1). If the roughing-line diameter is based on this step, it is certain to be more than adequate for the preceding steps.

A drop of 20% in pump speed due to line loss is considered reasonable. If one assumes an available 14-liter/sec pump (30 cfm), the net speed for the final roughing stage is 6.6 liters/sec (Table 3.1). Therefore, the resultant speed S_v is 80% of the 6.6 liters/sec, or 5.3 liters/sec. The conductance of a line that would provide this resultant speed is obtained from the system equation

$$\frac{1}{S_v} = \frac{1}{C_L} + \frac{1}{S_{mp}}.$$

By solving for $1/C_L$ and inserting the values for S_v and S_{mp}, one obtains

$$\frac{1}{C_L} = \frac{1}{5.3} - \frac{1}{6.6}; \quad C_L = 29 \text{ liters/sec.}$$

This is the minimum line conductance for roughing. Therefore the required conductance for roughing is about half of that required for backing during crossover and the $1\frac{3}{4}$-in. tubing is more than adequate.

If the net speed of 5.3 liters/sec is used in the pumpdown-time equation, the time for reaching a pressure of 0.01 torr from atmosphere is 5.25 minutes, instead of 4 minutes.

Foreline Materials. For lines of the size indicated, copper is the usual choice. It can easily be hard-soldered or soft-soldered, and it cleans readily. Thin-wall copper tubing is light in weight and little difficulty is encountered in working it with hand or machine tools. Solder fittings, such as elbows, tees, crosses, etc., are readily available. Demountable joints are simple to make by using brass flanges with machined O-ring grooves. The flanges can be soldered to the tubing ends, as shown in Fig. 2.33.

Appendix L contains a table listing the dimensions of flanges that can be used on metal tubing.

Mild steel, stainless steel, and aluminum are also acceptable materials for forelines. Glass pipe can also be used, especially where an electrical nonconductor is needed.

Valves. The backing valve and the mechanical-pump valve will be exposed to the same conditions, so they are often the same type of valve. Several valve types can be used: gate, globe, angle, or ball valves. All these are available in sizes to suit lines 2 inches in diameter and smaller. (On systems with vacuum plumbing larger than 2 inches, either gate or angle valves are used.) Most manufacturers supply these valves to suit a variety of installation methods, including threaded joints (tapered pipe threads), flange joints (O-ring or pipe-flange gaskets), or solder joints. The pressure on either side of both valves will seldom be lower than 1 micron. This allows some latitude in sealing materials. O rings or flat rubber gaskets are used for sealing the valve port; O-ring, Wilson, or chevron seals are used for the stem seal, and O rings and flat gaskets on the bonnet seal.

For the roughing valve the same valve types are used, with the possible exception of the ball valve. This type has no provision for increasing the sealing pressure on the port in the event of leakage, a lack which could be troublesome. The roughing valve has one side exposed to the high-vacuum region. Thus the sealing materials used on this side must satisfy the same conditions of use as the other seals in that region. For this reason the valve is normally installed with the port seal toward the high vacuum. The stem seal and the bonnet seal do not "see" this area; therefore, two possible sources of leakage are eliminated. When this method of installation is not possible, a bellows-sealed valve is recommended. The bellows seals only the stem, which still leaves the bonnet seal as a possible leakage source. But at least this arrangement does keep an air-covered shaft from entering the high-vacuum region. Globe and angle valves can be obtained that have a bellows-sealed stem.

All four types of valves can be converted to solenoid-controlled operation. Many manufacturers supply them with the conversions made. Opening or closing a valve can thus be accomplished by an electrical signal which makes it possible to provide fail-safe operation in the event of a power failure, or to interlock the entire pumpdown sequence. Gate valves are available in brass, aluminum, and stainless steel. Angle valves are cast in brass and aluminum or are machined from aluminum, stainless steel, or brass bar stock. Large sizes (12 inches or more) are fabricated from rolled plate aluminum, mild steel, or stainless steel. Globe valves are cast from brass or stainless steel, and ball valves are cast from brass, aluminum, and stainless steel. Figures 2.25–2.31 show several types of vacuum valves.

Gages. The gage used in the forevacuum region is normally a thermal-conductivity gage. The operating range of this gage covers the pressures encountered (see Fig. 2.15). The thermocouple type of gage with a metal tube is used most often because it is sturdier than the Pirani. Also the thermocouple gage is cheaper and quite adequate for the job. The gage tube is usually located near the junction of the backing and roughing lines, where it can serve the dual purpose of monitoring both backing and roughing pressures. Do not install the gage tube where it will act as a sump for the condensate that may collect in the foreline. In a horizontal section the tube should extend upward from the top of the line. In a vertical section a 90-degree elbow is used and the tube is extended upward from this, parallel to the axis of the line. Thermocouple gages having metal tubulations are supplied with $\frac{1}{8}$-inch national pipe connections. A common method of installation is to coat all but the first two threads with "Glyptal," then screw the tube into a pipe coupling previously soldered or welded to the line. An alternate method, which makes changing the tube less difficult, is to use a quick-disconnect coupling. The gage tube can be attached to one half of this coupling with the help of soft-solder, "Glyptal," or vacuum wax. Then the mating half is soldered or welded to the line. With this method, a spare gage tube with fitting installed can be kept nearby, which makes the replacement of a bad tube quick and simple, with less probability of a leak. Figure 3.16 shows typical installations.

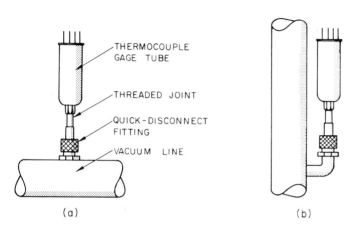

THERMOCOUPLE
GAGE TUBE

THREADED JOINT

QUICK-DISCONNECT
FITTING

VACUUM LINE

(a)   (b)

Fig. 3.16. Foreline gage installation. (a) Installation in a horizontal section (b) in a vertical section.

Thermocouple-gage power supplies can be obtained that have a provision for interlocking or fail-safe circuits. An electrical impulse is triggered when the gage reading reaches a preselected point. This impulse, by the use of relays, can be used to shut down a diffusion pump or close a valve in the event of a pressure rise. It can also be used to prevent the diffusion pump from being turned on until the pressure is below a selected level.

Special Outlets. An outlet in the foreline to which a leak-detecting device can be attached is a recommended feature (outlet A in Fig. 3.15). If this outlet is placed near the junction of the backing and roughing lines — where it is bounded by the roughing, backing, and mechanical-pump valves — the leak-detecting device can be attached to the system without shutting the system down. The three valves are closed, the connection made, the line pumped down by opening the mechanical-pump valve, and then the leak detector can be used. Another advantage of this location is that the leak-detecting instrument can be exposed to separate sections of the system in turn, which facilitates the location of leaks.

An outlet (outlet B in Fig. 3.15) should be installed in the foreline between the mechanical-pump valve and the mechanical pump. (The consequences of stopping the mechanical pump without venting it to atmosphere have been mentioned.) With this outlet the mechanical pump can be let up to air without disturbing the remainder of the system. If the outlet is the same size as that used to install the thermocouple gage, it provides a convenient means of checking the base pressure of the mechanical pump. Both these outlets should be provided with a demountable joint — an O-ring-sealed flange or a quick-disconnect fitting.

Vibration Damping. Since a mechanical pump vibrates, vibrations will be transmitted along the forevacuum line to the base plate. In addition to causing unnecessary stress on the line joints, vibrations upset jigs and fixtures in the bell jar and cause work pieces to shake loose and fall. To isolate the vibrations of a mechanical pump from the remainder of the system, a section of foreline is made either from thin-metal bellows or from rubber or plastic tubing. The walls of this section will be flexible and, in the case of rubber and plastic, may collapse. Heavy wire wound into an extended helical coil and inserted into the rubber or plastic tubing will prevent collapse. Heavy-walled rubber tubing and wire-supported plastic tubing for vacuum service are commercially available. The metal bellows, however, is strong in resisting radial pressure but weak in resisting axial pressure. The tendency is for the bellows to shorten in length, which causes equipment connected by a horizontal run to move together. This movement nullifies the vibration-damping effect of the bellows. To prevent such movement, the equipment should be independently secured. When bolting down is undesirable, the bellows can be put in a vertical run. Also, if a horizontal run is not self-supporting, it should be supported by a frame or bracket attached to the wall or floor to prevent sagging. (See Fig. 3.17 for typical installations.)

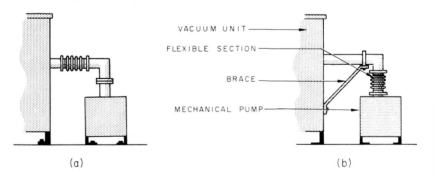

(a)   (b)

Fig. 3.17. Mechanical pump installation. (a) When the pump is connected by a horizontal run, both mechanical pump and vacuum unit should be bolted down. (b) Bolting down of equipment is unnecessary if mechanical pump is connected by a vertical run.

Foreline Trap. A foreline trap is inserted between the backing valve and the mechanical-pump valve. During roughing this trap collects migrating mechanical-pump oil and prevents it from entering the high-vacuum vessel. During backing the trap prevents the mechanical-pump oil from entering the diffusion pump, and vice versa. These two oils are very different in nature and purpose, so it is harmful to the operation of either pump to allow them to mix. These traps should be cooled well below the pour point of the oils, to prevent migration. The temperature of a mixture of dry ice (solid CO_2) and trichloroethylene, approximately $-78°$ C, will trap most diffusion pump oils and *all* mechanical-pump oils. Liquid nitrogen is also frequently used. Figure 3.18 shows the type of U-tube foreline trap

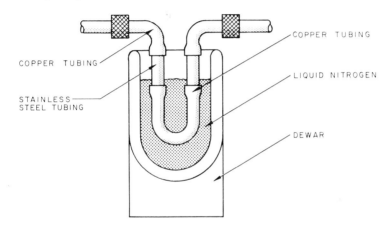

COPPER TUBING

COPPER TUBING

STAINLESS STEEL TUBING

LIQUID NITROGEN

DEWAR

Fig. 3.18. U-tube foreline trap using liquid nitrogen.

used on many systems of this size. An alternative is a molecular-sieve (zeolite) trap that operates at room temperature, but must be reactivated periodically by baking at 300 to 400° C, preferably in vacuum.

Protective Devices. Considerable damage can be done to high-vacuum equipment by mishaps such as power and cooling water failures.

One method of overcoming the difficulties caused by water failure is to put a interlock on the water line. The interlock cuts the power to the diffusion pump heater if the water flow is interrupted. Another form of protection is a thermoswitch similar to that used on domestic appliances. Mounted on a diffusion-pump boiler, a thermoswitch cuts the power to the diffusion-pump heaters if the boiler of the pump exceeds the preset maximum temperature. This occurs whether the excess heat is caused by interruption of coolant flow or by the coolant's being too hot. However, when the diffusion-pump boiler cools below the preset maximum, the power to the heaters will come back on. This may be an advantage or disadvantage, depending on the situation. A dropout relay may be provided to prevent this cycling.

When a power failure occurs it is advisable to: (1) isolate the vacuum vessel from the pumping system, (2) isolate the diffusion pump from the mechanical pump, (3) let the mechanical pump up to air, and (4) open all the electrical circuits. Since power will not be available to operate the valve mechanism in this event, the usual approach is to have air pressure or spring tension act to close the valve when the power is lost from the solenoid. In other words, this system fails safe.

To prevent damage due to an excessive pressure rise, the high-vacuum gages can be modified to operate an interlock that will cause the high-vacuum isolation valve to close.

One more protective device should be mentioned — in this case, one for the operator. Where high voltage is present in a continuously cycled system, such as an evaporator or electron beam welder, it is absolutely essential to interlock the high voltage with the vacuum. Thus, when the system is at atmospheric pressure the high voltage is off. This can be accomplished by mounting a microswitch on a bellows. The contraction of the bellows when the system is evacuated and the expansion of the bellows when the system is at atmospheric pressure actuates this microswitch. Power to the high-voltage supply is interrupted by the microswitch when the system is at atmospheric pressure. Interlocks of this type are available from several vacuum-equipment manufacturers.

Assembly and Test

Cleaning. The first step to consider in the assembly of the components into a functioning unit is cleaning. Each item, including manufactured components such as valves and pumps, must be cleaned thoroughly. Clean surfaces are an absolute necessity in vacuum work. Very small amounts of volatile solids or liquids will evolve enormous amounts of gas when pumped down in a vacuum system. The vapors produced may also contaminate pump oils, thus reducing the effectiveness of the pump or actually damaging the pump in some cases.

Even though surface deposits of grease and oil may have low vapor pressures they can contain large quantities of absorbed atmospheric gases. These gases are liberated slowly at low pressures, thus reducing the net speed of the pumps.

Visible deposits of such material as cutting oils, tapping compounds, polishing agents, etc. are usually removed by dissolving them with an appropriate solvent. Table 3.2 lists some commonly used solvents and the materials on which they can be used. Use of the solvent in a vapor-phase degreaser is the most effective method, but washing in a bath of solvent is generally adequate. When a solvent bath is used, however, the dissolved deposits are dispersed in solution throughout the bath. When the part is taken out, the solvent evaporates, leaving a thin residue of the dissolved deposit. Flushing with clean solvent is the best means of reducing the residue to a minimum. Ultrasonic agitation of the bath helps to reach the deposits in cracks and holes. Once the section has been cleaned, direct contact with the hands should be avoided and the clean section should be covered or sealed off to prevent recontamination.

Leak-testing Components. After cleaning is completed, the next step in the assembly procedure is to check each component individually for leaks. If there are any holes in the joints or in the walls of the vacuum system through which gas can leak, part of the pumping speed will be used to pump out leakage gas, and therefore the calculated gas-handling capacity of the system will not be available for the process. Locating these small leaks in the walls of a vacuum system can be one of the most troublesome and difficult phases of assembly. Finding leaks can be made less difficult if each component is tested separately before assembly. Just reducing the size and area concerned makes the leaks easier to locate and repair. In addition, with the tightness of each component assured, leak testing the assembled system becomes much less complex.

Instruments Used in Leak Testing. Leak testing generally involves use of a tracer gas. The gas is supplied on one side of the system and indicates a leak by its presence on the other side. Two instruments commonly used to detect the presence of a tracer gas are the halide leak detector and the mass-spectrometer leak detector.

The Halide Leak Detector. The tracer gas used with the halide detector is a halide gas, such as chloroform, carbon tetrachloride, "Freons," or trichloroethylene. The presence of this gas is indicated by the halide detector. This instrument uses the change in emission from a hot platinum filament to detect the presence of a halide. If a halide is present in the gas around the filament, the thermionic emission from the filament increases and registers on a sensitive galvanometer. The halide detector is also sensitive to pump fluids containing halides, so that if the mechanical pump or the diffusion pump uses these, the detector will be ineffective.

The Mass-spectrometer Leak Detector. The mass spectrometer is an instrument that distinguishes between elements by detecting differences in their masses. The mass-spectrometer leak detector is a simplified form of the mass spectrometer, sensitive only to the tracer gas, usually helium. Helium is used because its natural occurrence in the atmosphere is one part in 200,000, and the possibility of another gas being mistaken for it is small. Another advantage to helium is that it is light and diffuses readily into a

TABLE 3.2. PROPERTIES OF COMMONLY USED SOLVENTS.*

Solvent	Chemical formula	Vapor pressure at room temp (torr)	Boiling point (°C)	Flash point (°C)	Toxicity (max. allowable concentration in ppm)
Chlorinated hydrocarbons					
Trichlorethylene	C_2HCl_3	60	87	None	100
Carbon tetrachloride	CCl_4	88	77	None	10
Chloroform	$CHCl_3$	180	61	None	50
Aromatic hydrocarbons					
Benzene	C_6H_6	80	80	−11	25
Toluene	C_7H_8	23	110	·5	200
Xylene	C_8H_{10}	5	140	30	200
Petroleum hydrocarbons					
Stoddard solvent	—	25	155	40	500
Ethers					
Ethyl ether	$C_4H_{10}O$	440	35	−30	400
Ketones					
Acetone	C_3H_6O	180	56	−20	1000
Methyl ethyl ketone	C_4H_8O	71	80	−2	250
Alcohols					
Methyl (wood) alcohol	CH_4O	98	65	15	200
Ethyl (grain) alcohol	C_2H_6O	46	78	18	1000
Isopropyl alcohol	C_3H_8O	38	82	15	400
Fluorinated hydrocarbons					
Trichloromonofluoro-methane "Freon-MF"	CCl_3F	700	24	None	1000
Trichlorotrifluoro-ethane "Freon-TF"	CCl_2FCClF_2	284	48	None	1000
Tetrachlorodiluoro-ethane "Freon-BF"	CCl_2FCCl_2F	57	93	None	1000

*Source: Bulletin FS-6, Solvent Properties Comparison Chart, issued by E. I. du Pont de Nemours & Co., Inc., and used with permission.

Chlorinated hydrocarbons. Carbon tetrachloride is miscible with alcohol, chloroform, or ether. It is an excellent solvent for fats, oils, greases, and waxes. It may cause swelling of Neoprene and natural rubber if they are soaked in it for long periods.

Chloroform is similar in action to carbon tetrachloride, but less toxic and it has a higher evaporation rate.

Trichloroethylene is similar to carbon tetrachloride and chloroform in action but is less toxic and has a lower evaporation rate than either of them.

Aromatic hydrocarbons. Benzene is a solvent for fats, vegetable and mineral oils, rubber, and chlorinated rubber. It is quite toxic and very flammable.

Toluene is similar to benzene but safer to use. It is reported to be an acceptable solvent for the silicone oils.

Petroleum hydrocarbons. Stoddard solvent is a petroleum distillate of low flammability. Its main use is as a dry-cleaning agent.

Ethers. Ethyl ether has a very high evaporation rate and is exceptionally flammable.

Ketones. Acetone is miscible with water and with other solvents such as ether, methyl alcohol, ethyl alcohol, and esters. It will dissolve cellulose acetate, ethyl cellulose, vinyl and methacrylate resins, and chlorinated rubber. Methyl ethyl ketone is similar to acetone but has less solubility in and for water.

Alcohols. Methyl alcohol is miscible with water and most organic liquids. It will dissolve shellac and some vegetable waxes. It is quite toxic, and prolonged breathing of the vapors can cause blindness.

Ethyl alcohol is miscible with water and many organic liquids. It is a solvent for shellac, oils and animal greases. It is relatively nontoxic.

leak. In the operation of the mass-spectrometer leak detector, gas molecules from the system being tested are exposed to a mass analyzer, where they are bombarded with electrons from an incandescent filament and ionized. Any helium ions present are separated from the other ions by electric and magnetic fields and are counted. The output signal from the counter is directly proportional to the number of helium molecules present in the gas from the system being tested. This leak detector is thus a vacuum gage that measures the partial pressure due to helium.

Leak Testing Techniques. There are two general ways by which leaks can be located. One requires a positive pressure inside the part being tested, with atmospheric pressure on the outside. The other uses a vacuum inside the part, with atmospheric pressure outside. Both methods may be required to make a complete test. Often the first step in leak testing may be the pressure test.

Leak Testing with Inside Pressure. With the part pressurized on the inside, leaks can be located in several ways: one can listen for the hiss of escaping air, or, if the part is small enough, it can be submerged in water, and bubbles will show a leak. If the part is too large to dunk and a leak is too small to hear, a soapy solution painted over the test areas will form telltale bubbles. A special solution, "Leak-Tek," is made especially for this purpose. With this method, however, the leak must be large enough to form a bubble within a reasonable time.

When the methods outlined above do not uncover a leak, a halide leak detector may be used. The part is pressurized with a halide gas, and a probe is used to detect any gas that has leaked through. When used in this way, the sensing head, which is hand held, contains a small blower, by which gas from the area being tested is forced past the hot platinum filament. The presence of tracer gas is registered on a meter located in the sensing head.

The mass-spectrometer leak detector may be used in the same way, except that, in this case, the part is pressurized with helium. A sampling probe, consisting of a small needle valve, is used. The probe is connected to the vacuum manifold of the detector by a length of flexible tubing. The probe is moved about over the surface of the part. Helium that is present in the area surrounding a leak is drawn into the probe, through the line, and into the mass analyzer of the detector.

Isopropyl alcohol is similar to the other alcohols listed but is not quite as good a solvent.
Fluorinated hydrocarbons. As a group, these solvents are nonflammable, have a low toxicity, and are very stable. They have very little solvent effect on most plastics and elastomers and have little solubility in or for water. They dissolve most waxes, greases, and oils, including the silicones.
"Freon-MF" has the highest evaporation rate, almost equal to ether. "Freon-TF" is used most frequently, its evaporation rate is equivalent to that of acetone. The evaporation rate of "Freon-BF" is close to that for ethyl alcohol.

Leak Testing with Vacuum. When leaks are small enough to allow the part to be evacuated, the vacuum check is the preferred method, as it is more sensitive and, in many cases, can be quantitative.

It is possible to use the thermal conductivity and ionization gages to detect leaks (with the obvious limitation that the pressure in the part being tested must be within the range of the gage used). In using the thermal conductivity gage or the ionization gage to detect leaks in a component, the gage is first installed on the part. The part is then evacuated to a stable pressure and the surface probed with the selected gas or vapor (acetone, being a common laboratory liquid, is often used, but alcohol and some gases, such as CO_2 and argon, are also effective). A sudden change in the pressure indicated by the gage marks the presence of a leak. It should be borne in mind that the responses of these gages are different for different gases. Hydrogen or hydrogen-containing vapors such as acetone or alcohol will change the response of the gage. Also it should be remembered that if liquid is allowed to cover the leak, the leak may be stopped temporarily, causing a drop in pressure. The response of the ionization gage varies more than that of a thermal-conductivity gage with a change in gas; the ionization gage is therefore to be preferred if a gas is used as a tracer.

When the halide detector is used in vacuum checking, the heated platinum surface is located in a tube which may be attached to the part with a quick-disconnect fitting. The preferred location for the tube is in a region where all the gases must pass. In most cases it is installed in the line leading to the vacuum pump. Halide gas is sprayed over the outside of the part with a small nozzle, which reduces the area being sprayed at one time. If there is a leak, the presence of the halides inside the part will be indicated by the meter, which measures the emission from the hot platinum filament in the tube. To use the mass-spectrometer leak detector on an evacuated part, a line is installed between the part and the vacuum manifold of the detector. Leaks are hunted with a jet of helium, using a probe with a small orifice at the tip to restrict the area covered by the gas. If the part has a leak, the helium on the outside of the part enters and is pumped through the leak detector along with the residual gases from the part. The mass analyzer in the detector will measure the partial pressure of the helium on the leak-rate meter. If a leak is present, the meter reading will increase an amount proportional to the leak rate; thus, not only is a leak indicated, but also its relative size. The percentage concentration of helium over the leak will affect this reading; for best results this concentration should be close to 100%.

When using any mass-spectrometer leak detector, it should be remembered that its performance will be to a great extent dependent on the condition of its own vacuum system. The detector should be used only to detect leaks and never to pump down the part being tested. It should be protected against contamination, and the best standards of cleanliness should be maintained.

Leak Testing a Typical Component. To illustrate a testing procedure in some detail, a description of the complete leak testing of a typical component, the baffle, will be given. Figure 3.19 shows the set-up required. The steps are as follows:

Pumping the Component Down. Attach the baffle to the hookup line and install the necessary temporary cover plates. The same care should be taken in making up these joints as in the assembly of the system itself.

With valves A, B, C, and D closed, start the auxiliary pump. If a thermocouple gage is provided between valve B and the auxiliary pump, the base pressure of the pump is noted for later reference.

Open valves B and D to reduce the pressure in the test volume (the baffle housing).

Assuming that the auxiliary pump has a capacity equal to that used in the system example, the pressure in the baffle should be within range of the thermocouple gage (about 500 microns) within 5 minutes. If this pressure is obtained within this time, proceed to the mass-spectrometer leak check, p. 107.

If the pressure is not within this range within 5 minutes, a large leak may be responsible. Close valve B and stop the mechanical pump for a moment. In a quiet area it is sometimes possible to locate a large leak by tracing its sound.

If no leak is heard, restart the auxiliary pump and open valve B. Attach a second pump to the leads of the internal coil of the baffle. If the leak is in this coil, the pressure in the housing will drop as the coil is pumped down.

If there still is no change in the housing pressure, recheck all gasketed joints for tightness and alignment, and make sure there is a gasket in each joint. Sometimes a joint is assembled without a gasket to check alignment and then forgotten. There is also the possibility that there is water in the baffle — this will keep the pressure above several torr for some time. If none of these steps uncovers a leak, a pressure test will be necessary.

Air Pressure Test. Make sure the component can withstand the internal pressure necessary to make a good test. Attach an air supply to the part and pressurize the part to approximately 5–10 psig, depending on system pressure limits. Paint surfaces of the housing with "Leak-Tek" solution and watch closely for bubble formation. Leaks found in this way should be repaired, and the system pumped down again. If a pressure below 500 microns is obtained, proceed to testing with the mass-spectrometer leak detector. If no bubbles form, a helium pressure test is indicated.

Helium Pressure Test. This method should be approached with care, since helium will be used later for vacuum checking with the mass-spectrometer leak detector. If, during a pressure check, helium is trapped inside the test connections or the part being tested, later vacuum test results could be masked by residual helium. The sampling probe or sniffer is used for this check. The part to be tested is pressurized with helium. (Valve D in Fig. 3.19 must be closed.) The sampling probe is attached to valve C. With valve D closed and the sampling probe closed, open valve C and B and pump down the probe line. With the leak detector in operating condi-

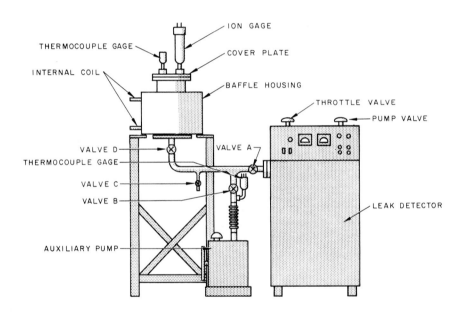

Fig. 3.19. Typical setup for leak checking a component.

tion, open the throttle valve. Close auxiliary-pump valve B. Adjust the probe opening to a stable leak-detector pressure of 0.1 micron. Slowly move the probe over the pressurized component. When a leak is located, a small hood is secured over that local area so that the tracer gas coming from it will not interfere with further testing. Testing is continued following this procedure for each leak until no positive localized response is found. The leaks found are then marked and the component is removed from the test station for repairs. (Note: before the part is removed the leak detector throttle valve should be closed. It should be closed whenever changes are made in the hookup line.)

When repairs have been made, the part is reinstalled on the test station and pumped down with the auxiliary pump preparatory to further checking.

Vacuum Testing with the Mass-spectrometer Leak Detector. If the part is sufficiently leak free (either originally or by repair) to sustain a pressure of approximately 500 microns, the next step is a vacuum test with the mass-spectrometer leak detector.

With the leak detector in operating condition (see Appendix K for operating instructions) and assembled with the component to be tested as shown in Fig. 3.19, the pump valve should be open and the throttle valve closed.

With the filament off, open the throttle valve slowly. With 500 microns in the baffle, only a slight opening of the valve is needed to provide operating pressure in the leak detector. Adjust the valve opening until the gage (of the leak detector) reaches the operating pressure recommended (usually 0.1 micron). Once a steady reading is obtained, turn the filament on and begin checking for leaks.

Begin checking at the top of the part. Helium, which is lighter than air, will move upward, and if one starts at the bottom, there is a chance of the probe's indicating a false leak from helium drifting up from a lower part previously checked. By starting at the top and making temporary seals for any leaks found, there is less chance of a false reading. Under the existing conditions (a pressure of 500 microns in the test piece and the throttle valve just barely open) response will be slow.

The probe must be moved slowly along joints such as the top circumferential weld on the baffle housing. When a response is noted (seen or heard), the spot is marked and the probe removed until the detector ceases to respond. When it clears, begin at this mark and work backward at the same speed until the response is heard again. This spot is also marked. The leak should lie close to the midpoint between the two marks.

One method of testing a small joint, such as those around the leads to the internal coil, is to hood the complete joint with sheet-plastic and masking tape, taking care to exclude the opening of the leads from the hood. By filling the hood with helium, the entire joint is tested at once. If there is no response, the hood is moved to the next small joint. If there is a response the hood is removed and the probe moved back and forth over the region that was under the hood, in order to locate the spot that gives maximum response. If leaks could be sealed as they were found, conditions would improve steadily as the check progressed, and testing would be simple. However, to remove the part and reweld or resolder each leak as it was found would be a long, drawn-out process. The alternative, use of temporary sealing materials, is not recommended because the sealing materials may lodge in the leak, making satisfactory permanent repair difficult. The best compromise is to locate several leaks and then remove the part for repair of these leaks. An acceptable temporary seal can be made by placing a small piece of aluminum foil or sheet plastic over the leak and then applying vacuum putty or vacuum wax, or even "Glyptal," over that.

As leaks are stopped, the pressure in the part being tested drops, and the throttle valve can be opened further without exceeding recommended operating pressure. The response time and recovery time will be shortened; this improves testing conditions. As more leaks are stopped and the pressure in the part drops still farther, the auxiliary pump is throttled until it is closed. Response and recovery times are again shortened, with further improvement in testing conditions.

With the throttle valve wide open and the auxiliary pump closed off, the helium flow from the probe can be greatly reduced and small leaks can be pinpointed. By submerging the probe tip in water, the number of bubbles emerging per unit time can be counted. This provides a rough estimate of the flow of helium; one or two bubbles per second is generally adequate. Leaks are pinpointed by moving the probe slowly around the suspected region until the maximum response is indicated by the leak detector. The location of this spot is noted and the probe is removed until the leak detector clears. Then the probe is placed directly on that spot. If there is a leak, the detector should respond immediately.

In some situations it may be possible to improve testing conditions further by throttling the leak detector's pump valve. Just as the throttle valve controls the pressure drop between the test part and the leak-detector analyzer, the pump valve controls the pressure drop between the analyzer and the leak detector pumps. If, with the auxiliary pump closed off and the throttle valve wide open, the pressure in the leak detector falls below the recommended level, adjustment of the pump valve will bring the pressure up.

Assembly. When all the system components have been checked out as leak-tight, they are ready to be assembled into a unit. If this is done with care, the completed unit will also be leak-free. There are a few specific areas that require special care:

The surfaces against which gaskets seal should be inspected closely for scratches that carry across the sealing area from the vacuum to the atmosphere side.

Check gaskets carefully; when stretched, they should snap back into shape. Old gaskets are not resilient and may have surface checks (cracks). Both these conditions can cause leaks.

Note the dimensions of the O-ring groove. Most standard O rings come in several cross-sectional diameters. This dimension should be about 30% greater than the depth of the groove in which it is to fit (see Appendix L).

Rubber gaskets should be greased with a low vapor-pressure grease, such as Dow Corning high-vacuum grease, or "Apieson L." The grease should be used sparingly. It is not intended as a seal, but serves only to lubricate the gasket so that it will slide into and around surface imperfections. (Grease is of no value on self-lubricating materials such as "Teflon.")

Check the alignment of demountable joints by making a trial assembly without gaskets. Misaligned joints usually leak if they are forced into position instead of being reworked to fit.

The components of most vacuum systems are assembled in the order of convenience. In the construction of the "typical" system the base plate is the support for all other components. Consequently the first step is to secure the base plate to the frame. The valve is then assembled to the base plate, and the baffle to the valve. The diffusion pump is filled with the correct amount of oil and is bolted to the baffle. With the mechanical pump in position, all forevacuum plumbing can be installed. The lead-ins are installed in the base plate, and then the placement of bell jar and hoist completes the assembly. Once the necessary utilities are provided (electricity, water, and compressed air), the system is ready to run.

Startup. A final leak check is made in conjunction with the initial startup. The joints just made up must be tested, and also, since the pumping system will produce a much lower pressure in the bell jar than did the leak detector, some small leaks in this region may be revealed that had previously been masked by the higher pressure.

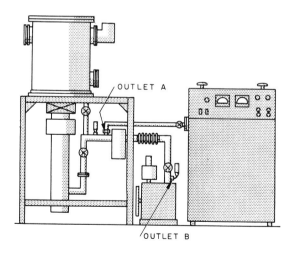

Fig. 3.20. Leak checking the vacuum system.

The leak detector is attached to the forevacuum line of the system at outlet A (see Fig. 3.20). The initial startup procedure is as follows:

(1) Close all valves.

(2) Start the mechanical pump and check the direction of rotation immediately. If the direction is wrong, correct the wiring to the motor.

(3) Determine the base pressure of the mechanical pump by installing a thermocouple-gage tube at outlet B (see Fig. 3.20). A single-stage pump should have a base pressure between 1 and 2×10^{-2} torr; a compound pump between 1 and 5×10^{-3} torr.

(4) Open the mechanical-pump valve. Since the volume of the foreline is small, the pressure in this region should be very close to the base pressure of the mechanical pump in less than a minute, if there are no leaks. If it is necessary to check for leaks, the possibility of leakage through the seat of a backing or roughing valve should be kept in mind, since this would not be detected by probing on the outside.

(5) Open the backing valve. In less than a minute the diffusion pump should be pumped down to near the base pressure of the mechanical pump. The desorption of atmospheric gases contained in the fresh diffusion-pump oil could prolong the first pumpdown of the diffusion pump. This may cause the pressure to level off at some value above the base pressure of the mechanical pump, thus giving a false indication of a leak. However, if gassy diffusion-pump oil is the cause, the pressure should begin to drop again in a short time, continuing until the pressure is very near the mechanical-pump base. If it does not, the reason could be a leak through the seat of the high-vacuum valve, or a leak in a joint.

(6) Close the backing valve and open the roughing valve. Under normal conditions for this system it should take no more than 5 to 7 minutes to reach a pressure near the base of the mechanical pump. If the pressure stops dropping considerably above this, a leak is indicated. This leak could be a virtual leak, however, caused by heavy outgassing of the large surface area presented by the walls of the bell jar. Mild heating (up to 80° C) of the walls of the bell jar should cause a substantial pressure rise. This rise should level off within 15 to 30 minutes and then begin to drop again. The bell jar is then allowed to cool; the pressure should then drop to near the mechanical pump's base pressure. If it does not, the bell jar must be tested with the leak detector.

Most of the joints in the bell-jar region will have been tested except for the lead-ins to the base plate. Since these lead-ins are usually very close together, helium drift can be reduced during testing by constructing a gas-tight cup which can be placed over each lead-in in turn and filled with helium.

(7) When the bell-jar pressure is close to the base pressure of the mechanical pump, the roughing valve is closed and the backing valve opened.

(8) Turn on the diffusion-pump heaters and open the control valve for the diffusion-pump cooling water. Fresh diffusion-pump oil contains a large amount of gas absorbed from the atmosphere during storage. When the oil is heated for the first time, this gas is evolved rapidly, creating a pressure increase in the forevacuum line. A rise of 200 microns is not uncommon. In 5 to 10 minutes the diffusion-pump boiler should be at operating temperature (approximately 200° C). At this point the flow rate of the diffusion-pump cooling water should be adjusted. Most pumps have an optimum cooling-water flow rate based on an inlet water temperature of about 20° C.

The setting of the thermal switch, which shuts off electric power to the diffusion-pump heaters if the pump becomes overheated, should also be made at this time. This switch contains a bimetal strip or similar device which controls the opening and closing of a set of contact points. When the temperature of the thermal switch reaches a preset point, the contacts open, de-energizing a relay, which cuts the heater power. When the temperature drops below this point, the contacts close and manual resetting of the relay will restore power to the heater. The relay prevents undesirable cycling of the boiler heater in the absence of an operator. The temperature at which the points open and close is adjusted by a control screw. The thermal switch is mounted on the casing just above the boiler, and must be in good thermal contact with the casing to operate reliably.

Before the thermal switch is set, the control screw must be turned to its high-temperature limit. The coolant flow rate is then adjusted to the recommended level and the diffusion pump is operated long enough to reach equilibrium temperature.

To set the thermal switch, turn the control screw toward the low-temperature setting until its contacts open, thus shutting off diffusion-pump heater power. Quickly back off one-eighth to one-quarter of a turn on the screw, before the temperature changes. The contacts should close and the power come back on when the relay is reset. With the screw in this position, the diffusion-pump heater should remain on during normal operation.

To test the setting, turn off the cooling water. The heater power should be cut off in about 2 minutes by the thermal switch. A small adjustment of the screw may be necessary to obtain this time lag. When a satisfactory setting is obtained, the screw is locked in position.

(9) Open the high-vacuum isolation valve. If the diffusion pump is operating properly, the pressure in the backing line should increase, because of the increased flow of gases from the bell jar. If the pressure does not

increase, close the valve immediately and check the condition of the pump. (See Chapter 2 for a discussion of diffusion-pump malfunctions.)

(10) If the diffusion pump is operating correctly, the pressure in the bell jar should begin to drop rapidly through the 10^{-4} torr range, slowing as it reaches the middle of the 10^{-5} torr range.

(11) At this time the bell jar and liquid-nitrogen thimble trap can be heated to accelerate degassing of the walls. This can be accomplished by a hot-air blast on the outside walls or by electrical heating tape wrapped around the outside. (Caution: rubber gaskets should not be heated above 100° C.)

(12) The high-vacuum portion of the system is given a final check for leaks. With a clean system and the pressure in the region of 10^{-6} torr, conditions are ideal for leak hunting. Extremely small leaks can be found under these conditions. For high-vacuum leak checking, both the probe and the hood are used. The probe is used first to pinpoint any individual leaks still existing. The hood is used to determine the total leakage of the high-vacuum region.

Probe Method. The leak detector is attached at outlet A as before (see Fig. 3.20). With all but the smallest leaks located and sealed, it will be possible to close the mechanical-pump valve and back the diffusion pump with the leak detector alone. Frequently it is also necessary to partially close the leak detector's pump valve to bring the pressure at the analyzer up to the optimum (usually about 0.2 micron of Hg). The pump valve should not be closed completely, however, as this would result in a measurement of the rate of rise of helium pressure and not an equilibrium rate of leak. Even when the pressure at the analyzer is far below the recommended value, the leak detector will still indicate the presence of helium.

When both the system and the leak detector have been arranged for optimum testing conditions, the high-vacuum portion of the system is probed with the helium nozzle. A minimum flow of helium from the nozzle is used (1 bubble per second), and the probing must be conducted slowly and methodically.

When it is impossible to obtain a response by probing, an evaluation of the total residual leak rate can be made with the hooding method.

Hooding Method. It is virtually impossible to eliminate completely all leaks in a vacuum system. In most practical cases there will be some maximum acceptable total in-leakage. This limit of acceptability is based on such factors as the pumping capacity at the desired operating pressure, process requirements, and the expected gas load. It is quite common to require a minimum leak rate based on the smallest leak detectable by the available detector. By using the mass-spectrometer leak detector to probe for individual leaks, one can establish only that no single leak exists that is equal to or greater than 1×10^{-10} atm-cc/sec. There could be several leaks of some lower value whose combined leakage could exceed the maximum acceptable quantity. To measure this combined leakage with the mass-spectrometer leak detector, the entire outer surface of the vacuum system is covered by helium. On the example system, which is a relatively small unit, this can be accomplished by enclosing the system in a bag or hood made of a gas-tight material such as plastic sheeting. Helium is forced into the bag, displacing the air. On a larger unit this method is usually impractical. On a large unit, however, it is sometimes possible to hood a surface in sections; then all sections are filled with helium to determine the total system leakage.

With the leak detector backing the system and the hood filled with helium, the total in-leakage of the system will register on the leak-rate meter of the detector. This is a relative reading only. To be quantitative it must be compared to a leak of known value. A factory-calibrated leak or a calibrated adjustable leak may be used. In evaluating total leakage by hooding, the calibrated adjustable leak will give more realistic results, since it will be exposed to the same concentration of helium as the unknown leak. The calibrated leak is attached to the system where it will be exposed to conditions approximating as closely as possible any actual leaks. For the system being tested, a bell-jar port will provide an adequate location.

A valve is installed between the calibrated leak and the system. With this valve closed, the hood is filled with helium. If the leak detector has not responded after several minutes the system can be considered acceptably leak-tight. However, it is advisable to test the sensitivity of the leak detector (before uncoupling it from the system) by opening the valve to the calibrated leak. (Note: depending on the size of the calibrated leak, it may be necessary first to pump out the volume between the valve and the leak.)

If the leak detector *does* respond when helium is admitted to the hood, this response is allowed to reach a steady value on the leak-rate meter. The reading is noted and the valve to the calibrated leak is opened. After the response has again become stable, the new reading is noted and the valve is closed. If the leak detector is operating correctly, the meter indication should drop back to the first level. The first reading noted is due to the unknown leak in the system. The second reading minus the first reading is due to the calibrated leak. Since the reading on the leak-rate meter is directly proportional to the amount of helium leaking into the system, then:

$$\frac{\text{the first reading}}{\text{the second reading minus the first reading}} = \frac{\text{unknown leak}}{\text{calibrated leak}},$$

from which the value of the unknown leak rate can be calculated. This leak rate is for helium only and must be converted if the leak rate for air is desired. If this value is low enough to be acceptable, the system is ready to be put into operation. If it is above the acceptable limit, more leak hunting is in order. Since it is assumed that all individual leaks large enough to register on the leak detector have been eliminated, further leak hunting must be done by hooding the system in separate sections. This localizes the leaking region.

After the total in-leakage rate of the system is within acceptable limits, the system should be thoroughly degassed. All surfaces in the high-vacuum region above the diffusion-pump baffle should be raised in temperature to a point just below that which could cause damage (see Chapter 5). This temperature should be held for several hours, or overnight if possible. At the end of the degassing period the cold trap is chilled, and the system is ready for a performance check.

Performance Check. The performance check will determine whether the system meets the required specifications. If the results are recorded and kept with the unit, they will provide an excellent reference for tracing troubles which may occur later. The time to reach the crossover pressure (roughing time) and the time to reach working pressure can be obtained by a test pumpdown of the bell jar. If the system is then left pumping for several hours, the pressure obtained can also be noted and considered as the practical ultimate. Testing the system speed requires some additional preparation.

The system specifications call for a gas throughput of $Q_{process} = 5 \times 10^{-3}$ torr-liters/sec at 1×10^{-5} torr. The system speed therefore should be 500 liters per second. From Eq. (1.8):

$$Q = PS$$
$$5 \times 10^{-3} = (1 \times 10^{-5})S$$
$$S = 5 \times 10^2 = 500 \text{ liters/sec.}$$

A speed-run test must be made to determine if the system requirements have been met.

Figure 3.21 shows schematically a typical arrangement for determining the pumping speed of a vacuum system. The diffusor is a tube that extends well into the vacuum chamber and points away from the pump. Its purpose is to make the leak nondirectional, thus simulating an actual gas load as closely as possible. The leak valve is usually a needle valve by which gas flow can be very closely controlled. It is used to adjust the rate of leak into the chamber. The manometer provides the means of measuring the amount of gas admitted to the chamber. The manometer is usually graduated in milliliters (1 milliliter equals 1 cc). The atmosphere valve is a simple shutoff valve; when it is closed, the gas leaking into the system through the needle valve will be drawn from the trapped volume above

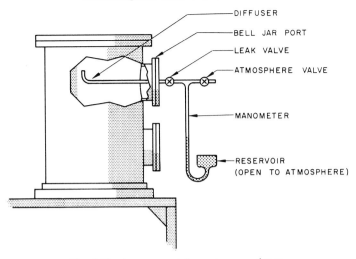

Fig. 3.21. Arrangement for system speed test.

the fluid level in the manometer. As the manometer fluid rises to replace the air drawn into the vacuum chamber it indicates the volume of gas that has entered. The volume entering per unit time can be measured with a stopwatch.

With the leak valve closed and the atmosphere valve open, the system is allowed to reach its equilibrium base pressure. When the leak valve is opened (slowly, to avoid stalling the pump), the pressure will rise as the pump seeks to reach equilibrium with the leak. The leak valve is adjusted until the pressure in the chamber reaches the level at which the test is to be made. After waiting a short time to be sure the pump and the leak are in equilibrium, the atmosphere valve is closed. Since the air is now being drawn from the manometer tube, the fluid in the manometer will rise to replace it. The volume of fluid that rises in the manometer tube per unit of time provides a measure of the amount of air leaking into the system per unit of time. Since the pressure and the volume of the entering air and the pressure in the vacuum chamber are known, the volume of air pumped out of the chamber can be calculated from the equation:

$$P_1V_1 = P_2V_2,$$

where

P_1 = atmospheric pressure,

V_1 = volume of air admitted at P_1,

P_2 = pressure in the vacuum chamber,

V_2 = volume of gas pumped by the vacuum system.

The speed of the leak S_1 is obtained from time t that it takes for the measured volume V_1 to enter the vacuum chamber, that is

$$S_1 = \frac{V_1}{t} \quad \text{and} \quad S_2 = \frac{V_2}{t}$$

Since Q is constant throughout the system,

$$P_1 S_1 = P_2 S_2$$

or

$$S_2 = \frac{P_1 S_1}{P_2}.$$

If S_1 is measured in liters per second and P_1 and P_2 are in the same units of pressure, S_2 is obtained in liters per second.

Example: With a given system it takes 25 minutes (1500 seconds) to displace 10 cc of air (0.01 liter) in the manometer. With the pressure in the chamber at 1×10^{-5} torr, then

$$S_1 = \frac{1 \times 10^{-2} \text{ liter}}{1.5 \times 10^3 \text{ seconds}}$$

or

$$6.67 \times 10^{-6} \text{ liter/sec.}$$

Since P_1 is 760 torr and P_2 is 1×10^{-5} torr,

$$S_2 = \frac{P_1 S_1}{P_2} = \frac{760}{1 \times 10^{-5}} \times 6.67 \times 10^{-6} = 500 \text{ liters/sec.}$$

The following precautions are necessary when this method of measuring the rate of leak into the vacuum chamber is used.

A light fluid, such as a low vapor-pressure degassed oil (specific gravity of 1 or less), should be used in the manometer in preference to mercury.

As much as possible of the total volume of air trapped between the oil and the leak valve should be displaced for each run.

The temperature should not change by more than $3°$ C in any one speed run.

Ideally, the manometer fluid should have the same density as air; if not, the fluid — as it rises in the tube to displace air being drawn out — causes the pressure in the trapped volume to be decreased by an amount equal to the static head (difference in levels) of the fluid. Since a manometer fluid having a density equal to that of air is not available, a fluid of low vapor pressure and low density, such as "Octoil" (specific gravity 0.98) or butyl phthalate (specific gravity 1.04) is used (certainly not mercury, which has a specific gravity of 13.6). Therefore, in the equation

$$S_2 = \frac{P_1 S_1}{P_2}$$

P_1 will not be atmospheric pressure but somewhat less. This could be accounted for quite simply by correcting the value of P_1 in the equation. However, this is not the only effect that the lower pressure has on the trapped volume.

If the trapped volume in the manometer, before the oil begins to rise, is quite large compared to the volume displaced during the speed run, more air will be drawn into the chamber than is measured with the manometer. This causes the calculated speed to be erroneously low. This can best be explained by an example.

Assume a trapped volume of 100 cc. A displacement of 10 cc is recorded for a test run, causing the oil to ride 13.6 cm above the level in the reservoir. A static head of 13.6 cm of oil with a specific gravity of 1 indicates a pressure in the trapped volume of 1 cm Hg (10 torr) less than atmospheric (the specific gravity of mercury is 13.6). If atmospheric pressure is taken as 750 torr, then the amount of gas in the trapped volume before the run was 750 torr $\times$ 0.1 liter (100 cc), or 75 torr-liters. The amount withdrawn was 0.01 liter (10 cc); thus there is 0.09 liter (90 cc) remaining in the volume at a pressure of 750 minus 10, or 740 torr. The amount of gas remaining is 740 $\times$ 0.09, or 66.6 torr-liters. The amount of gas that has entered the chamber during the run is therefore 75 torr-liters minus 66.6 torr-liters, or 8.4 torr-liters. The volume of 8.4 torr-liters of gas at S.T.P. is

$$\frac{8.4 \text{ torr-liters}}{750 \text{ torr}}$$

or, 0.0112 liter (11.2 cc), which is 12% greater than the measured displacement. Thus the actual pump speed is 12% greater than that calculated with the uncorrected volume.

A change in temperature will also have an effect on the measurement of displacement. The volume of gas is proportional to its absolute temperature. Therefore, a temperature change of 2.73° C means a volume change of 1%. If, for example, the trapped volume is 100 cc as above, the 1% change would be 1 cc. Depending on the rate of temperature change, the observed displacement could be in serious error.

Operation. For any vacuum system, it is advisable to establish at the outset safe operational procedures that will satisfy the requirements of the process. Once established, these procedures should be made routine. This will prevent errors that might cause equipment failure and will help keep the system functioning at its best. The sequence of operation may vary somewhat with different systems. The following general procedures should suit most standard installations.

(1) *Starting the mechanical pump*

(a) Turn on the mechanical-pump switch. Be sure the pump starts and not just the motor. Pumps often seize during shutdown periods and this condition is not noticed until startup. If it is a new installation be sure the pump is rotating in the right direction.

(b) Open the mechanical-pump valve.

(c) Wait until the foreline pressure reaches 50 microns, chill the foreline trap, and then proceed to the next step.

(2) *Starting the diffusion pump*

(a) Open the backing valve.

(b) When the pressure reaches about 50 microns, turn on the diffusion-pump heaters and open the valves for the pump-casing cooling water and baffle cooling water.

(c) Allow the diffusion pump to reach operating temperature. The time required varies with the size and make of pump. (It will be given in the pump's operating instructions or in the manufacturer's catalogs.)

(3) *Pumping down the vessel*

(a) Close the backing valve and open the roughing valve.

(b) When the vessel pressure is below 50 microns, close the roughing valve, open the backing valve, and open the high-vacuum isolation valve. As the isolation valve is opened and the diffusion pump begins working, there will be a noticeable increase in the forepressure. This increase is normal, but it can be reduced by roughing the vessel to a lower pressure.

(c) When the forepressure drops to its previous level, the vessel pressure should be within range of the high-vacuum gage, which can then be turned on.

(d) If the system has not been operated for some time, it may be advisable to heat the walls of the vessel mildly (within the temperature limit of the materials used in its construction) to accelerate degassing.

(e) If the system has a thimble trap, it is chilled when the pressure appears to stop dropping, or, if the vessel is heated for degassing, when the heat is removed.

(4) *Complete shutdown*

A system should be shut down completely only when absolutely necessary. The conditions of the mechanical pump, diffusion pump, and vessel are improved by continued pumping. Continual starting up and shutting down lead to burned out heaters, leaky oil drains on the diffusion pump, and frequent oil changes for the mechanical pump. Also, minimum exposure of the vessel to atmosphere reduces pumpdown time, improves base pressure, and reduces maintenance requirements.

When a location is subject to frequent power failures, the vacuum system must be completely shut down when unattended, unless it has fail-safe protection.

The sequence for a complete shutdown of the vacuum system is as follows:

(a) Shut off the power supply to the high-vacuum gages.

(b) Close the high-vacuum isolation valve and vent the bell jar.

(c) Remove the refrigerant from the cold trap and allow the trap to warm up. If it is a thimble trap it must be removed from the system, warmed, cleaned, and replaced.

(d) Shut off the diffusion-pump heater and allow it to cool to at least 80° C, preferably to room temperature.

(e) Shut off the pump-casing cooling water and the baffle cooling water.

(f) Close the mechanical-pump valve and vent the diffusion pump.

(g) Shut off and vent the mechanical pump.

(5) *Partial shutdown*

To gain access to the vessel requires only a partial shutdown, as follows:

(a) Turn off the high-vacuum gage.

(b) Close the high-vacuum isolation valve.

(c) Vent the vessel. A reduction in the time required for subsequent pumpdown is possible if the venting is done with dry nitrogen.

(d) If a thimble trap is used, it should be removed, cleaned, and replaced.

(6) *Startup from partial shutdown*

The starting sequence from a partial shutdown is the same as step (3). When a partially shutdown system is to be idle for an hour or more, it is advisable to pump the vessel back to the base pressure. This helps to keep surfaces clean. For shorter periods pumpdown may be impractical. However, the vessel should always be closed (bell jar lowered into sealing position) while it is not being worked on, to exclude dust and moisture-laden air.

Troubleshooting. The prevention, detection, and correction of troubles that occur in vacuum systems will be easier if the performance of the system under normal conditions is known; that is, if the base pressure, pumpdown time, rate of pressure rise in the valved-off vessel, etc., are known for the system when it is clean, dry, and leak-tight, and when the pumps are operating properly.

Comparisons will frequently indicate the region of difficulty. For example, if roughing down takes longer than the normal time, the system may be dirty, there may be a leak, or the mechanical pump may be failing. If, after crossover, the base pressure with the diffusion pump included compares favorably with the normal value, the first two possibilities are unlikely. If the forepressure at this time is higher than that recorded, the mechanical pump would appear as the most likely cause of the difficulty.

A daily record of pumpdown time and base pressure will also be extremely helpful. Any deterioration of a system with time will be apparent and provide the opportunity to practice preventive maintenance.

A rate-of-pressure-rise measurement in the valved-off vessel when the vessel is known to be clean, dry, and leak-tight will provide a basis for comparison of the condition of the vessel. This rate-of-rise measurement should be taken from the base pressure of the vessel.

To correctly diagnose faulty system performance, it will be necessary to have a thorough knowledge of the function and characteristics of all the system components. For example, if the roughing time is satisfactory but the decrease in vessel pressure is slow after crossover, a faulty diffusion pump is indicated. By knowing what could cause such a condition, it is possible to locate the trouble quickly and make corrections.

By having these data on normal system performance and knowledge of system components, it is possible to locate the malfunctioning portion of a system by the proper manipulation of valves.

Assuming a frequently encountered condition, that of a higher-than-normal base pressure in the vessel, and a higher-than-normal forepressure, a useful procedure is as follows: close the mechanical-pump valve. On a gage installed between this valve and the mechanical pump, one of three conditions will be noted:

The pressure does not change. This could be due to:

(a) A bad gage (check this by replacing it with a tested gage and power supply).

(b) A leak between the mechanical pump and the valve. This possibility must be investigated by using a leak detector.

(c) A faulty pump. Changing the oil may be a cure, but if several changes do not correct the difficulty, an overhaul or replacement is indicated.

The pressure starts dropping slowly.

(a) If it stops before reaching the base of the mechanical pump, usually dirty oil is indicated.

(b) If it reaches the base of the mechanical pump very slowly, a leaky seal or blocked oil line could be the cause.

The pressure starts dropping rapidly to the base of the mechanical pump. This indicates that the problem lies upstream of the mechanical-pump valve. If the difficulty does seem to be upstream, open the mechanical-pump valve and allow the pressure to return to its previous level. Close the backing valve and note the pressure indicated by the forepressure gage.

If the forepressure does not change, the cause may be:

(a) A leak in the foreline. This can be determined with a leak detector.

(b) A faulty gage. Check this possibility by substituting one that is known to read correctly.

If the pressure drops, the cause may be:

(a) A leak in the diffusion pump.

(b) A gas load from the vessel.

This situation can be resolved by further tests upstream. Open the backing valve and allow the pressure to reach the level it had prior to the closing of the valve. Close the high-vacuum isolation valve.

If the forepressure does not change, the cause may be:

(a) A leak in the diffusion-pump region, including the baffle housing. This possibility must be checked with the leak detector. The seal on the diffusion-pump drain is a common cause of such leaks.

(b) High-vapor-pressure substance in the oil, or excessively decomposed oil. The fluid must be drained and replaced (check the amount of fluid; this could be a contributory factor). The odor of cracked or contaminated oil is distinctive, but difficult to describe.

A slow drop in the forepressure usually indicates that the diffusion pump is working, but below normal. Check those conditions that could cause a slow pump, such as low heater power, coolant too cold, thermal switch out of adjustment, poor thermal contact between heater and boiler, etc.

A rapid drop of the forepressure indicates that the diffusion pump is operating properly and is working on a gas load from the system. The gas load could be due to heavy degassing from the system or to leaks.

(a) If the system is at all dirty, it should be cleaned. Even if contamination is not the primary cause, leaks will be easier to find with a clean system.

(b) If a leak is indicated, check first the areas where changes have been made recently. Check sealing surfaces for scratches, check gaskets for debris, and then use the leak detector to localize the leak.

An excessive rate of pressure rise in the vessel (compared with the rate of rise known to exist when the vessel is clean and tight) indicates either a leak into the vessel or excessive volatile contaminants in the vessel. Rate of rise can be measured with a stopwatch and a pressure gage.

REFERENCE

1. 1960 Seventh Annual Symposium on Vacuum Technology Transactions, Pergamon Press, New York, 1961, p. 372.

CHAPTER 4

Ultrahigh Vacuum

An ultrahigh vacuum system is usually considered one that will pump to pressures of 10^{-9} torr and below. The need for these low pressures lies mainly in the field of scientific research.

For instance, in the study of plasmas (fully ionized gases), it is necessary to keep the impurity (nonplasma) gases to an irreducible minimum. Otherwise the hot ions of the plasma, confined by a magnetic field, could be neutralized by exchange of electrons with impurity-gas molecules. The neutralized ions would then be lost to the walls of the system. Furthermore, if the system walls were not degassed (as they must be to achieve ultrahigh vacuum), the collisions of the neutralized ions with them would liberate quantities of adsorbed gas, and thus increase the concentration of impurity gases.

Another area in which ultrahigh vacuum is needed is that of semiconductor research. In this field, surface studies of thin films deposited on very clean surfaces (substrates) are made to determine semiconductor characteristics. Since the work function of a semiconductor changes drastically with the amount of gas adsorbed on its surface, it is important to control this amount closely. At a pressure of 10^{-6} torr, the minimum time for one monolayer (a layer one molecule thick) of gas to form on the clean surface is one to two seconds; at 10^{-9} torr it is about half an hour; in the 10^{-10} torr range, it is a matter of hours. Thus the advantage, if not the actual necessity, of operating at ultrahigh vacuum pressures when doing surface studies is apparent.

Still another area of scientific investigation that uses ultrahigh vacuum is space research. To simulate an altitude of 300 miles at room temperature, for instance, requires a pressure on the order of 10^{-9} torr.

As stated in Chapter 2, vacuum systems can be classified according to the range of pressure they can produce and in which they operate. These categories were rough vacuum, low vacuum, high vacuum, very high vacuum, and ultrahigh vacuum.

Rough vacuum (760 to 1 torr) and low vacuum (1 torr to 10^{-3} torr) can be produced by rotary pumps alone. Relatively high vapor-pressure organic sealing materials such as "Glyptal," vacuum wax, or rubber gaskets lubricated with vacuum grease may be used, and construction materials are almost unlimited.

Fig. 4.1. Ultrahigh vacuum pumping system. 1. Diffusion pump; 2. Elbow trap and baffle; 3. Liquid nitrogen level controller; 4. All-metal gate valve; 5. Pumping manifold.

Diffusion pumps backed by rotary mechanical pumps will produce high vacuum (10^{-3} to 10^{-6} torr). Organic seals are still acceptable, but are used with more care, and construction materials with low vapor pressure are preferred.

A very high vacuum (10^{-6} to 10^{-9} torr) will be produced by a diffusion pump backed by a rotary mechanical pump, if the diffusion pump is well trapped. Only a few of the organic sealing materials are acceptable, and their use is held to a minimum. Only low-vapor-pressure construction materials are used.

Ultrahigh vacuum (10^{-9} torr and below) can also be produced by a diffusion pump backed by a rotary mechanical pump. Both pumps must be extremely well trapped, and metal gaskets are used instead of elastomers; construction materials are selected to withstand the system bakeout that is usually necessary. (See Fig. 4.1.) It is important to note that the same

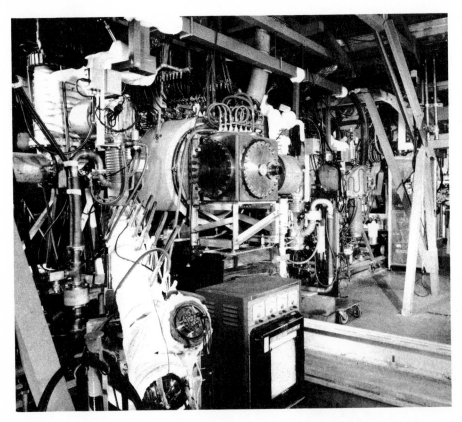

Fig. 4.2. Ultrahigh vacuum pumping system in use on a plasma physics experiment.

type of equipment that produces the high and very high vacuum can produce an ultrahigh vacuum. There is nothing inherently mysterious or exotic about ultrahigh vacuum; the difference between obtaining high vacuum and ultrahigh vacuum lies in the techniques and materials used.

Figure 4.2 shows an ultrahigh vacuum pumping system used on a plasma experiment.

The characteristics of any vacuum system in equilibrium can be described as follows: a box representing a vessel, as shown in Fig. 4.3, has a gas flow into it represented by Q_l, leaking from the atmosphere; Q_o outgassing from surfaces, Q_{bs}, backstreaming from the pumping system; and

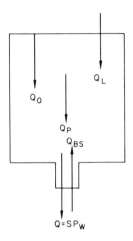

Fig. 4.3.

Q_p, gas evolved from the process. The gas flow *out* of the box can be represented by the product of the speed S of the system and the operating or working pressure P_w. That is,

$$Q_l + Q_o + Q_{bs} + Q_p = SP_w$$

or

$$P_w = \frac{Q_l + Q_o + Q_{bs} + Q_p}{S}.$$

Since control over the process gas is limited, efforts in producing a minimum base pressure are confined to control of Q_l, Q_o, Q_{bs}, and S. The base pressure of the system is

$$P_b = \frac{Q_l + Q_o + Q_{bs}}{S} \tag{4.1}$$

It is these four factors Q_l, Q_o, Q_{bs}, and S that will be considered in the following sections.

GAS LEAKAGE

Gas leakage (Q_l in Eq. (4.1)) may occur through the system walls, through joints, or across seals. Leakage through the system walls is negligible for such metals as aluminum or 304 stainless steel. These materials are often used in ultrahigh vacuum construction. Glass is permeable to helium to some extent; however, this leakage is low enough to allow ultrahigh vacuum to be obtained in glass systems.

Joints

Joints in ultrahigh vacuum systems are made to stringent specifications. Joining may be accomplished by welding (usually inert-gas-shielded tungsten arc welding) or by brazing with alloys of very low vapor pressure. In either case great care must be taken with cleanliness and proper fit in the preparation of the joint. The connections must also, of course, be

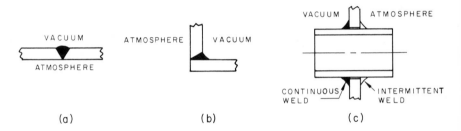

(a)   (b)   (c)

Fig. 4.4. Weld joints for ultrahigh vacuum use. (Also see Appendix N.)

cleaned thoroughly after the joint is made. The joints are checked to leak rates less than 10^{-10} atm-cc/sec on the leak detector. Figure 4.4 shows some recommended welding configurations for joints. See Appendix N for further details.

Seals

Seals for ultrahigh vacuum systems are of two types: static or fixed seals for demountable joints and dynamic seals to accommodate the passage of rotary or reciprocating motion through the walls of the vacuum system.

Ultrahigh vacuum sealing materials are either elastomers or metals. The use of elastomers is restricted to systems in which they will not be heated to over 200° C; some hydrocarbon elastomers begin to decompose at 100° C. "Viton" and "Kel-F" are fluorocarbon elastomers of low vapor pressure. Silicones have the lowest vapor pressure of any of the elastomers, but they are also the most permeable. In an application such as a valve seat, however, this limitation could be unimportant. When seal temperatures exceed 200° C, metal is the sealing material used. Although it is far more difficult to make a seal with metal than with elastomers, metal seals are used because of their low vapor pressure, low permeability, and ability to withstand bakeout. Copper, copper-nickel, aluminum, and gold are the metals used most frequently.

Static Seals. In general, the static seal is accomplished by plastically deforming an elastic material into the nonuniform surface of a mating flange, thus reducing the leakage below the limit of detectability. The design of static seals has been the subject of much research and development, and there are many different types in use. The design of static seals using fluorocarbons resembles that of the usual O-ring application, with the exception of those using "Teflon," which will cold-flow and must have positive restraint. There are also designs using Buna-N and Butyl that can accommodate bakeout. The flanges of these seals are water-cooled and the seals perform well after bakeout if they are refrigerated to reduce out-

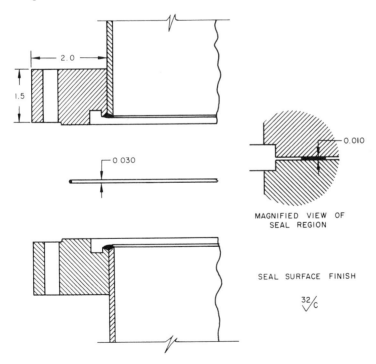

MAGNIFIED VIEW OF
SEAL REGION

SEAL SURFACE FINISH

$\frac{32}{\sqrt{}}$C

Fig. 4.5. Aluminum O-ring seal for ultrahigh vacuum.

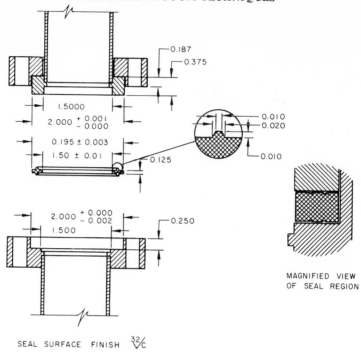

SEAL SURFACE FINISH $\sqrt[32]{\text{C}}$

Fig. 4.6. Coined copper seal.

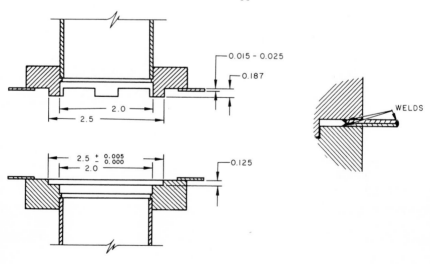

Fig. 4.7. Take-apart weld seal. (From ORNL Rept. CF 59.8.80.)

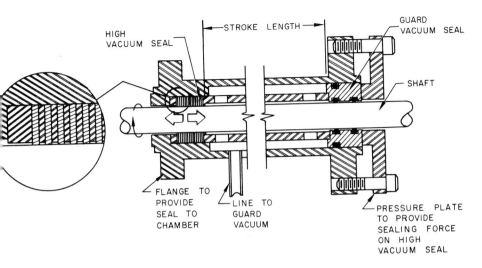

Fig. 4.8. Differentially pumped dynamic seal.

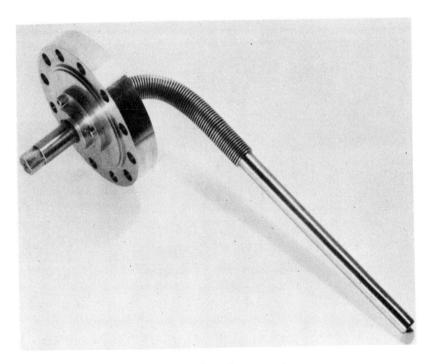

Fig. 4.9. All-metal rotary seal.

gassing and permeation. Some examples of metal-seal designs are shown in Figs. 4.5, 4.6, and 4.7. Appendix L gives a more comprehensive treatment of some static seal designs.

Dynamic Seals. The design of an ultrahigh vacuum dynamic seal employing elastomers should include provisions for differential pumping, as shown in Fig. 4.8. A guard vacuum is supplied to reduce the pressure differential across the seal. In a differentially pumped elastomer seal used for reciprocating motion, the distance between the high-vacuum seal and the guard-vacuum seal should be equal to or greater than the length of the stroke, to prevent air from being carried into the system on the surface of the rod. If the seal is to be used for rotary motion only, the distance between the differentially pumped seals need not be so great. If the system is to be baked, the differentially pumped seal must be cooled during this time.

Dynamic seals using metal (see Fig. 4.9) can be made by means of metal bellows. These seals will withstand high-temperature bakeouts without having to be cooled. Another means of transmitting motion through the wall of a vacuum system is by the magnetic drive shown in Fig. 4.10. The available torque is limited, however, and slippage may occur.

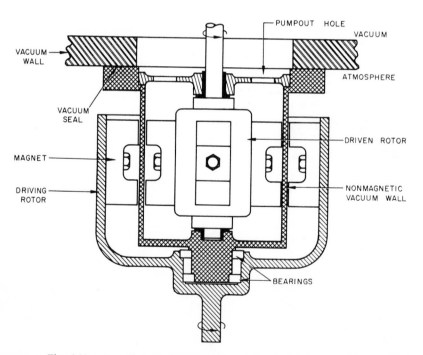

Fig. 4.10. Magnetic drive for rotary motionthrough the vacuum wall.

In general, then, leakage gas can be kept to a minimum (less than 10^{-10} atm-cc/sec) if construction materials are chosen carefully, welded or brazed joints are sound, static and dynamic seals are designed properly, and if all materials and components can withstand bakeout temperatures.

OUTGASSING

The gas load due to outgassing (Q_0 in Eq. (4.1)) comes from the surfaces in the vacuum. It can be kept to an acceptable minimum by carefully selecting the materials to be used in the vacuum and by keeping these materials clean. Materials such as stainless steel, copper, bronze, steel, and aluminum have low vapor pressures and are good ultrahigh vacuum construction materials. They have an equilibrium outgassing rate near 10^{-10} torr-liter/sec per square centimeter. After a bakeout at 400° C, stainless steel and aluminum go to less than 10^{-12} torr-liter/sec per square centimeter. Cadmium and zinc, often found in hard solders and brazing alloys, should not be used in ultrahigh vacuum construction, as they have vapor pressures of at least 0.1 torr at 400° C. Magnesium is another metal with high vapor pressure at bakeout temperature.

Large amounts of gas are pumped out of a system during a long bakeout (of 48 hours, for instance). It can be shown that the amount of gas pumped out is greater than the amount that could have been adsorbed onto the system walls. This indicates that much of the pumped gas must result from diffusion out of the metal, rather than desorption from its surface.

Most elastomers have a room-temperature vapor pressure of less than 10^{-6} torr, but they have poor heat resistance, and liberate large quantities of gas as they decompose. The hydrocarbons generally begin to decompose at 100° C. Of the fluorocarbons, "Viton" begins to decompose at 250° C and "Teflon" at about 325° C.

Lubrication

Proper lubrication is a problem in all high and ultrahigh vacuum systems at very low pressures because ordinary lubricants either become ineffective or evaporate. Dry lubricants, such as molybdenum disulfide, must be used at very low pressures. Molybdenum disulfide will form molybdenum trioxide at about 500° C in the atmosphere, but in vacuum, where there is little oxygen available, decomposition is negligible. Two lubricants of this type are "Electrofilm 1005" (molybdenum disulfide and glass frit in xylene) and "Molykote X-15" (molybdenum disulfide in a sodium-silicate solution). "Electrofilm 1005" is applied by air brush and is baked on in vacuum at 1100° F for up to an hour. "Molykote X-15" can be applied by brush or spray, then is air-dried.

Cleaning

Cleaning of materials to be placed in the vacuum is essential. Satisfactory cleaning methods include the vapor-phase degreaser, the ultrasonic bath, or simply washing with detergent and water, followed by a water rinse. Generally, the cleaning method depends on the kind of deposit to be removed. In extreme cases, and where the material to be cleaned will survive such treatment, boiling in hydrogen peroxide or firing in a hydrogen atmosphere is very effective.

BACKSTREAMING

Gas emanating from the pumping system (Q_{bs} in Eq. (4.1)) is the largest source of gas at the base pressure. There are three main sources of vapors and gases from the pumping system: pump-fluid vapor that backstreams, pump fluid that migrates along the walls of the system, and back-diffusing gases from thermally cracked pump-fluid.

Pump-fluid vapors that backstream can be stopped by traps. Two types of trap are used in ultrahigh vacuum systems. In the liquid-nitrogen trap shown in Fig. 4.11 surfaces maintained at liguid-nitrogen temperature block

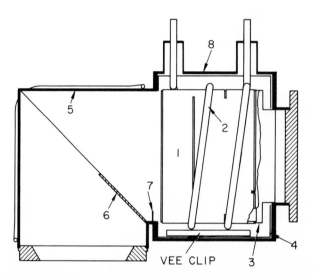

VEE CLIP   3

Fig. 4.11. Combination elbow baffle and liquid nitrogen trap. 1. Trap; 2. Liquid nitrogen coil; 3. Oil migration barrier; 4. Heat shields; 5. Water-cooled below; 6. Line-of-sight baffle with drain hole; 7. Dam to prevent condensed oil on elbow from draining into trap housing; 8. Trap housing with re-entrant filler tubes.

the straight-line path from pump to vessel. To get into the vessel from the pump, all gases must strike a cold surface at least once. In another type, the so-called "room-temperature" trap, shown in Fig. 4.12, the blocking surfaces are covered with adsorbent materials such as artificial zeolite or

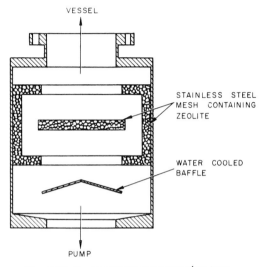

Fig. 4.12. Room-temperature sorption trap.

aluminum oxide. The adsorbents must be reactivated periodically by baking at temperatures up to 350° C under vacuum.

Another source is the pump fluid that migrates along the walls of the system. This migration is arrested either by a surface cooled with liquid nitrogen or by adsorption into the zeolites or aluminas mentioned above. In the liquid-nitrogen-cooled trap, a surface cooled by liquid nitrogen is used as a barrier over which the fluid cannot creep (see Fig. 4.11). In the adsorbent-type trap the barrier is covered with adsorbents.

Actually, in a well-designed system, it is found that the pump fluid itself contributes little to the total vapor pressure in the vessel. Some pump oils, for example, have vapor pressures at room temperature of the order of 10^{-8} torr; some of the polyphenyl ethers have vapor pressures at room temperature as low as 10^{-10} torr. The objectionable gas probably comes from fractions of the pump fluid cracked in the diffusion-pump boiler. Most of these fractions are hydrogen and hydrocarbons such as methane and ethane, whose vapor pressures even at liquid-nitrogen temperatures are quite high (several torr). Some of these gases may come from mechanical-pump oil that has backstreamed into the diffusion-pump boiler, where it is cracked at boiler temperatures. This latter condition can be minimized by putting a trap in the foreline between the mechanical pump and the diffusion pump.

The use of getter-ion pumps is an effective way to avoid the problems associated with backstreaming. Since they use no oil, they do not require a trap between pump and vessel. They do not backstream in the usual sense, but do exhibit about the same base pressure on a baked system as a trapped diffusion pump. A system pumped by a getter-ion pump and backed and roughed by sorption pumps has the unique advantage of not involving any hydrocarbons in the pumping process. However, there are disadvantages to such a system. For instance, it is difficult to pump noble gases, such as argon and helium. Several millitorr of helium are left in a system roughed by the sorption pump and must be consumed by the getter-ion pump.

Molybdenum gettering is a fairly recent ultrahigh vacuum technique. The vessel is first pumped down to pressures below 10^{-8} torr by the usual method (trapped diffusion pumps, for instance). Molybdenum, in the form of wire filaments (see Fig. 4.13) is raised to about 1700° C by resistance heating to drive out absorbed gases. The temperature is then increased until a coating of molybdenum is deposited on the walls of the vessel. Active gases in the vessel, such as oxygen, hydrogen, and nitrogen, will be

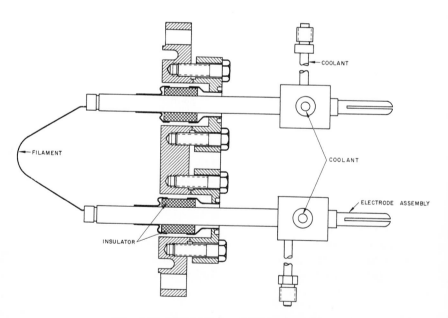

Fig. 4.13. Molybdenum evaporator assembly.

gettered on the surface of this newly deposited molybdenum. High pumping speeds at very low pressures have been obtained with this method; gas can be removed at the rate of 2 to 4 liters/sec per square centimeter of surface. A particular advantage of molybdenum over other active metals, such as titanium, is that it can be more thoroughly degassed.

Cryogenic (low-temperature) pumping is useful in specific ultrahigh vacuum applications but has not been used extensively. The principle of cryogenic pumping, of course, is not new; it has been used for years in cold traps and cold thimbles. One technique being investigated is the use of a cryogenic fluid, such as helium, to solidify oxygen, carbon dioxide, or nitrogen on a surface held at a temperature less than 11° K. This surface is then used to adsorb hydrogen at pressures well below the equilibrium vapor pressure of hydrogen at this temperature. The pumping rate for hydrogen is 20 liters/sec per square centimeter. However, as soon as a monolayer of hydrogen forms on the cryogenic surface, the speed for hydrogen falls off rather rapidly.

PUMPING SPEED

The last of the four factors that affect the base pressure is the pumping speed (S in Eq. (4.1)). This must be maximized to get the lowest possible base pressure. The conductance of the connections between the diffusion pump and the vessel must be as high as possible, but not at the expense of allowing backstreaming pump fluid to reach the vessel. The system should have a full-opening valve, a low-impedance but efficient trap, and a low-impedance baffle. Such a system is shown in Fig. 4.1. It has a valve, trap and baffle between the pump and the vessel, and provides an over-all pumping efficiency of about 30%. That is, for a 1500-liter/sec pump the system speed is about 450 to 500 liters/sec. The valve is all metal, full-opening, has a high conductance, and is bakeable to 400° C. The trap design is also unique (see Fig. 4.11). There is no reservoir in the system; liquid nitrogen is simply circulated through a tube from a Dewar flask. There is also a migration barrier between the trap and the flange body. There is no water baffle as such, but there is an elbow which is water-cooled and also radiation-cooled by the liquid nitrogen-temperature trap surfaces. All fluid emanating from the diffusion pump must first hit this elbow, which is at cooling-water temperature or below. In this way the vapor pressure of the fluid "seen" by the liquid nitrogen-cooled surface is the vapor pressure consistent with the temperature of the cooled elbow. Therefore, very little fluid is transferred to the trap; most of it drains back into the pump.

The technology of ultrahigh vacuum is well developed; nowadays it is a routine matter to reach pressures of the order of 10^{-10} torr. Further progress will depend on improvements in components. For instance, few bakeable high-conductance valves having reasonable reliability are available commercially. Gages offer the problem of calibration; there is currently no means for absolute calibration of ionization gages in the ultrahigh vacuum range. Faster diffusion pumps would be an advantage, but these seem difficult to develop. Actually, a reduction in the amount of gas emanating from the pump would have the same effect. To this end, development of oils with a lower vapor pressure and a higher resistance to cracking would be helpful. Lastly, it should be possible to reduce the amount of gas evolving from the walls of the vacuum system. This entails the development of materials and seals that would withstand higher temperatures during bakeout, and perhaps very low temperatures during operation.

CHAPTER 5

Properties of Materials Used in Vacuum Systems

To obtain the lowest pressures and gain the most satisfactory service from any vacuum system, the materials of which it is made must be chosen with care: such properties as their outgassing rate and permeability must be considered. There are also the problems associated with joining the materials in a vacuum-tight working unit; possible chemical reactions between different materials must be guarded against, and proper welding or brazing techniques must be used. Finally, the cost of the material must be taken into account. In most cases a compromise between quality, economy, and feasibility must be accepted. Here again, a thorough knowledge of the properties of materials will make the compromise most satisfactory.

Outgassing

The gases evolved from a material under vacuum stem from three sources: evaporation (or chemical decomposition), desorption from surfaces, and diffusion out of the material. The evaporation rates and equilibrium vapor pressures of the elemental metals can be calculated from thermodynamic relationships. (Values for the more frequently used metals are listed in Appendix J.) Evaporation rates for alloys are not as predictable as for elements, although the rates for the metallic elements of which the alloy is composed provide a basis for estimating. The evaporation rates of chemical compounds, organic ones in particular, are quite difficult to predict. These compounds are also subject to decomposition.

The amount of sorbed (that is, either absorbed or adsorbed, or both) gases released from the surface and from the interior of a material will vary widely with the type of material and with its history. As a result, it is impractical to estimate the outgassing rates on the basis of calculations alone.

Instead, tests are made on samples of a given material under controlled conditions. By exposing a significant number of samples to the same set of conditions, an average value of outgassing rate is obtained. In this way the total gas evolved by the sample, whether by desorption or by diffusion, can be determined. The amount of gas released from a known surface area at a given temperature and pressure per unit time is known as its air-equivalent outgassing rate. This rate is usually measured in torr-liters/sec per square centimeter. Such measurements have been made on a wide selection of materials by many experimenters. Several of the more recent reports on these measurements are listed in Appendix C.

Permeability

The permeability of a material is a measure of how much of a given gas (at a given temperature) will diffuse through it per unit time. It is difficult to arrive at an absolute value for a material, because the pressure difference across it, its temperature, its purity, and the condition of its surface all affect its permeability. Tests under controlled conditions, similar to those made to determine outgassing rates, are made to establish the permeability of materials. While permeability is usually important only in ultrahigh vacuum systems, any material that has a high permeability to helium will be unsuitable for systems that are checked with a mass-spectrometer leak detector.

Joining Properties

The properties of a material that will affect the techniques of joining are of definite interest in vacuum work. One should know whether the material can be welded, brazed, and/or soldered to form a vacuum-tight seal. What types of fluxes, braze alloys, or solders to use in joining should be known. Some materials react chemically with others when joined in a system; these should be known and special care taken in their use.

Economy

As mentioned above, the choice of a material is often a compromise between quality, economy, and feasibility. For instance, a material may be low in initial cost, but the cost of machining may be prohibitively high.

ELEMENTAL MATERIALS AND ALLOYS

Aluminum

Aluminum is a strong, light-weight, corrosion-resistant metal with a low vapor pressure. Aluminum is inexpensive, easy to work, and readily available in most common forms, such as pipe, tubing, plate, sheet, foil, bars, and various extruded shapes. For these reasons it is widely used as a construction material for vacuum systems. Although pure aluminum is sometimes used, aluminum alloys with higher strengths are usually preferred. Aluminum is joined by inert gas-shielded tungsten arc welding. It is difficult to make vacuum-tight joints with some aluminum alloys; both 6061 alloy and pure aluminum, however, allow vacuum-tight joints. Joints can be made by soldering or brazing, but they are frequently porous and are to be avoided, if possible.

Antimony

Antimony is a constituent of some low-melting alloys used for soft soldering. Its use in vacuum systems should be avoided where possible because it has a high vapor pressure (10^{-4} torr at 400° C) and is difficult to remove once it enters a vacuum system.

Brass

Brass is essentially a copper-zinc alloy, although there are variations containing other elements. It is widely used as a construction material, although the zinc limits its use to situations where it will not be heated above 200° C. Brass is easy to machine and is easy to join by using soft solder or silver solder. After being heated to silver-solder melting temperature (500° C or over), it becomes soft and deforms easily. It is available in most forms, including pipe, tubing, plate, sheet, foil, bar, and extruded shapes. Flanges for the demountable joints in the foreline are generally of brass; the lines are also frequently brass tubing.

Bronze

Bronze is essentially a copper-tin alloy. From the standpoint of vapor pressure, it is far better than brass as a construction material. Cast bronze fittings are sometimes porous, so that forged fittings are preferred. Soft solder and hard solder are used for joining. Bronze is easy to machine; many valve bodies are made of it.

Cadmium

Cadmium is a soft metal with a low melting point and a high vapor pressure (2.5 torr at 450° C). It is used in many soft-solder and hard-solder alloys, and these alloys should be avoided in the vacuum systems for that reason. Cadmium plating is a standard finish for many mild steel parts. Either such parts should not be used, or the cadmium plating should be removed before the part is used.

Carbon

In its usual form, carbon is a black porous solid, is easily machined, and has good dimensional stability. These features make it useful for jigs and fixtures for use at high temperatures. Carbon has a low vapor pressure, but a temperature of 1800° C for several hours is necessary to degas it. Carbon becomes stronger at high temperatures. A combination of low thermal expansion and high thermal conductivity results in good resistance to heat shock. Cracking with a sudden increase in temperature or spalling is rare. It has a slightly negative temperature coefficient of electrical resistivity — that is, it conducts electricity better when it is hot.

Copper

Copper is a low vapor-pressure metal that can be machined and formed easily. It can be hardened only by cold-working and is annealed at 500° C. Forevacuum plumbing is predominantly copper — mainly because fittings such as ells, tees, crosses, etc., are readily available. Copper is soft- or hard-soldered with ease and can, with care, be joined by inert gas-shielded tungsten arc welding. If it is to be brazed in hydrogen, oxygen-free, high-conductivity copper must be used, because the hydrogen reacts with any oxygen contained in the copper, leaving it brittle and porous. Copper is used as a gasket material, and is a constituent in many soldering and brazing alloys.

Chromium

Chromium is used frequently as an electroplated coating over steel, brass, or copper. In this use it is satisfactory for vacuum service, although there is absorbed hydrogen in the metal, due to the electroplating process. Chrome-plated items are difficult to join by soldering, brazing, or welding. Chromium is also used as a constituent of some high-temperature, high-strength brazing alloys.

Gold

Gold is one of the "noble" metals and does not corrode in the atmosphere, even at high temperature. It can be used as a gasket material and is used in many soldering and brazing alloys.

Iron

The vapor pressure of pure iron is low, but it oxidizes easily. The oxide readily absorbs water vapor, which makes it troublesome in high-vacuum applications.

Indium

Indium is used as a gasket material. It has a low melting point (155° C), but it also has a low vapor pressure. As a gasket seal it has limitations at high temperatures, but it performs well at low temperatures. It has been used as a seal for an all-metal valve; the indium is melted each time the seal is opened or closed. Indium will "wet" glass. It is frequently used in soldering and brazing alloys.

"Kovar"

"Kovar" is a proprietary alloy composed of 53.7% iron, 29% nickel, 17% cobalt, and 0.3% manganese. Its melting point is approximately 1450° C and its vapor pressure is about 10^{-5} torr at 1000° C (very low). Its main use is in metal-to-glass seals for vacuum service. It can be soft-soldered with the same flux used for nickel, but for hard-soldering a preplate of copper is recommended. It can be heliarced (arc welded in a helium atmosphere) to itself and to stainless steel.

Lead

Lead is sometimes used as a gasket material for joints not requiring bakeout. It is used in low melting-point solders.

Magnesium

Magnesium has a high vapor pressure, about 5×10^{-3} torr at 450° C. It is sometimes included in special bronzes.

Mercury

Mercury is a metallic element, liquid at normal temperatures and pressures. It is used as a diffusion-pump fluid and in vacuum gages, such as the U-tube manometer and the McLeod gage. Electronic gages are adversely affected by mercury vapors and should be protected from them by traps. Mercury vapor is extremely toxic; before working with it the hazards should be clearly understood. The vapor pressure of mercury at room temperature is about 1 micron.

Molybdenum

Molybdenum is one of the refractory (high-melting-point) metals. (Its melting point is 2620° C.) It is frequently used as a heating element for vacuum furnaces and is also used for filaments, boats, and crucibles from which materials can be volatilized (evaporated) for deposition in vacuum. Another use is for active-metal pumping at very low pressures. Molybdenum oxidizes rapidly when heated in air. It is tough but machinable, and can be shaped by modified sheet-metal practices.

"Nichrome"

There are several alloys called "Nichrome," composed of nickel, chromium, and iron. All of them melt at about 1400° C. "Nichrome" can be spot-welded, but soft- and hard-soldering is difficult. At atmospheric pressure, it is used extensively in electric heaters, ovens, and furnaces. It can also be used for heating elements in vacuum, up to about 850° C.

Nickel

The corrosion resistance of nickel is excellent. Also, it welds, solders, and brazes without difficulty and machines and forms easily. It is often used to plate surfaces needing protection from mercury amalgamation. "Electroless" nickel-plating, a dip process, is very convenient for difficult plating geometries. Nickel is frequently used in brazing alloys.

Palladium

Palladium is one of the noble metals; however, it does oxidize to some extent when heated in atmosphere. Palladium is permeable to hydrogen at a rate depending on the temperature. This characteristic is used to advantage when a source of pure hydrogen or a variable hydrogen leak is desired. Palladium is sometimes used in high-temperature brazing alloys.

Platinum

Platinum is a noble metal of very high ductility (that is, it can be drawn into a very fine wire). It can be heated in an oxidizing atmosphere without harm and is frequently used for windings in furnaces operating at such conditions. Platinum's resistance to oxidation also makes it useful for boats and crucibles in which metallic oxides can be volatilized in vacuum. Platinum is attacked by metallic salts. It is permeable to hydrogen to a lesser degree than palladium, but it can be used in the same way. It is used in some high-temperature brazing alloys. Thin platinum foil can be used as a flux in spot-welding molybdenum or tungsten.

Silver

Silver is well known as the chief constituent in the brazing alloys referred to as hard or silver solders. Silver alone is often used for brazing. It tarnishes (forms silver sulfide) in air at room temperature. It machines and forms easily.

Steel

Mild steel (sometimes called cold-rolled steel) is simply a low-carbon, nonheat-treatable steel and does not identify any one particular steel. Those types of mild steel with low sulfur content are preferred for use with vacuum. Mild steel is available in many different shapes and can be joined by welding, brazing, or soldering; all these operations are straightforward. The vapor pressure of steel is low enough for vacuum work, but it corrodes easily and the corrosion absorbs water vapor. It is frequently used for forevacuum plumbing, especially on mercury-pump systems, because it is not measurably affected by mercury vapor. Mild steel is easy to work, both with hand and machine tools.

Stainless Steel

Stainless steel, often listed as corrosion-resistant steel, is an alloy of chromium and plain carbon steel. Stainless steel is strong and moderately easy to work both with hand and machine tools. It is available in many forms, such as tubing, extrusions, plate, and forgings. It can be joined by welding, brazing, or soldering. If welded, inert-gas-shielded tungsten arc welding is preferred. For vacuum work, 303 stainless steel is not acceptable because it contains sulfur, which makes it unsatisfactory for vacuum-tight welded joints. Stainless steel of the 300 series is used quite often in the construction of ultrahigh vacuum systems. Its electrical and thermal conductivity is low. It is nonmagnetic, although cold working at room temperature will increase its magnetic permeability slightly. It will withstand high temperature, but above 1200° C the chromium will evaporate slightly. In fact, one satisfactory method of producing chromium films by deposition in vacuum is by the resistance heating of a stainless steel wire filament. Stainless steel is frequently used in constructing shields to reduce thermal losses in vacuum where the temperature of the shield does not exceed 1000° C.

Tantalum

Tantalum is one of the refractory (high-melting-point) metals; its melting point is 2996° C. It is more ductile than molybdenum and tungsten, and also much more expensive. It is easy to work with hand tools, and, although it is tough, it can be worked with machine tools. Tantalum has a high resistance to attack by acids. It acts as a getter from 600 to 1000° C. Tantalum is used for heat shielding and heating elements in vacuum furnaces. It is also used for boats, crucibles, and filaments in vacuum deposition of thin films. As a thin foil (0.001 inch), it can be used as a flux in spot welding molybdenum or tungsten.

Tin

Although tin melts at a quite low temperature (232° C), it has a low vapor pressure (10^{-5} torr) at about 800° C. For this reason it is used as a soft solder, and in soldering and brazing alloys. It has low strength; joints must be designed to avoid stress on the solder. Bakeable metal or glass valves have been designed using tin as a seal; the tin is melted each time the seal is opened or closed.

Titanium

Titanium is light, strong, resistant to corrosion, and has a relatively high melting point (1725° C) and a low vapor pressure (less than 10^{-5} torr at 1000° C). It absorbs large quantities of gas when heated above 400° C and must be in a vacuum or in an inert gas atmosphere if it is to be heated, as in brazing, heat treating, welding, etc. It is workable both with hands and machine tools. It is frequently used for active-metal pumping. Wire filaments of titanium are electrically heated and evaporated onto the walls of a chamber. The evaporated titanium reduces pressure in the chamber by sorbing gases. The active metal in most ion-getter pumps is titanium.

Tungsten

Tungsten has the highest melting point of any metal (3382° C). It is very difficult to work, but is available in annealed sheet and wire that can be cold-worked to form strip heaters and filaments. It retains its strength at high temperature and is often used as a spring at temperatures of 2000° C or more. It can be machined, to a degree, with carbide-tipped tools, but grinding is the usual machining method. Ultrasonic and electronic machining devices can be used in some cases. Tungsten oxidizes rapidly when heated in atmosphere. It is an emitter of electrons at temperatures from 2000° C up and is the most frequently used filament material in ionization gage tubes.

Zinc

Zinc is a soft metal with a low melting point and a fairly high vapor pressure (0.1 torr at about 400° C). Because of its high vapor pressure, the use of zinc in a high-vacuum system should be avoided if possible. It is alloyed with copper to make brass and is also found in many of the standard solder and brazing alloys used in torch brazing.

Zirconium

Zirconium has a moderately high melting point (2127° C). The pure metal is quite ductile, but extremely small quantities of impurities destroy its ductility. It is similar to titanium in absorption of gases. Some explosive hazards exist with finely divided zirconium, especially in the presence of water. Before machining zirconium, it is advisable to consult one of the many handbooks that cover the subject.

CERAMICS

Ceramics are used mainly for high-temperature thermal and electrical insulation. They are stronger than glass and will withstand higher operating temperatures. In the construction of vacuum furnaces, they are useful for supporting heating elements and work pieces. Very satisfactory vacuum-tight electrical lead-ins can be constructed by using ceramic bushings with O-ring seals between the ceramic and the vacuum wall, and between the ceramic and the electrical conductor. Ceramics can be joined to metal by metallizing the ceramic, then electroplating the metallized region. The metal is then brazed to the electrodeposit. Several manufacturers have a stock of ceramic-to-metal seals in a wide range of sizes; some produce seals that are satisfactory for ultrahigh vacuum service. *Glazed* ceramics are preferred for electrical insulators in vacuum, as it is easier to remove any conductive deposits.

Many different ceramics are used in vacuum applications. A few of the most frequently used ceramics are alumina, porcelain, steatite, lava and sapphire.

Alumina

Alumina is a single-oxide refractory ceramic. It is the most frequently used ceramic for electron tubes, furnace structures, and other vacuum applications. The ceramic used in most ceramic-to-metal terminals or lead-ins is alumina. The mechanical strength and insulative properties of alumina are very good at high temperatures. The safe maximum operating temperature for alumina is considered to lie between 1600 and 1800° C.

So-called "soft-fired alumina" is available in a pressed and partially fired state. In this condition it can be machined easily. After machining, it is finish-fired to obtain its high-temperature properties. It shrinks about 25% on firing, which poses some difficulties. Machining after firing is accomplished by grinding with diamond wheels.

Sapphire

Sapphire is a very pure form of aluminum oxide. It can be obtained in transparent form to use as vacuum windows and will stand temperatures of 1900° C. The infrared transmission of sapphire is better than that of fused silica. Sapphire is produced in the form of single crystals. Also, it can be sealed to glass.

Porcelain

Porcelain has three main ingredients: clay, feldspar, and flint. The proportions are varied to make up ceramics that emphasize certain properties, such as thermal-shock resistance, dielectric strength, or mechanical strength. Porcelain standoff insulators are stocked by most ceramic suppliers. These are available in standard diameters and lengths and have threaded holes in the ends. They are very useful in making jigs and fixtures to be used in vacuum. Porcelain tubing is also a commonly stocked item. The maximum safe operating temperature of porcelain is about 1000° C.

Steatite

Steatite is a ceramic made up of a mixture of talc and clay, to which alkali or alkali-earth oxides have been added. After firing, it consists mainly of magnesium metasilicate. Standoff insulators and tubing similar to those made of porcelain are available in steatite. The maximum safe operating temperature for steatite is about 1000° C.

Lava

Lava is a ceramic made from natural talc. It is obtainable in several grades. It is simple to machine before firing. After firing it becomes hard; further working can be accomplished only by grinding. A dimensional change is caused by firing — either expansion or contraction, depending on the grade of lava. The maximum safe operating temperature for lava is from 1000 to 1200° C.

Boron Nitride

Boron nitride is sometimes called white graphite because of its similarity to graphite. Under some circumstances it can be used for self-lubricating bushings. It has very good insulating properties, even at high temperature. It is easy to machine to close tolerance and remains machinable even after heating to high temperature. Boron nitride absorbs water vapor and should be slowly and carefully degassed at elevated temperatures for vacuum service.

"Pyroceram"

"Pyroceram" is a new ceramic material prepared in much the same way as glass. It can be converted into a crystalline ceramic by heat-treating at about 1250° C.

Glass

Glass is a very useful material for vacuum service. One obvious reason is its transparency to visible light. While glass has poor impact resistance and low mechanical strength, it has a low vapor pressure and is very resistant to chemical attack. It is a good insulator and can be fused to most metals to form electrical lead-ins. Glass is available in plate stock, tubing, and pipe and is readily worked into various shapes.

Of the many different types of glass that exist, only a few are of predominant interest in general vacuum service. Soft glasses such as lead glass or soda-line are often used as tube envelopes. Hard glasses such as "Nonex" or "Pyrex" have greater strength than the soft glasses and are often used for such purposes as observation ports and bell jars. Hard glass will withstand higher temperatures than soft and is therefore preferred if bakeout is anticipated. Fused silica, or quartz, as it is more commonly called, will withstand very high temperatures, but is quite permeable to gases. This characteristic is used to advantage in constructing leaks for calibrating or testing purposes.

Although glass can be sealed to metal, care must be taken to match expansion coefficients. Much information on this subject is contained in a book, "Materials and Techniques for Electron Tubes" by W. H. Kohl (Reinhold Publishing Corp., New York, 3rd edition in prep.)

Mica

Natural mica is a mineral deposit of complex silicates. The two types associated with vacuum applications are muscovite and phlogopite. Phlogopite is not as hard as muscovite, but will withstand a higher temperature (phlogopite, 800° C; muscovite, 600° C). Both are excellent insulators, resist chemical attack and mechanical and thermal shock.

Mica is used to make insulating spacers in evacuated electronic devices (such as windows in waveguide equipment) and in the construction of high-temperature capacitors. It can be worked with hand or machine tools, but the edges fray easily. Holes cannot be drilled or punched close to the edge without causing splitting or delamination (separation of layers). Mica can be split easily into thin flexible sheets. The larger the sheet size, the higher the cost. Sheets 3 by 5 inches are quite common. With care, sheets as thin as 0.00005 inch can be obtained by separating the laminations of thicker sheets. To prepare natural mica for use in a vacuum it should be washed in acetone, rinsed in alcohol (sometimes soaked), and air-dried in an oven at 100 to 200° C.

A synthetic mica, whose electrical and thermal properties are superior to those of natural mica, is also obtainable. The safe operating-temperature range for this type is 850 to 900° C. It has a low vapor pressure, but is difficult to split into thin sheets.

A glass-bonded natural mica is obtainable which has many of the electrical and thermal characteristics of normal mica but it cannot be split. It can be machined easily and some types are moldable. A glass-bonded synthetic mica is also available.

PLASTICS

Plastic materials may contain some water vapor, solvents, and plasticizers (to a degree dependent on the past history of the material). Generally it is the evolution of these constituents in vacuum that gives plastics the reputation of having a high vapor pressure. However, some plastics may provide satisfactory service as construction materials when the initial outgassing has subsided. If plastics are the materials to be processed in the vacuum system, however, fresh material will be added continuously, and this initial outgassing must be considered in the design of the system. The vapor pressure of many of the plastics is sufficiently low to allow their use as construction material for high vacuum systems. Properly treated, some are satisfactory for limited use in ultrahigh vacuum systems.

The acceptability of plastic materials in a vacuum system depends very much on the conditions of use. Some considerations are: the quantity to be used, how or where it is to be used (as a bearing, as a part of the vacuum wall, or as a structural member), the temperature to which it will be exposed, whether or not there is radiation involved, the range of vacuum in which it is to be used, and whether it is to be a permanent part of the system or only temporary.

Obviously, with a dynamic system, if the total outgassing expected from the plastic is small compared with the speed of the pumps, the plastic is acceptable unless the vapors liberated have a damaging effect on the pump fluid. If the plastic is to be used as a part of the vacuum wall, its rate of permeation plus the outgassing rate must be small compared to the pump speed.

The usefulness of a plastic material will also vary with the range of vacuum in which it is to be used. In rough vacuum most plastics are acceptable, unless their vapors react with the pump fluid. However, starting with the low-vacuum range, the outgassing rate versus pump speed must be taken into account. For although the outgassing rate of the material does not change appreciably at lower pressures, more speed is required at lower pressures to handle the same outgassing rate.

Acrylics

"Plexiglas" and "Lucite" are trade names of two popular acrylics. They can be obtained in forms that are transparent to visible light and are easy to form with either machine or hand tools. Thus they are often used as substitutes for glass — on observation ports, for example, or even as small vacuum chambers. The acrylics are good electrical insulators but cannot be used where they may become hot, since they will soften at 70 to 80° C. They are resistant to attack by weak acids and caustics, but are attacked by esters, ketones, and aromatic hydrocarbons. They are also permeable to helium.

Acrylics are available in the form of tubing, rod, flat stock, and extruded or cast shapes. Joining of acrylic sections can be accomplished by gluing with a solution made of acrylic chips dissolved in ethylene dichloride or by "Duco" cement.

When working acrylics, cutting tools must be sharp and they must be kept cool; otherwise, the plastic at the cut becomes soft, the tool is clogged, and cutting action stops. The clogged tool rubbing on the surface creates more heat, thus making the condition worse. The excess surface heat created also permeates crazing or checking (fine cracking) of the material.

Phenolics

Two common phenolics are known by the trade names "Micarta" and "Bakelite." They can be used at higher temperature than acrylics, up to 150° C. They have very good electrical resistivity, and are easy to work into desired shapes with hand or machine tools; therefore, they are frequently used as insulators for vacuum service. The best strength is displayed by the fiber-reinforced phenolics, but with these it is important to do the machining properly. It is not advisable to remove the glaze from the surface to be exposed to vacuum, as leakage will occur along the imbedded fibers if the surface is part of the vacuum wall. Machined surfaces are difficult to clean properly. The glaze can be reapplied, but the additional time and trouble nullify much of the initial advantage in using this material. A quick method of providing an insulated lead-in is to use a "Micarta" or "Bakelite" flange over a port with the conductor mounted in a hole drilled in the flange. Gasket grooves should not be cut in the phenolic, as leakage across the seal will occur along the fibers. By placing the gaskets on the vacuum side, against the glazed surface, the cut surfaces of the flange will be on the atmosphere side and will not affect the vacuum.

Fluorocarbons

Of all the fluorocarbons, "Teflon" and "Kel-F" are perhaps the best known. These plastics have very good electrical properties. Their slick, wax-like surface makes them useful as self-lubricating bearing materials. They have a low outgassing rate and therefore are quite frequently used as sealing materials for vacuum-tight joints. They are not harmed by temperatures as high as 300° C. Solvents such as alcohol, the ketones, and the hologenated hydrocarbons do not affect them. They resist attack by acids such as aqua regia, hydrofluoric, sulfuric, and nitric. They also resist strong caustics.

"Teflon" and "Kel-F" are easily worked with either machine or hand tools, but the cutting edges must be kept sharp. If not, the material will deform around the tool, making it difficult to control dimensions.

These fluorocarbons will cold-flow under pressure. Consequently, if they are to be used as bearings or gaskets, the support or retainer must be designed to restrain their movement, or provision must be made for periodic take-up of the joint.

There are filled fluorocarbons available, such as "Rulon" or "Fluorosint," that have reduced cold-flow characteristics. These also have better properties for use as bearings in vacuum than unfilled fluorocarbons.

A tape made of "Teflon" and glass fiber has recently been developed. It is useful as a sealant on pipe threads. To provide a vacuum-tight joint, the threads must be clean and smooth. Slightly more than a full wrap of tape is wound on the male thread before assembly.

Some fluorocarbon plastics have been developed recently. Of these, a product called "Viton" has been tested and found to have many properties useful in vacuum. Its resistance to acids, caustics, and solvents is similar to that of the parent fluorocarbon. It is not harmed by temperatures up to 250° C. It is resilient and has a low permeability and outgassing rate. It has a lower electrical resistance than such materials as neoprene or Buna-N and is more likely to take a permanent set.

HYDROCARBONS

Natural Rubber

Vulcanized natural or gum rubber swells and softens in oils, carbon disulfide, or carbon tetrachloride, but is resistant to attack by acids. It has a high resistance to permanent set and a high abrasion resistance.

Synthetic Rubbers

Nitrile (commonly called Buna-N) has good resistance to petroleum oils, aromatic hydrocarbons, dilute acids, and caustics; but poor resistance to solvents such as acetone. Buna-N ages more rapidly than other hydrocarbons and should not be stored for long periods, especially in sunlight. Its resistance to permanent set is good. Abrasion resistance is also good. "Hycar" is the trade name for Buna-N compounds.

Neoprene. Neoprene (also called chloroprene) has a fairly good resistance to attack by most oils and acids; it is attacked by solvents such as acetone. It resists abrasion, but resistance to permanent set is only fair. It has outstanding resistance to aging.

Butyl. Butyl has a very low permeability to gases, and excellent resistance to aging or overheating. Resistance to attack by acids is good; by solvents and oils, only fair. It has a low resistance to permanent set.

GR-S. (Butadiene-styrene rubber, now called SBR) Low resistance to attack by solvents and oils. Medium resistance to permanent set. Excellent abrasion resistance. Fair resistance to aging.

TABLE 5.1 SEALANT MATERIAL CHARACTERISTICS*

	Flange temperature 6° C			Flange temperature −25° C		
Type of rubber	Lowest pressure attained (10^{-9} torr)	No. of runs	Ranges of values (10^{-9} torr)	Lowest pressure attained (10^{-9} torr)	No. of runs	Ranges of values (10^{-9} torr)
Butyl	1.0	5	0.8–1.2	0.17	2	0.15–0.20
Natural rubber	4.5	2	4.0–5.0	1.2	2	1.0 –1.4
Neoprene	2.1	6	2.0–2.4	0.12	2	0.20–0.22
Buna-N	3.8	4	3.6–4.0	0.48	2	0.46–0.50
Silicone (red)	220	2	210–230	—	—	—
Silicone (green)	320	2	240–400	—	—	—
"Viton-A"	1.3	3	1.2–1.4	0.56	2	0.55–0.57
"Teflon"	4.2	4	4.0–4.4	1.0	2	0.9 –1.1

TABLE 5.2 MATERIAL OUTGASSING RATES OF RUBBER O RINGS*†

Material of vacuum system O ring	Pressure with empty chamber after 24-hr pumping (10^{-9} torr)	Material of test O ring	Pressure with test O ring in chamber after 24-hr pumping (10^{-9} torr)	Outgassing rate of test O ring with entire surface exposed (10^{-5} micron-liter/sec/cm²)
Butyl	1.0	Neoprene	46	5.40
Neoprene	2.0	Silicone (red)	5.8	0.44
Neoprene	2.0	Silicone (green)	5.8	0.44
Butyl	1.0	"Teflon"	22	2.52
Butyl	1.0	Butyl	10	1.08
Butyl	1.0	"Viton-A"	18	2.04
Neoprene	2.0	Natural rubber	20	2.16

*Taken from "Improved Elastomer Seal Designs for Large Metal Ultrahigh Vacuum Systems Permitting Ultimate Pressures in the Low 10^{-10} torr Range," by Imre Farkass and E. J. Barry (1960 7th National Symposium on Vacuum Technology Transactions, Pergamon Press, Inc., New York, 1961) p. 35.

†All tests conducted at room temperature.

Silicones. The most outstanding property of silicone plastics is their resistance to temperature extremes. They will, in general, withstand temperatures as high as 350° C for short periods, and 250° C under sustained conditions. They will also remain flexible at temperatures as low as −80° C. They have lower strength and abrasion resistance than most other plastics, and a higher permeability to gases. Resistance to strong acids is low; resistance to aging or weathering is high.

"Silastic" is a tradename for several silicone compounds. Standard O rings are available as well as several RTV (room-temperature vulcanizing) compounds which can be used for encapsulating or molding special shapes. See tables on following page for further data.

Epoxies. In general, epoxies are satisfactory for vacuum service, providing there is little or no plasticizer used and provided the reinforcing material, if any, is not exposed to the vacuum but is covered by a glaze of pure epoxy.

Glossary

Absolute Pressure: Pressure measured above the zero value of a perfect vacuum; absolute pressures are often designated psia (pounds per square inch absolute).

Absolute Zero: The zero point on the absolute temperature scale ($0°$ K).

Absorption: The "taking in" of gas molecules into a material.

Adsorption: The adhesion of gas molecules to the surface of a material.

Angle Valve: A valve in which the inlet and outlet are at right angles to one another.

Atmospheric Pressure: The pressure exerted by a mercury column 760 millimeters high at $0°$ C under a standard acceleration of gravity of 980.665 cm/sec^2. (14.7 psi at sea level).

Avogadro Law: One of the gas laws. The Avogadro law states that equal volumes of different gases at the same pressure and temperature contain the same number of molecules.

Backstreaming: The drift of the working fluid of a pump upstream toward the vessel being exhausted.

Baffle: A system of cooled surfaces placed near the inlet of a pump to condense backstreaming vapor and return it to the pump.

Bakeout: The heating of a system to drive out adsorbed or absorbed gases to accelerate outgassing.

Ball Valve: A valve whose disk consists of a drilled ball which rotates to allow or cut off flow.

Base Pressure: Lowest pressure a pump can produce; also the lowest pressure to which a system can be pumped.

Boyle's Law: One of the gas laws. Boyle's law states that pressure and volume in a gas are inversely proportional (assuming constant temperature and mass).

Calibrated Leak: A leak whose value is variable; used for speed measurements and in leak detection.

Charles' Law: One of the gas laws. Charles' law states that pressure and temperature in a gas are directly proportional (assuming constant temperature and mass).

Chevron Seal: A motion seal using a V-shaped gasket.

Condensation: Change of phase from vapor to solid or liquid.

Conductance: The capacity of a vacuum line to conduct gas. Defined as

$$C = Q/(P_1 - P_2).$$

Dalton's Law: A gas law that states that in a mixture of gases in which the gases do not react chemically each gas exerts its own pressure independently of the other gases.

Degassing: The evolution of adsorbed or absorbed gas in vacuum by external means (frequently by heating).

Dewar Flask: An insulated container.

Diffusion Pump: A vapor pump having a boiler pressure of a few torr and capable of pumping gas with full efficiency at intake pressures not exceeding about 20 microns and forepressures not exceeding 500 microns.

Ejector Pump: A vapor pump having a boiler pressure of more than a few torr and capable of pumping gas with full efficiency at intake pressures of more than about 20 microns and discharge pressures (forepressures) exceeding 500 microns.

Elastomer: An elastic, rubber like substance.

Electrical Conductivity: A measure of the ability of a substance to conduct electricity.

Evaporation: The change of phase from a solid or liquid to a vapor.

Forepressure: Pressure at the outlet of a diffusion pump.

Gage Pressure: Pressure measured from atmospheric pressure as a reference point. Gage pressures are often designated psig (pounds per square inch gage).

Gas (Permanent): A substance that exists in the gaseous phase at room temperature and atmospheric pressure.

Gas Ballast: The technique of admitting a controlled amount of dry gas at the compression stage of the pumping cycle of a rotary pump. The ballast gas mixes with the gas being pumped and reduces the compression necessary to exhaust the gases, thereby reducing the condensation.

Gate Valve: A valve in which the disk moves back into a lateral extension of the body in a plane perpendicular to the direction of gas flow.

Getter Pumping: Pumping by means of an "active metal." In getter pumping gas reacts chemically with a getter metal, such as molybdenum or titanium. The compound so formed has a very low vapor pressure in comparison with the free gas.

Gram Mole: A measure of the mass of gas in a given sample. A gram mole contains approximately 6×10^{23} molecules.

High Vacuum: 10^{-3} torr to 10^{-6} torr.

Halide Leak Detector: A leak detector using halide gas as a tracer gas.

Ideal Gas Law: One of the gas laws. The ideal gas law relates pressure, volume, mass, and temperature. It states that $PV = nRT$.

Ion-Getter Pump: A pump that combines the operating principles of the getter pump and the ion pump. Molecules are ionized and attracted to an active-metal cathode, where they are buried and "sputter" active metal molecules onto the system walls. The active metal thus sputtered getters gas.

Inlet Pressure: The pressure at the inlet of a pump.

Inline Trap: A trap placed in a vacuum line.

Kinetic Theory: A mathematical theory that explains gas behavior.

Leak (Actual): Any break in the wall of a vacuum system that allows external gas to flow into the system.

Leak (Virtual): A source of gas or vapor within the system which gives an indication similar to an actual leak.

Leak Detector: An instrument that is sensitive to a tracer gas, used in leak hunting.

Low Vacuum: 1 torr to 10^{-3} torr.

Mass Flow Rate (Sometimes called throughput): The amount of gas flowing past a given point per unit time. The mass flow rate (designated Q) is proportional to the mass of gas flowing past the point per unit time.

Mass-Spectrometer Leak Detector: A modified form of the mass spectrometer, used in leak hunting.

Maximum Permissible Inlet Pressure: Highest pressure at which a pump can operate.

Maximum Tolerable Forepressure: Highest pressure against which a pump can exhaust.

Mean Free Path: The average distance a gas molecule can travel before colliding with another gas molecule. The mean free path is dependent on the density of the gas and the diameter of the gas molecule.

Mechanical Booster Pump: A rotary mechanical pump that operates on the principle of the Roots blower.

Micron: A unit of pressure defined as 10^{-3} torr.

Millimeter of Mercury (abbreviated mm Hg): A unit of pressure defined as that pressure that will support a column of mercury one millimeter high.

Molecular Flow: A gas flow regime that occurs at low pressures and that is characterized by its relative randomness.

Needle Valve: A valve with a needle-shaped disk.

Outgassing: The natural evolution of adsorbed or absorbed gas in vacuum.

Organic vapors, seals, etc.: Refers to organic (carbon-containing) compounds such as rubber, plastic, and oil.

Partial Pressure: The pressure a gas exerts in a mixture of gases. The total pressure of a mixture of gases is the sum of the partial pressures of its constituents.

Phase: A state of matter — solid, liquid, or gas.

Plasma: A completely ionized gas.

Poiseuille's Equation: An equation for determining the rate of gas flow in the viscous flow regime.

Poppet Valve: A valve in which the disk forms a kind of baffle.

Pressure: The force per unit area a gas exerts. It can be measured in torr, microns, psia, or millimeters of mercury.

Process: The operation for which the vessel is evacuated.

Pumpdown Time: The time needed to pump from a given pressure to another given pressure.

Pump Speed: The volumetric flow rate measured at the pump inlet; designated S_p.

Pumping Speed: The volumetric flow rate at any point in the system; designated S.

Rate of Rise: Rate of pressure rise in the valved-off vessel, used to determine total vessel leakage.

Resistance: The impedance a connecting passage presents to gas flow. Defined as $Z = (P_1 - P_2)/Q$.

Rough Vacuum: 760 torr to 1 torr.

Sorb: To adsorb or absorb.

Sorption Trap: A trap containing sorbent surfaces.

Standard Leak: A leak of fixed, known value, used to calibrate a leak detector.

S.T.P.: "Standard temperature and pressure," that is, 0° C and atmospheric pressure.

Temperature: A measure of relative hotness or coldness. Temperature is usually measured in degrees Fahrenheit (°F), degrees centigrade (°C), or degrees absolute (°K).

Thermal Conductivity: A measure of the ability of a substance to conduct heat.

Torr: A unit of pressure defined as 1/760th of atmospheric pressure.

Trap: A device to condense any vapors present in the vacuum, thus reducing the partial pressure in the vacuum caused by these vapors.

Turbulent Flow: A gas flow regime characterized by the disparity between an individual molecule's velocity and the net gas velocity.

Ultimate Pressure: The lowest pressure obtained after enough pumping time has elapsed to establish that further reduction in pressure would be negligible.

Ultrahigh Vacuum: 10^{-9} torr and below.

Vacuum: A space filled with gas at a pressure less than atmospheric pressure. Vacuums can be classified according to the range of pressure: rough, low, high, very high, and ultrahigh vacuum.

Vacuum Pump: A pump which can produce a vacuum in a vessel by either removing gas molecules or changing their phase.

Vacuum System: Pump, vessel, and the necessary "plumbing" and vacuum-measuring equipment.

Vacuum Vessel: The container in a vacuum system that is evacuated and in which the process is carried on.

Vapor: The gaseous phase of a substance normally a solid or liquid.

Vapor Pressure: The partial pressure of a vapor at a condition of dynamic equilibrium.

Vapor Pump: A vacuum pump that pumps by means of a directed stream of vapor.

Very High Vacuum: 10^{-6} torr to 10^{-9} torr.

Viscous Flow: A gas flow regime characterized by its smoothness and order.

Volume: A measure of space. In vacuum work volume is measured in cubic feet or in liters.

Volumetric Flow Rate: Volume of gas flowing past a given point per unit time; designated S.

Wilson Seal: A motion seal made by an elastomer washer fitted snugly over a shaft.

Appendixes

APPENDIX A: The Metric System

The metric system is a system of weights and measures used in scientific work throughout the world. The basic unit of length in the metric system is the *meter*, equivalent to 39.4 inches. Other units of length in the system are expressed in terms of this basic unit; the *centimeter* is 1/100th of a meter, the *kilometer* is 1000 meters.

The basic unit of mass in the metric system is the *kilogram*. The kilogram is equal to 2.2 pounds. Other units of mass in this system are expressed in terms of the kilogram; the *gram* is equal to 1/1000th of a kilogram, etc.

Note that the various units are related to one another by multiples of *ten*. This aspect of the metric system makes it easy to convert from one unit to another. The number of multiples of ten of the basic unit is given by a prefix on the unit in question. The prefixes are

$$
\begin{aligned}
\text{mega-} &= 1{,}000{,}000 \\
\text{kilo-} &= 1{,}000 \\
\text{deca-} &= 10 \\
\text{centi-} &= 1/100 \\
\text{milli-} &= 1/1{,}000 \\
\text{micro-} &= 1/1{,}000{,}000
\end{aligned}
$$

Thus a *kilo*gram = 1000 grams, a *micro*gram = 1/1,000,000th of a gram, a *milli*meter = 1/1000th of a meter, etc.

APPENDIX B: Temperature Scales

There are three temperature scales commonly used in scientific work: the Fahrenheit, the centigrade, and the absolute scales.

The *Fahrenheit* scale (temperatures on this scale are designated °F) is in common use in England and the United States and is standard in engineering usage in these two countries.

The *centigrade* scale (temperatures on this scale are designated °C) is the scale most often used in scientific and technical work throughout the world. Zero on this scale corresponds to freezing point of water (at a pressure of 1 atmosphere) and 100° C corresponds to the boiling point of water.

The *absolute* scale (temperatures on this scale are designated °K) is the same as the centigrade scale except that its zero point is 273 degrees below the centigrade zero. That is, 0° K = −273° C. The temperature 0° K is referred to as absolute zero.

To convert Fahrenheit temperatures to centigrade, subtract 32 from the Fahrenheit temperature and then take 5/9 of the result, that is,

$$t_{\text{centigrade}} = 5/9(t_{\text{Fahrenheit}} - 32)$$

To convert centigrade temperatures to Fahrenheit, take 9/5 of the centigrade temperature and add 32 to the result. That is,

$$t_{\text{Fahrenheit}} = 9/5\, t_{\text{centigrade}} + 32$$

Absolute temperatures are easily obtainable from centigrade temperatures by adding 273 degrees to the centigrade temperature:

$$t_{\text{absolute}} = t_{\text{centigrade}} + 273$$

and

$$t_{\text{centigrade}} = t_{\text{absolute}} - 273$$

APPENDIX C: Degassing-Rate Reports

1. B. B. Dayton, "Transactions of the 8th National Vacuum Symposium," Pergamon Press, Inc., New York, 1962, p. 42. This report covers the effect of baking on outgassing rates.

2. B. B. Dayton, "6th National Symposium on Vacuum Technology Transactions," Pergamon Press, Inc., New York, 1960, p. 101. Discusses degassing rates, sorption coefficients, permeability, solubility. Includes data from several sources. Both metallic and nonmetallic materials are covered.

3. K. A. Ray, "7th National Symposium on Vacuum Technology Transactions," Pergamon Press, Inc., New York, 1961, p. 243. Discusses sublimation of organic materials at low pressures.

4. P. H. Blackman, F. J. Clauss, C. E. Ledger, and R. E. Mauri, "Transactions of the 8th National Vacuum Symposium," Pergamon Press, Inc., New York, 1962, p. 1244. Discusses evaluation of performance of lubri-

cants, bearings, organic adhesives, and electrical contacts under low-pressure conditions.

5. B. D. Power and D. J. Crawley, "Proceedings of the First International Congress on Vacuum Techniques," 1958, Pergamon Press, Inc., New York, 1960, p. 206. Contains an evaluation of gas evolution from construction materials.

6. B. G. Hogg and H. E. Duckworth, *Rev. Sci. Instr.*, **19:** 331 (1948). Discusses vacuum properties of dielectrics.

APPENDIX D: Exponents and Scientific Notation

EXPONENTS

Exponents are a form of mathematical abbreviation. In the expression 5^4, the number 4 placed above and a little to the right of the 5 is called the *exponent*. The 5 is called the *base*, and the expression is read "5 to the fourth power." The exponent tells the number of times 5 is to be used as a factor: that is, $5^4 = 5 \times 5 \times 5 \times 5 = 625$.

Multiplying numbers with exponents. Powers with the same base may be multiplied by adding the exponents, then raising the base to the exponent obtained: $5^3 \times 5^2 = 5^{3+2} = 5^5 = 5 \times 5 \times 5 \times 5 \times 5 = 3,125$.

Dividing numbers with exponents. Powers with the same base may be divided by subtracting the exponent of the divisor from that of the dividend. Thus, $5^4/5^2 = 5^{4-2} = 5^2 = 25$.

Special cases. $4^3/4^3 = 4^{3-3} = 4^0$. But $4^3/4^3 = 1$, so that $4^0 = 1$. *Any number to the zero power = 1.*

$7^2/7^4 = 7^{-2}$. But $7^2/7^4 = \dfrac{7 \times 7}{7 \times 7 \times 7 \times 7} = 1/7^2$. Thus, *any number to a negative power equals the reciprocal of the number* with the sign of the exponent reversed.

SCIENTIFIC NOTATION

Powers of ten provide a convenient method of expressing very large or very small numbers in an abbreviated form, known as scientific notation. For example,

$$56,000 = 56 \times 1000 \text{ or } 56 \times 10^3$$
$$= 5.6 \times 10,000 \text{ or } 5.6 \times 10^4$$
$$1,270,000 = 127 \times 10,000 \text{ or } 127 \times 10^4 \text{ or } 1.27 \times 10^6$$
$$0.00007 = 7 \times 0.00001 \text{ or } 7 \times 10^{-5}$$
$$0.0000016 = 1.6 \times 0.000001 \text{ or } 1.6 \times 10^{-6}$$

To change a number written in scientific notation back to ordinary notation, if the exponent of ten is positive, move the decimal place to the right the number of places indicated by the exponent. If the exponent of ten is negative, move the decimal place to the left the number of places indicated by the exponent. For example, 3.1×10^4 equals 31,000; 4.3×10^{-3} equals 0.0043.

To multiply numbers expressed in scientific notation, multiply the ordinary numbers as usual, then add the exponents of 10: $(2 \times 10^3) \times (3 \times 10^4) = 6 \times 10^{3+4} = 6 \times 10^7$. To divide numbers expressed in scientific notation, divide the ordinary numbers as usual, then subtract the exponents of 10: $(6 \times 10^4)/(3 \times 10^5) = 2 \times 10^{4-5} = 2 \times 10^{-1}$.

Calculations involving very large or very small numbers are simplified if the numbers are first expressed in terms of scientific notation. For example,

$$\frac{0.000597}{0.00232} \text{ becomes } \frac{5.97 \times 10^{-4}}{2.32 \times 10^{-3}} = 2.57 \times 10^{-4+3} = 2.57 \times 10^{-1} \text{ or } 0.257.$$

Similarly,

$$\frac{275,000}{0.00048} = \frac{2.75 \times 10^5}{4.8 \times 10^{-4}} = 0.573 \times 10^{5+4} = 0.573 \times 10^9 = 573,000,000.$$

To add or subtract numbers expressed in scientific notation, first change the numbers so that they have the same power of ten: Then add or subtract. Thus

$$5.6 \times 10^3 + 7 \times 10^2 = 56 \times 10^2 + 7 \times 10^2 = 63 \times 10^2 \text{ or } 6.3 \times 10^3,$$

$$4.8 \times 10^7 - 3.0 \times 10^5 = 4.8 \times 10^7 - 0.03 \times 10^7 = 4.77 \times 10^7$$

APPENDIX E: Molecular Weight and Mean Free Path of Some Gases

Gas	Molecular weight (atomic mass units)	Mean free path at 10^{-3} torr and room temp (cm)
Hydrogen	2	9.1
Helium	4	14.3
CH_4 (methane)	16	
Water vapor	18	3.5
Neon	20	10.2
Nitrogen	28	5.1
CO (carbon monoxide)	28	
Air	29	5.2
Oxygen	32	5.4
Argon	40	5.0
CO_2 (carbon dioxide)	44	3.2
Mercury	201	6.3

APPENDIX F: Organic Diffusion-Pump Fluids

Organic pump fluids are of several types:

(1) The esters, which are stable under normal operating conditions but are less resistant to breakdown by overheating than other fluids.

(2) The chlorinated hydrocarbons, which are used to obtain high limiting forepressures because they will stand higher boiler pressures with less thermal decomposition than other fluids.

(3) The hydrocarbons, which are general-purpose fluids.

(4) The silicones, which are more stable than the others and will better stand exposure to air while hot.

Trade name	Vapor pressure at room temp. (torr)	Type	Pour point (°F)	Boiling point at 0.5 torr (°C)	Specific gravity
"Apiezon" A	10^{-5}	Petroleum hydrocarbon	10		0.872
"Apiezon" B	10^{-7}	Petroleum hydrocarbon	10		0.873
"Apiezon" C	10^{-8}	Petroleum hydrocarbon	15		0.880
"Apiezon" J	10^{-8}	Petroleum hydrocarbon	45		0.916
"Apiezon" K	10^{-9}	Petroleum hydrocarbon	50		0.921
"Convaclor" 8	2×10^{-4}	Chlorinated hydrocarbon	20	122	1.447
"Convaclor" 12	2×10^{-4}	Chlorinated hydrocarbon	50	130	1.538
"Convoil" 10	2×10^{-3}	Petroleum	−10	135	0.91
"Convoil" 20	8×10^{-6}	Petroleum	16	190	0.86
"Narcoil" 10	3×10^{-4}	Chlorinated hydrocarbon	50		1.538
"Narcoil" 40	1×10^{-6}	Ester	−25		0.973
"Octoil"	2×10^{-7}	Ester	−61	183	0.983
"Octoil" S	5×10^{-8}	Ester	−69	199	0.912
"DC 702"	5×10^{-8}	Methyl polysiloxanes	−40	175	1.071
"DC 703"	2×10^{-8}	Methyl polysiloxanes	−33	180	1.089
"DC 704"	1×10^{-8}	Methyl polysiloxanes	−36	190	1.066
"DC 705"	very low		−15	245	1.095
"Convalex"	very low	Polyphenyl ether			1.2

APPENDIX G: Vacuum Lubricants

VACUUM GREASES

Listed in the following table are greases suitable for use on elastomer seals (such as O rings), stopcocks, and similar items.

Trade name	Melting point	Vapor pressure at room temp (torr)
"Apiezon" L	47° C	$< 10^{-10}$
M	44° C	$< 10^{-7}$
N	43° C	$< 10^{-8}$
T	125° C	10^{-8}
"Celvacene," light	90° C	—
"Celvacene," medium	120° C	—
"Celvacene," heavy	130° C	—
Dow-Corning stopcock grease	Constant viscosity from	$< 10^{-6}$
Dow-Corning high-vacuum grease	-40 to $200°$ C	$< 10^{-6}$

SOLID LUBRICANTS

These lubricants resist evaporation and may be used to lubricate bearings, etc. under high vacuum.

"Electrofilm 1005." This lubricant consists of molybdenum sulfide plus glass frit suspended in xylene. Before application the parts are *cleaned thoroughly*. The solution is best applied to the parts with an air brush. These parts are then air dried and baked in vacuum at 1350° F for four hours. A powdery film of molybdenum trioxide is formed by the reaction of the molybdenum disulfide with small amounts of absorbed oxygen. This film is abrasive and should be removed. Metals that have been coated in this way are molybdenum, 304 stainless steel, and tungsten carbide.

"Molykote X-15." This lubricant consists of molybdenum disulfide and graphite in a sodium silicate solution. Before application the parts are *cleaned thoroughly* (a mild surface abrasion actually increases wear life). The solution is applied to the parts by brushing or spraying. It will air-dry in one hour at room temperature, but wear life is increased by air-drying for 30 minutes and then baking at 180° F for one hour.

Molybdenum Disulfide. A quick approach to lubrication for temporary service is to mix molybdenum disulfide in a slurry with acetone, alcohol, or water and paint it on the surfaces to be lubricated. The coating must be renewed frequently.

"Fluorosint." This is "Teflon" plus filler materials to improve the physical properties. It machines easily, and dimensions can be held close. It can be supplied in molded form by specification. It has less cold flow than "Teflon," and low surface friction. It is resistant to attack by acids (except hydrofluoric). It is a good insulator and stands temperatures up to 250° C.

"Teflon." This product has good lubrication qualities at low surface speeds but will "ball up" at high speeds. It cold-flows easily. See Chapter 5 for other physical properties.

APPENDIX H: Cements and Adhesives

Compound	Description	Application temp. (°C)	Max. recommended service temp. (°C)	Vapor pressure at room temp. in torr	Melting point (°C)
"Apiezon" Q	A sealing compound of putty-like consistency made of a mixture of graphite and the low-vapor-pressure residue of paraffin oil distillation. It can be used to make a temporary vacuum seal by pressing into place with the fingers. It is soluble in kerosene and most other hydrocarbon solvents.	Room temp.	30	10^{-4}	45
"Apiezon" W-40, W-100, and W	A black sealing wax useful for sealing joints that will not withstand soldering temperature. Three kinds are available: soft (W-40), medium (W-100), and hard (W). To apply, the joint is heated and the wax is rubbed over the hot surface. When the wax has flowed into place the joint is cooled. The wax is soluble in benzene and carbon tetrachloride.	50 80 100	30 50 80	10^{-3} (at 180°C) 10^{-3} (at 180°C) 10^{-3} (at 180°C)	45 55 85
"Araldite"	Type I (thermosetting) is supplied in powder or stick form. It is heated in contact with the joint until it melts. It cures upon cooling and bonds to most metals.	150	115	10^{-6}	120
"Araldite"	Type 101 (cold-setting) is supplied as viscous liquid with an accompanying hardener to be added and mixed just before use. It sets at room temperature and bonds to most metals.	Room temp.	—	—	—
"Eastman" 910	A cyanoacrylate monomer modified with a thickening agent and plasticizer. A polymerization reaction occurs when it is squeezed between two surfaces and a rapid set results. It will bond to an extremely wide variety of materials. It is not particularly toxic but it adheres to the skin extremely well.	Room temp.	100	—	Softens at 165
Dekhotinsky cement	This is composed of shellac and pitch. It will not dissolve in water, benzene, or turpentine. It is	150	100	10^{-4}	140

APPENDIX H: Cements and Adhesives (cont.)

Compound	Description	Application temp. (°C)	Max. recommended service temp. (°C)	Vapor pressure at room temp. in torr	Melting point (°C)
Dekhotinsky cement (cont.)	slightly soluble in acetone. It sticks best to clean, hot surfaces.				
"Glyptal" (red)	A viscous enamel used as a temporary seal. It adheres to clean metal. It is sometimes used to seal pipe threads. It is somewhat soluble in acetone methyl ethyl ketone, or xylene.	Room temp.	125	10^{-5}	—
"Picein" 50 and "Picein" 80	A black wax, soluble in either benzene or turpentine. It is a good electrical insulator and can be used to seal small leaks and is insoluble in alcohol or water. It will seal glass to metal.	55 90	45 95	10^{-6} 10^{-6}	80 105
"Sauerisen"	A suspension of ceramic powder in sodium silicate solution. It sets hard after air-drying for several hours. It can be used for cementing glass or ceramic to metal but is not vacuum-tight.	Room temp.	590	Low	—
Silver Chloride	Used to cement glass or ceramic to metals. It must be heated to make a joint, then cooled slowly or it will crack. It is insoluble in water, alcohol, benzene, or acids but is soluble in sodium thiosulfate (or ammonium hydroxide).	470	400	1×10^{-2} at 800	455
"Resiweld"	A two-component plastic. It can be compounded to set hard or resilient. It is useful in making temporary or semipermanent seals on metal or plastic. It resists acids, caustics, and solvents, and is difficult to remove.	Room temp.	150	Med. low	—
"Silastic RTV" 731	This product is ready to use as supplied. No catalyst or heat is required. Curing begins as soon as it is applied, by reaction with the moisture in the air. It bonds to metal, glass, and plastics. Its bond strength can be improved with a special primer.	Room temp.	250	Low	—

APPENDIX I: Soldering and Brazing

SOFT SOLDER

There are a number of lead-tin alloys known as soft-solders. One of the most satisfactory of these for vacuum applications is the 50–50 lead-tin alloy; other solders are shown in the table.

SOFT SOLDERS

Solder	Composition tin (%)	lead (%)	Liquidus* (°C)	Solidus† (°C)	Comments
Tin	100	—	232	232	Pure tin. Has a low vapor pressure but poor wetting characteristics.
Eutectic	62	38	183	183	This alloy has the highest melting point. Has a high tensile strength but poor wetting and flowing characteristics.
Half and half	50	50	212	183	Most widely used.
Fine solder	40	60	238	183	Most ductile.
Plumber's solder	30	70	257	183	
Lead	--	100	327	327	Pure lead.

Fluxes

Solution of $ZnCl_2$, NH_4Cl, and H_2O
Paste of NH_4Cl and petroleum jelly
Solution of resin and alcohol (noncorrosive; used mainly in electrical work)

*Lowest temperature at which the alloy is liquid.
†Highest temperature at which the alloy is solid.

To make vacuum-tight joints with soft solder, the surfaces to be joined must first be cleaned. The surfaces are then heated and a thin coating of solder applied. The "tinned" sections are then joined and the joint area heated until the solder melts and flows.

Satisfactory joints for vacuum service are possible only if the surfaces are first cleaned thoroughly. Gross contaminations such as corrosion or oxidation are removed from the surfaces by an abrasive such as a file or emery cloth. Greasy deposits are removed by solvents. A flux is then brushed or wiped on and the surface is heated (the purpose of the flux is to break up oxide layers on the base metal and to keep both the solder and the base metal from oxidizing while they are being heated). With the solder in contact with the surface to be tinned, heat is applied with the soldering iron or torch until the solder melts and runs. Using a damp cloth, the molten solder is wiped around until the surface is completely coated with a thin layer of solder. Both surfaces are treated in this way, then joined and reheated until the solder melts and flows. More solder is added if necessary to make a smooth fillet around the joint. This keeps the solder from drawing away as it cools, leaving an opening in the seam. Clearance between the parts to be soldered should be kept at a minimum to insure a sound joint. The joint should not be disturbed until the solder cools and becomes entirely solid.

After the joint is complete it must be cleaned before it is put in a vacuum system. By intent, most fluxes are corrosive. If they are not completely removed from the joint and surrounding areas, a corrosive action will continue to undermine the joint, causing holes in the metal. Residue of most fluxes has a high vapor pressure and is harmful to pump oils. The proper cleaning technique depends to some extent on the type of flux. Liquid fluxes can be removed by very hot water (180° F). The addition of bicarbonate of soda to the first wash will help to neutralize the acid quickly. When extreme cleanliness is required, the joints should be boiled in several changes of water. Oil or resin fluxes are removed by several rinses in a degreasing agent — alcohol, for example. A grease-paste flux is removed by washing with a degreasing agent, another wash in hot water and detergent, followed by several hot-water rinses.

HARD SOLDERS AND BRAZING

Hard soldering (also called silver soldering) generally refers to soldering in air with a hand torch using alloys containing mainly silver and copper plus smaller amounts of other metals. These other metals are used to control the melting and flowing range and also the wetting characteristics of the alloy. Many of the alloys have additive metals with high vapor pressures (cadmium and zinc, for example), which restricts their use in high vacuum, especially if the joint is to be exposed to bakeout temperature. The constituents of some frequently used hard-solder alloys are given in the table.

A standard procedure for making hard-solder joints with a hand torch is outlined in Handy and Harman's Bulletins 17 and 20 (Handy & Harman Brazing Products Div., 82 Fulton St., New York). In making a vacuum-tight hard-soldered joint, however, some points deserve special emphasis.

Precleaning must be thorough, using abrasives for removing corrosion and oxidation, and solvents for greasy deposits. Joint clearance should be between 0.001 inch and 0.003 inch, which will allow capillary forces to draw the solder into the joint as a uniform continuous film. All sharp edges over which solder is to flow should be broken (a 0.005-inch radius is adequate) because solder resists flowing over sharp edges.

Before assembly, all surfaces of the joint to be wetted by the solder are coated with a thin layer of flux. Rotating the pieces (in the case of tubing) after assembly will help spread the flux evenly. If an oxyacetylene torch is used for heating, adjust it to a slightly reducing flame. Keep the torch moving in a slow fanning motion so that the heat will be increased uniformly over the entire joint area. When the temperature is slightly above the melting point of the solder, dip the solder into the flux to give it a thin protective coat of flux and press it firmly against the joint at the junction of the parts. In a few seconds, if the temperature is correct, the solder will melt and flow into the joint. If the joint is small, one inch in diameter or so, the solder need be fed at one point only. It will flow throughout the joint, provided the temperature is uniform. On larger joints the solder is made to flow by fanning the flame ahead of the molten solder and pulling the solder along with the heat, feeding additional solder when necessary. Overheating must be avoided because it causes the solder to alloy excessively with the metal of the parts. This causes a decrease in the flowing qualities of the solder and changes its melting point. It may also make the joint porous and brittle.

It is especially important that the heating be uniform. When the heating is uniform, it is possible to draw the solder completely through the joint to form a continuous fillet on the inside. With a continuous fillet on the inside there are no exposed cracks or pockets in which flux could be trapped. Flux is objectionable because it attracts and holds water vapor, thus creating a virtual leak. It may also cover an actual leak long enough to hide it during a leak test, and it may contaminate pump fluids. For the same reasons, flux removal after the joint is completed must be thorough. Flushing the joint inside and out with very hot water (180° F if possible) will usually dissolve most fluxes used in hard soldering.

SOLDERING AND BRAZING ALLOYS

The information supplied by the manufacturers of soldering and brazing alloys usually lists temperature data as well as the composition. The temperature data most frequently provided are the solidus and liquidus of the alloy. The solidus temperature is defined as the highest temperature at which all of the alloy is completely solid. The liquidus temperature is defined as the lowest temperature at which all of the alloy is completely liquid. These two points define the temperature limits within which the alloy changes from a solid to a liquid. The range within these limits is called the melting range. Some alloys will have a wide melting range during which they are mushy rather than fluid. These are most useful in building up fillets or filling gaps. Other alloys have a narrow melting range which may not even be noticeable during brazing. These are most useful in obtaining good capillary flow. With certain compositions the solidus and liquidus occur at the same temperature. This is called a eutectic composition. In general, a short melting range is preferred for vacuum joints.

At temperatures above 800° C it becomes difficult to make a good vacuum-tight joint with a torch. Oxidation of the metal being joined becomes more severe and it is hard to maintain uniform temperature at the joint. Joints seldom have their maximum strength, because the molten alloy is usually in contact with the metals being joined for a longer time than is recommended. This promotes joint corrosion and erosion. Several satisfactory alternatives are available. Induction heating in air after using a flux will provide a uniform and brief high temperature. Furnace brazing in air after using a flux also provides a uniform heat. Furnace brazing in a controlled atmosphere is the most satisfactory alternative. The usual atmosphere is hydrogen, although disassociated ammonia is also used. The vacuum furnace is a type of atmosphere furnace that is becoming quite popular.

The source of heat in furnace brazing may be induction coils or resistance elements. Electron-bombardment heating is also possible in vacuum. One excellent source of information on furnace brazing is "Materials and Techniques for Electron Tubes," by W. H. Kohl (Reinhold Publishing Corp., New York, Third edition in prep.)

When a high-temperature joint must be made and special equipment to do it is not available, the use of one of the nickel-based brazing alloys containing chromium, boron, and silicon may provide an answer. Several of these alloys are available from the American Platinum and Silver Division of Englehard Industries, Inc. They can be obtained in a paste form that has the powdered alloy suspended in a flux which remains on the joint in a molten state at temperatures up to 1200° C. One of these alloys, "LM-Nicrobraze," has a solidus of 954° C and a liquidus of 993° C. It can be used to braze stainless steel and nickel-base metals for parts operating at high temperature or in corrosive conditions.

HARD SOLDERS

Composition					
% silver	% copper	% other	Solidus (°C)	Liquidus (°C)	Comments
(1) 50	15.5	16.5 Zn; 18 Cd	620	636	This can be used on both ferrous and non-ferrous metals. It has a narrow melting range and good flow characteristics. The zinc and cadmium content must be considered if this alloy is used on a vacuum unit
(2) 35	26	21 Zn; 18 Cd	607	702	This has the same general characteristics as (1) above. It has a wider melting range and is therefore preferred for building up fillets and bridging gaps.
(3) 15	80	5 P	641	704	This is primarily intended for use on copper or copper alloys. It can be used on silver, tungsten, and molybdenum. It should not be used on ferrous metals because it forms brittle joints. A flux is not required for making joints on copper although flux will improve joint quality, especially on large pieces. It has a wide melting range.
(4) 60	30	10 Sn	600	715	This can be used on ferrous or non-ferrous metals. It has a wide melting range. It has a low vapor pressure, and is hard and very strong.
(5) 72	28		779	779	This mixture of silver and copper has the lowest melting point. It is excellent for joining copper to copper. It has a low vapor pressure and high strength. It can be used on stainless steel and Inconel.
(6) 63	27	10 In	635	705	This is similar in characteristics to (4) above but has a narrower melting range.

APPENDIX J: Vapor Pressure Data for the Solid and Liquid Elements*

Symbol	Element	Data temp. range, °K	Temperatures (°K) for vapor pressures (torr)														
			10^{-11}	10^{-10}	10^{-9}	10^{-8}	10^{-7}	10^{-6}	10^{-5}	10^{-4}	10^{-3}	10^{-2}	10^{-1}	1	10^1	10^2	10^3
Ac	Actinium	1873, EST.	1045	1100	1160	1230	1305⊙	1390	1490	1605	1740	1905	2100	2350	2660	3030	3510
Ag	Silver	958-2200	721	759	800	847	899	958	1025	1105	1195⊙	1300	1435	1605	1815	2100	2490
Al	Aluminum	1220-1468	815	860	906	958	1015	1085	1160	1245	1355	1490	1640	1830	2050	2370	2800
Am	Americium	1103-1453	712	752	797	848⊙	905	971	1050	1140	1245	1375	1540	1745	2020	2400	2970
As	Arsenic (s)		323	340	358	377	400	423	447	477	510	550	590	645	712	795	900
At	Astatine	EST.	221	231	241	252	265	280	296	316	338	364	398	434	480	540	⊙620
Au	Gold	1073-1847	915	964	1020	1080	1150	1220	1305	1405⊙	1525	1670	1840	2040	2320	2680	3130
B	Boron	1781-2413	1335	1405	1480	1555	1640	1740	1855	1980	2140	2300	2520⊙	2780	3100	3500	4000
Ba	Barium	1333-1419	450	480	510	545	583	627	675	735	800	883	984⊙	1125	1310	1570	1930
Be	Beryllium	1103-1552	832	878	925	980	1035	1105	1180	1270	1370	1500	1650⊙	1830	2080	2390	2810
ΣBi	Bismuth		510	540	⊙568	602	640	682	732	790	860	945	1050	1170	1350	1570	1900
ΣC	Carbon (s)	1820-2700	1695	1765	1845	1930	2030	2140	2260	2410	2560	2730	2930	3170	3450	3780	4190
Ca	Calcium	730-1546	470	495	524	555	590	630	678	732	795	870	962	1075	1250	1475	1800
Cd	Cadmium	411-1040	293	310	328	347	368	392	419	450	490	538	593	⊙665	762	885	1060
Ce	Cerium	1611-2038	1050	1110⊙	1175	1245	1325	1420	1525	1650	1795	1970	2180	2440	2780	3220	3830
Co	Cobalt	1363-1522	1020	1070	1130	1195	1265	1340	1430	1530	1655⊙	1790	1960	2180	2440	2790	3220
ΣCr	Chromium	1273-1557	960	1010	1055	1110	1175	1250	1335	1430	1540	1670	1825	2010⊙	2240	2550	3000
ΣCs	Cesium	300- 955	213	226	241	257	274	297	322	351	387	428	482	553⊙	643	775	980
Cu	Copper	1143-1897	855	895	945	995	1060	1125	1210	1300	1405⊙	1530	1690	1890	2140	2460	2920
Dy	Dysprosium	1258-1773	760	801	847	898	955	1020	1090	1170	1270	1390	1535	1710⊙	1965	2300	2780
Er	Erbium	1773, EST.	779	822	869	922	981	1050	1125	1220	1325	1450	1605	1800⊙	2060	2420	2920
Eu	Europium	696, 900	469	495	523	556	592	634	682	739	805	884	981	1100⊙	1260	1500	1800
Fr	Francium	EST.	198	210	225	242	260	280	306	334	368	410	462	528	620	760	980
Fe	Iron	1356-1889	1000	1050	1105	1165	1230	1305	1400	1500	1615	1750	1920⊙	2130	2390	2740	3200
Ga	Gallium (l)	1179-1383	755	796	841	892	950	1015	1090	1180	1280	1405	1555	1745	1980	2300	2730
Gd	Gadolinium	EST.	880	930	980	1035	1100	1170	1250	1350	1465⊙	1600	1760	1955	2180	2580	3100
ΣGe	Germanium	1510-1885	940	980	1030	1085	1150	1220⊙	1310	1410	1530	1670	1830	2050	2320	2680	3180
Hf	Hafnium	2035-2277	1505	1580	1665	1760	1865	1980	2120	2270⊙	2450	2670	2930	3240	3630	4130	4780
Hg	Mercury	193-575	170	180	190	201	214	229	246	266	289	319	353	398	458	535	642
Ho	Holmium	923-2023	779	822	869	922	981	1050	1125	1220	1325	1450	1605	1800	2060	2410	2910
In	Indium (l)	646-1348	641	677	716	761	812	870	937	1015	1110	1220	1355	1520	1740	2030	2430
Ir	Iridium	1986-2600	1585	1665	1755	1850	1960	2080	2220	2380	2560⊙	2770	3040	3360	3750	4250	4900
K	Potassium	373-1031	247	260	276	294	315	338	364	396	434	481	540	618	720	858	1070
La	Lanthanum	1655-2167	1100	1155⊙	1220	1295	1375	1465	1570	1695	1835	2000	2200	2450	2760	3150	3680
Li	Lithium	735-1353	430	452⊙	480	508	541	579	623	677	740	810	900	1020	1170	1370	1620
Lu	Lutetium	EST.	1000	1060	1120	1185	1260	1345	1440	1550	1685⊙	1845	2030⊙	2270	2550	2910	3370
Mg	Magnesium	626-1376	388	410	432	458	487	519	555	600	650	712	782	878⊙	1000	1170	1400
Mn	Manganese	1523-1823	660	695	734	778	827	884	948	1020	1110	1210	1335⊙	1490⊙	1695	1970	2370
Mo	Molybdenum	2070-2504	1610	1690	1770	1865	1975	2095	2230	2390	2580	2800⊙	3060	3390	3790	4300	5020
Na	Sodium	496-1156	294	310	328	347	370	396	428	466	508	562	630	714	825	978	1175

Nb	Niobium	2304-2596	1765	1845	1935	2035	2140	2260	2400	2550	2720	2930 ○	3170	3450	3790	4200	4710
Nd	Neodymium	1240-1600	846	895	945	1000	1070	1135	1220 ○	1320	1440	1575	1770	2000	2300	2740	3430
Ni	Nickel	1307-1895	1040	1090	1145	1200	1270	1345	1430	1535	1655	1800 ○	1970	2180	2430	2770	3230
Os	Osmium	2300-2800	1875	1965	2060	2170	2290	2430	2580	2760	2960	3190	3460	3800	4200	4710	5340
P	Phosphorus (s)		283	297	312	327	342	361	381	402	430	458	495	534	582	642	715
Pb	Lead	1200-2028	516	546	580 ○	615	656	702	758	820	898	988	1105	1250	1435	1700	2070
Pd	Palladium	1294-1640	945	995	1050	1115	1185	1265	1355	1465	1590	1735 ○	1920	2150	2450	2840	3380
ΣPo	Polonium	711-1286	332	348	365	384	408	432	460	494	537 ○	588	655	743	862	1040	1250
Pr	Praseodymium	1423-1693	900	950	1005	1070	1140 ○	1220	1315	1420	1550	1700	1890	2120	2420	2820	3370
Pt	Platinum	1697-2042	1335	1405	1480	1565	1655	1765	1885	2020	2180	2370	2590	2860	3190	3610	4170
Pu	Plutonium (ℓ)	1392-1793	931	983	1040	1105	1180	1265	1365	1480	1615	1780	1975	2230	2550	2980	3590
Ra	Radium	EST.	436	460	488	520	552	590	638	690	755	830	920 ○	1060	1225	1490	1840
Rb	Rubidium		227	240	254	271	289	312 ○	336	367	402	446	500	568	665	802	1000
Re	Rhenium	2494-2999	1900	1995	2100	2220	2350	2490	2660	2860	3080	3340	3680	4080	4600	5220	6050
Rh	Rhodium	1709-2205	1330	1395	1470	1550	1640	1745	1855	1980	2130	2310 ○	2520	2780	3110	3520	4070
Ru	Ruthenium	2000-2500	1540	1610	1695	1780	1880	1990	2120	2260	2420	2620	2860 ○	3130	3480	3900	4450
ΣS	Sulfur		230	240	252	263	276	290	310	328	353	382 ○	420	462	519	606	739
ΣSb	Antimony	693-1110	477	498	526	552	582	618	656	698	748	806	885 ○	1030	1250	1560	1960
Sc	Scandium	1301-1780	881	929	983	1045	1110	1190	1280	1380	1505	1650 ○	1835	2070	2370	2780	3360
ΣSe	Selenium	550- 950	286	301	317	336	356	380	406	437	472	516 ○	570	636	719	826	972
ΣSi	Silicon	1640-2054	1090	1145	1200	1265	1340	1420	1510	1610	1745 ○	1905	2090	2330	2620	2990	3490
Sm	Samarium	789- 833	542	573	608	644	688	738	790	853	926	1015	1120	1260	1450 ○	1715	2120
Sn	Tin (ℓ)	1424-1753	805	852	900	955	1020	1080	1170	1270	1380	1520	1685	1885	2140 ○	2500	2960
Sr	Strontium		433	458	483	514	546	582	626	677	738	810	900	1005 ○	1160	1370	1680
Ta	Tantalum	2624-2948	1930	2020	2120	2230	2370	2510	2680	2860	3080	3330 ○	3630	3980	4400	4930	5580
Tb	Terbium	EST.	900	950	1005	1070	1140	1220	1315	1420	1550	1700 ○	1890	2120	2420	2820	3370
Tc	Technetium	EST.	1580	1665	1750	1840	1950	2060	2200	2350	2530	2760 ○	3030	3370	3790	4300	5000
Te	Tellurium	481-1128	366	385	405	428	454	482	515	553	596	647	706 ○	791	905	1065	1300
Th	Thorium	1757-1956	1450	1525	1610	1705	1815	1935	2080	2250	2440	2680 ○	2960	3310	3750	4340	5130
Ti	Titanium	1510-1822	1140	1200	1265	1335	1410	1500	1600	1715	1850	2010 ○	2210	2450	2760	3130	3640
Tl	Thallium	519- 924	473	499	527	556 ○	592	632	680	736	803	882	979	1100	1255	1460	1750
Tm	Thulium	809-1219	624	655	691	731	776	825	882	953	1030	1120	1235	1370	1540	1760 ○	2060
U	Uranium	1630-2071	1190	1255	1325	1405 ○	1495	1600	1720	1855	2010	2200	2430	2720	3080	3540	4180
V	Vanadium	1666-1882	1235	1295	1365	1435	1510	1605	1705	1820	1960	2120	2320	2560	2850	3220	3720
W	Tungsten	2518-3300	2050	2150	2270	2390	2520	2680	2840	3030	3250	3500 ○	3810	4180	4630	5200	5900
Y	Yttrium	1774-2103	1045	1100	1160	1230	1305	1390	1490	1605	1740 ○	1905	2105	2355	2670	3085	3650
Yb	Ytterbium	EST.	436	460	488	520	552	590	638	690	755	830	920 ○	1060	1225	1490	1840
Zn	Zinc	422-1089	336	354	374	396	421	450	482	520	565	617	681	760 ○	870	1010	1210
Zr	Zirconium	1949-2054	1500	1580	1665	1755	1855	1975	2110 ○	2260	2450	2670	2930	3250	3650	4170	4830

Legend: ○ Melting point
s Solid
ℓ Liquid
Σ Indicates more than one species of gas for this element.

From R. E. Honig, RCA Rev., Vol XXIII, No. 4, Dec. 1962. Used with permission.

APPENDIX K: The Mass-Spectrometer Leak Detector

A block diagram of the vacuum system of a typical detector is shown in Fig. K.1. The throughput of the diffusion pump and the mechanical pump (these pumps are always in series) is controlled by the pump valve. This provides a means of controlling the pressure in the analyzer. The throttle valve controls the pressure drop between the system under test and

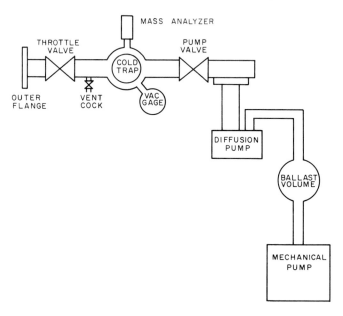

Fig. K.1

the analyzer to allow the analyzer to operate at its normal pressure of 1×10^{-4} torr. The analyzer is kept as clean as possible by connecting it to the system at the cold trap. The output signal of the analyzer due to helium is registered on a meter on the front panel. This signal can be amplified and used to power a small electric horn so that a leak gives both visible and audible warning of its presence. A vacuum gage is also connected at the cold trap to measure the total pressure in this area. This gage is a Philips cold-cathode ionization gage.

OPERATIONAL PROCEDURES FOR THE LEAK DETECTOR

Startup

(1) Close the throttle valve and check the manifold vent cock if any to see that it is closed.

(2) Open the pump valve all the way.

(3) With all switches on the control panel in the "off" position, connect the power cord to a 105- to 125-volt, 60-cycle supply.

(4) Turn on the forepump switch.

(5) When the forepump begins to run quietly (it is noisy during pump-down), turn on the diffusion pump.

(6) Allow approximately 15 minutes for the diffusion pump to come to operating temperature and turn the gage on.

(7) If the gage indication is off scale, turn it off, wait a few minutes, and then recheck. Once the pressure indication is less than full-scale the gage can be left on. The indicated pressure should be less than 0.2 micron within 30 minutes of the time that the diffusion pump is turned on.

(8) When the pressure gage reads 0.2 micron, fill the cold trap with liquid nitrogen.

(9) When the pressure reading reaches 0.1 micron, the analyzer filament can be turned on. Frequently the initial outgassing of this filament will cause a pressure rise that cuts off the current to the filament. When this happens, wait for the pressure to again reach 0.1 micron and turn the filament back on. It may be necessary to do this several times before the filament will stay on.

(10) The leak detector is now ready to detect helium.

Shutdown Procedure

(1) Turn off the filaments, gage switch, and diffusion pump.

(2) Close the throttle valve and pump valve.

(3) Remove the cap screws from the cold-trap thimble (do not attempt to remove the thimble until the manifold is at atmospheric pressure).

(4) Bring the manifold up to atmospheric pressure, through either the throttle valve or the vent cock. If dry nitrogen is used for this purpose instead of atmospheric air, the time required for the next pumpdown will be reduced.

(5) As soon as the manifold is up to atmospheric pressure, remove the cold-trap thimble immediately and place a temporary cover over the opening in the manifold. Dispose of the refrigerant, bring the thimble to room temperature, and clean the outer surface of the thimble with acetone. *Note:* When disposing of liquid-nitrogen refrigerant, either pour it into a Dewar or throw it in a safe place. If spilled in quantity on the skin it can cause a severe case of frostbite.

(6) Reinstall the cold-trap thimble.

(7) When the diffusion pump boiler has cooled sufficiently to be just warm to the touch, turn off the forepump.

(8) Open the pump valve to let the pump section to atmospheric pressure, then close the pump valve again.

Note: When the leak detector is to be shut down for a short period, such as overnight, follow steps 1 through 6 as given in the complete shutdown (except do not shut down the diffusion pump) and then continue as follows:

(9) By using an auxiliary mechanical pump, evacuate the manifold section through the throttle valve.

(10) Close the throttle valve.

(11) Check to see that the following conditions exist: throttle valve closed, pump valve closed, vent cock closed, diffusion pump on, forepump on, gage switch off. Under these conditions it should be possible to resume operations with the leak detector in minimum time.

ASSOCIATED LEAK-HUNTING EQUIPMENT

Auxiliary Pumps

The leak detector must not be used to evacuate the system to be tested. Consequently, an auxiliary means of evacuating the system under test must be provided. The type of auxiliary system used depends on the volume of the system under test. Small systems, 20 to 30 liters in volume, can be brought to within range of the leak detector by a mechanical pump alone. For larger systems, or when the leakage rate is quite high, a system with a diffusion pump and mechanical pump is required. A pressure of 10^{-3} torr in the system under test allows the throttle valve of the leak detector to be full open; this results in better operating conditions.

Valves and Gages

There should be a valve between the system under test and the auxiliary pumps. This allows the auxiliary pumps to be valved out whenever possible, to increase the effectiveness of the detector. Quite often a valve is also placed between the leak detector and the system being tested. There should be adequate gaging on the system being tested, so that the leak can be evaluated with reference to the total system pressure.

Standard Leak

When used with a mass-spectrometer leak detector, a standard leak consists of a small reservoir, usually glass, filled with 100% helium. The reservoir has a tubulation by which it can be attached to a leak detector or to a system being tested. In the tubulation is a porous element that allows helium to flow from the reservoir. The rate of leakage (which is assumed to be constant, since it changes only a few percent per year) is measured when the leak is constructed, and is inscribed on the reservoir. Standard leaks are obtainable with leak rates ranging between 10^{-5} and 10^{-8} atm-cc/sec.

A standard leak is used to calibrate the output of the detector's leak-rate meter. Before attempting to define the rate of flow of an unknown leak, the reading on the meter must be tested against a known leak. Then, if the leak detector adjustment is not changed, the meter reading caused by the unknown leak will be directly proportional to that caused by the known leak.

To calibrate a leak detector, a standard leak is connected directly to the inlet flange of the detector or to the flange of the external trap, if there is one. (The connection must include appropriate valving for evacuating this section before opening the throttle valve.) With the leak detector operating, opening of the throttle valve will cause an immediate deflection on the leak-rate meter. With the throttle valve and the pump valve wide open, the reading of the leak-rate meter is allowed to reach a steady value.

The leak-rate meter of most detectors reads from 0 to 100. A meter range switch, or multiplier, with positions of $\times 1$, $\times 3$, $\times 5$, $\times 10$, $\times 100$, etc. cuts down the signal from the analyzer. This allows leak rates greater than one full-scale deflection to be registered. When the detector responds to the standard leak, the range switch is used to keep the deflection of the needle on-scale. The needle deflection shown on the scale times the multiplier (indicated by the range switch) will yield the total number of meter divisions being registered by a leak.

Thus, if a standard leak having a leak rate of 3.7×10^{-7} atm-cc/sec causes the needle of the leak-rate meter to indicate a steady 56 on the scale with the range switch set at the $\times 3$ position, the sensitivity of the leak detector will be

$$\frac{\text{Leak rate of standard leak}}{\text{Number of divisions of meter deflection}} \text{ or,}$$

$$\frac{3.7 \times 10^{-7}}{168} = 2.2 \times 10^{-9} \text{ atm-cc/sec per division.}$$

If the unknown leak causes a deflection of 60 with the range switch at $\times 10$ (both throttle valve and pump valve wide open), the total divisions (600) times the sensitivity of the detector (2.2×10^{-9}) indicates a leak rate equivalent to 1.32×10^{-6} atm-cc/sec of helium.

Adjustable Leak

The adjustable leak is essentially a needle valve with a relatively small port. This leak is made of metal and has a provision for locking the needle at the desired setting. Its purpose is to provide a controlled flow of a larger amount of gas than is possible with the glass standard leak. Adjustable leaks can be obtained with a range from 1 to 1×10^{-5} atm-cc/sec.

To calibrate an adjustable leak, the leak detector is first calibrated with the glass standard leak. The adjustable leak, with a 100% concentration of helium around it, is then set for the desired leak rate. (Note: A transparent plastic bag inflated with helium and tied over the leak will allow adjustment of the valve.)

The adjustable leak should be calibrated before and after every use because the setting is easily disturbed.

Sampling Probe (Sniffer)

To detect a gas on the outside of pressurized components, a line is first attached to the inlet flange, of the detector. Optimum detecting pressure is maintained in the detector by providing an adjustable valve (called a sampling probe or sniffer) on the end of the line. The inlet of the sniffer is moved slowly along the system walls around suspected areas. The concentration of gas that forms over a leak will be drawn into the detector through the sniffer and cause a response on the leak-rate meter. The efficiency of the sniffer can be tested with a glass standard leak.

Helium Supply

Several sizes of helium gas cylinders are available. The cylinder will require a regulator to reduce the high storage pressure down to a few pounds per square inch. To allow a fine jet of helium to be played over the surface of the system, a nozzle with an adjustable flow rate will be required. A length of light flexible tubing will also be required to connect the nozzle to the cylinder regulator.

Connecting Lines Between the Leak Detector and the System Under Test

These lines should have maximum conductance to allow short response and recovery times. They can be made of rubber, vinyl, or, preferably, flexible metal tubing. In no case should a rigid line be made up to the leak detector because of vibration. If rubber is used, helium should not be introduced into this line in concentration, because the rubber will absorb helium, thus giving delayed false readings.

APPENDIX L: Bakeable Ultrahigh Vacuum Flange Gaskets

PINCH GASKETS

The bakeable pinch gaskets described in this section have been developed by the Lawrence Radiation Laboratory's (Livermore) Sherwood Group, and are based on a redesigned Westinghouse seal.* The seals (see Fig. L.1) can be used when pressures on the order of 10^{-10} torr must be maintained or when system cleanliness is a requirement. Usual bakeout temperatures range from 200° C to 450° C; the seal does not set the temperature.

Three flange configurations are shown (Figs. L.2-L.4) in both tube and pipe sizes. Group I covers sizes through 10-in. I.P.S. Group II covers pipe diameters 12 inches through 24 inches; this group uses centering lugs on flange OD's to secure alignment. Group III is a clamped double seal with

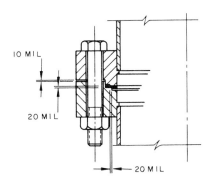

Fig. L.1

pumpout provision between seals. It is used as an alternative to Group II.

Flanges. Use 304 stainless steel in all cases. Typical weld preparation is shown. Welds are made using the inert-gas-shielded tungsten arc.

Fastenings. For flange Groups I and II use 5/16–24 UNF 302, 303, 304, or 316 cold-finished (cold rolled threads and cold headed) stainless steel cap screws per Federal Spec. QQ-S-763b having a yield strength at 0.2 percent offset of 80,000 psi (min.) and an ultimate strength of 115,000 psi (min.). Heat-treated A-286 stainless steel is preferred but is several times more expensive. "Unbrako" type 300 stainless steel (series 1960) socket head cap screws work satisfactorily. Torque fastenings to 400 lb-in. Use "Silver Goop" or equivalent as a thread lubricant.

*Westinghouse Research Laboratories Research Report 100FF1054-R1, December 31, 1956.

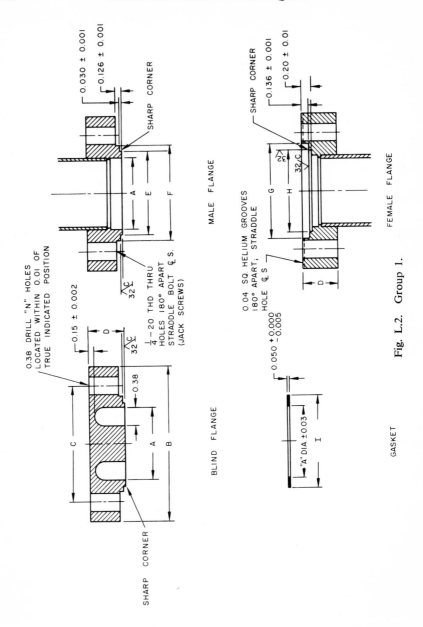

Fig. L.2. Group 1.

Gaskets. Use OFHC copper or annealed 90–10 cupro-nickel (preferred) sheet 45–50 mils thick. Avoid material with scratches, or else polish out scratches leaving a concentric lay.

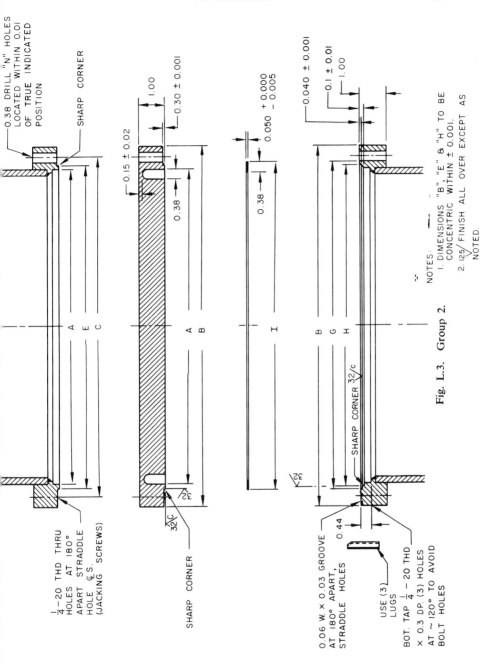

Fig. L.3. Group 2.

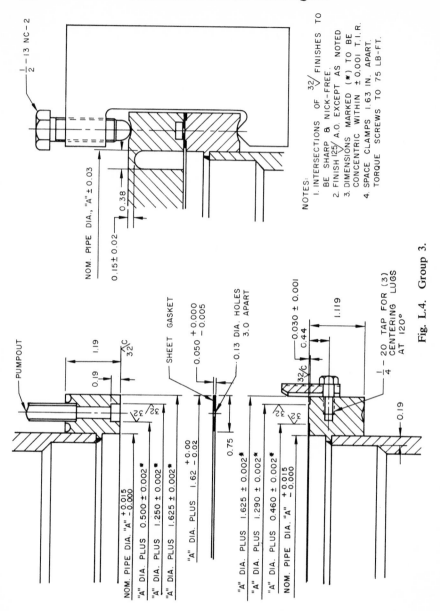

NOTES:
1. INTERSECTIONS OF $\sqrt{32}$ FINISHES TO BE SHARP & NICK-FREE.
2. FINISH $\sqrt{125}$ A.O. EXCEPT AS NOTED
3. DIMENSIONS MARKED (✱) TO BE CONCENTRIC WITHIN ± 0.001 T.I.R.
4. SPACE CLAMPS 1.63 IN. APART. TORQUE SCREWS TO 75 LB-FT.

Fig. L.4. Group 3.

ALUMINUM-FOIL GASKETS

While pinch gaskets are reliable flange seals for bakeable ultrahigh vacuum systems, they are asymmetrical, cumbersome, and very costly.

GROUP I

A pipe or tube size (OD)	B dia. ±0.03	C bolt circle	D dia. ±0.02	E dia. ±0.001	F dia. ±0.001	G dia. ∓0.001	H dia. ∓0.001	I dia. +0.00 −0.02	N No. of bolts
0.50	2.00	1.31	0.63	0.655	0.875	0.881	0.615	0.87	4
1.00	2.75	1.94	0.75	1.290	1.500	1.505	1.250	1.49	6
1.50	3.25	2.44	0.75	1.755	2.000	2.005	1.715	1.99	8
2.00	3.75	2.94	0.75	2.290	2.500	2.505	2.250	2.49	10
2.38	4.13	3.31	0.75	2.665	2.875	2.880	2.625	2.87	12
(2 in. I.P.S.)									
3.00	4.75	3.94	0.75	3.290	3.500	3.505	3.250	3.49	16
3.50	5.25	4.44	0.75	3.790	4.000	4.005	3.750	3.99	16
(3 in. I.P.S.)									
4.00	5.75	4.94	0.75	4.290	4.500	4.505	4.250	4.49	18
4.50	6.25	5.44	0.75	4.790	5.000	5.005	4.750	4.99	20
(4 in. I.P.S.)									
5.00	6.75	5.94	0.75	5.290	5.500	5.505	5.250	5.49	24
5.56	7.25	6.44	0.75	5.790	6.000	6.006	5.750	5.99	24
(5 in. I.P.S.)									
6.00	7.75	6.94	0.88	6.290	6.500	6.506	6.250	6.49	26
6.63	8.38	7.57	0.88	6.915	7.125	7.131	6.875	7.12	26
(6 in. I.P.S.)									
8.00	9.75	8.94	1.00	8.290	8.500	8.506	8.250	8.49	32
8.63	10.38	9.57	1.00	8.915	9.125	9.131	8.875	9.12	34
(8 in. I.P.S.)									
10.00	11.75	10.94	1.00	10.290	10.500	10.506	10.250	10.49	40
10.75	12.50	11.69	1.00	11.040	11.250	11.256	11.000	11.24	42
(10 in. I.P.S.)									

GROUP II

A Pipe or tube size (OD)	B dia. ±0.002	C bolt circle	D dia. ±0.001	G dia. −0.000 +0.005	H dia. 0.001	I dia. +0.00 −0.02	N No. of holes
12.0	13.750	12.94	12.290	12.500	12.250	12.49	46
12.75	14.500	13.69	13.040	13.250	13.000	13.24	50
(12 in. I.P.S.)							
13.0	14.750	13.94	13.290	13.500	13.250	13.49	50
14.0	15.750	14.94	14.290	14.500	14.250	14.49	54
15.0	16.750	15.94	15.290	15.500	15.250	15.49	58
16.0	17.750	16.94	16.290	16.500	16.250	16.49	60
17.0	18.750	17.94	17.290	17.500	17.250	17.49	64
18.0	19.750	18.94	18.290	18.500	18.250	18.49	68
19.0	20.750	19.94	19.290	19.500	19.250	19.49	72
20.0	21.750	20.94	20.290	20.500	20.250	20.49	76
22.0	23.750	22.94	22.290	22.500	22.250	22.49	82
24.0	25.750	24.94	24.290	24.500	24.240	24.49	90

Aluminum-foil flange seals are cheap and reliable, and the mating flanges are symmetrical and inexpensive to make. The simplicity of the seals approaches that of rubber O rings. These seals remain leak-tight from liquid-nitrogen temperatures to bakeout temperatures of 400° C — a temperature excursion of 600° C.

The aluminum-foil flange seal owes its ability to withstand thermal cycling to its flange design (see Fig. L.5 and L.6). The flange seal faces are machined at a small angle: as the bolts are tightened the flanges bend, until

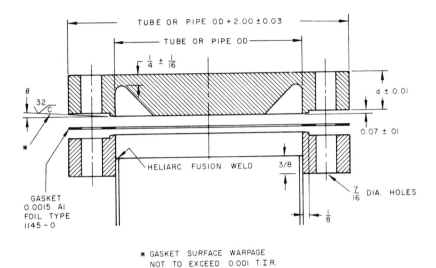

Fig. L.5. Aluminum-foil gasket flange for tubes and pipes up to 10 in. in diamter.

the opposing flange seal faces are very nearly parallel. The aluminum gasket is then under a very large load (2000 to 3000 pounds per inch of gasket) and considerable work energy is stored in the rotated flanges. This stored energy prevents flange unloading due to thermal changes.

Assembly. (1) Lay a sheet of 0.0015-in. aluminum foil (type 1145–O) over one of the mating flanges (3-mil foil may be easier to handle on very large flanges). The foil should extend beyond the outside diameter of the flange by about 1 inch. Press the sheet gently against the gasket surface to prevent wrinkling, and with a scalpel cut four small ears at 90° intervals. Tape each ear to the periphery. With the sheet thus secured cut out the bolt holes and remove the center section along the inside edge of the flange gasket surface.

(2) On smaller sizes (8-in. OD and under), which can be handled by hand, bring the two flanges together using two bolts to align them. On the

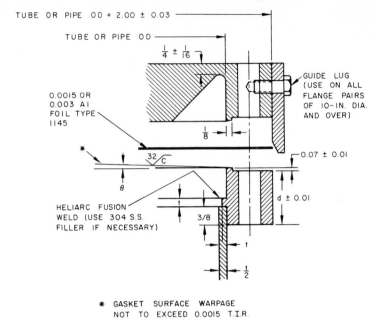

Fig. L.6. Aluminum-foil gasket flange for tubes and pipes 10 in. and over in diamter.

larger sizes use the three flange guides for alignment. Care should be taken not to mar the gasket when lining up the bolt holes.

(3) Install four bolts, nuts and washers at 90°. Press the mating gasket surfaces together and hand tighten the bolts. Install the remainder of the fasteners and uniformly torque all bolts in increments of fifty lb-in. The final torque should fall between 300 and 350 lb-in.

When bakeout temperatures exceed 350° C the foil tends to stick in places to the stainless steel. It is easily removed with an acid brush and hydrochloric acid. The acid is flushed away with water, followed by alcohol.

The tables give flange dimensions for tubes and pipes.

Notes:
  (a) Surface shall be 32 micro-inch concentric finish, made with a sharp, single-pointed tool.
  (b) Do not drag tool or burnish or polish after finish cut.
  (c) Provide cover to protect finished surface.

To reduce possibility of cutting through foil where angle is machined in seal face, acute corners should be rounded off to approximately 0.010-in. radius.

PIPE SIZES

Outside radius (in.)	Bolt circle radius (in.)	No. bolts	Bolt separation (in./bolt)	Gasket-face angle θ	Flange thickness d (in.)
0.6575	1.1575	4	1.82	$\frac{1}{2}° - \frac{3}{4}°$	0.50
1.1875	1.6875	6	1.768	$\frac{3}{4}° - 1°$	0.563
1.75	2.25	8	1.77	$\frac{3}{4}° - 1°$	0.688
2.25	2.75	10	1.73	$1° + 10'$ $- 0°$	0.75
2.778	3.28	12	1.72	$1\frac{1}{2}° \pm 10'$	0.813
3.313	3.813	12	2.00	$1\frac{1}{2}° \pm 10'$	0.875
4.3125	4.813	16	1.89	$2° \pm 10'$	0.938
5.375	5.875	20	1.85	$2° \pm 10'$	1.063
6.375	6.875	24	1.80	$2° \pm 10'$	1.125
12.00	12.50	40	1.962	$2° \pm 10'$	1.5
18.00	18.50	60	1.938	$2\frac{1}{2}° \pm 10'$	1.75

TUBE SIZES

0.50	1.00	4	1.57	$\frac{1}{2}° - \frac{3}{4}°$	0.5
1.00	1.50	6	1.57	$\frac{1}{2}° - \frac{3}{4}°$	0.6
1.50	2.00	8	1.57	$\frac{3}{4}° - 1°$	0.7
2.00	2.50	10	1.57	$\frac{3}{4}° - 1°$	0.8

Equations for Aluminum Foil Flanges. In Figs. L.7 and L.8, if $(r_2 - r_1)$ $\ll r_1$, the following equations are a good approximation of the maximum

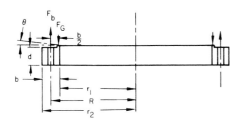

Fig. L.7

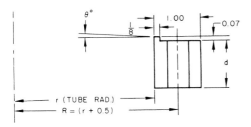

Fig. L.8. Equations for aluminum foil flanges.

stress and the rotational deflection due to the bolt load F_b and the gasket reaction F_G:

$$\sigma_{max} = \frac{MR}{Z} \tag{1}$$

$$\theta = \frac{MR^2}{EI} \tag{2}$$

where

$M = F_b \times b/2 = $ moment in lb-in. per inch,

$R = $ radius in inches to flange cross-section centroid,

$Z = \dfrac{bd^2}{6} = $ flange section modulus in in.^{3},

$I = \dfrac{bd^3}{12} = \dfrac{\text{moment of inertia of flange section normal to flange}}{\text{axis in in.}^4,}$

$E = $ modulus of elasticity (28×10^6 psi for 304 stainless steel).

Substituting into Eq. (1),

$$\sigma_{max} = \frac{3F_bR}{d^2} \text{ psi} \tag{3}$$

Substituting into Eq. (2),

$$\theta = \frac{6F_bR^2}{Ed^3} \text{ radians} \tag{4}$$

Combining Eqs. (3) and (4) and changing to degrees,

$$\theta = 4.09 \times 10^{-16} \sigma_{max} \frac{R}{D} \text{ degrees} \tag{5}$$

Calculations are based on the following:
  (1) Mating flanges are identical
  (2) Nuts, bolts, washers and flanges are 304 stainless steel
  (3) Bolt torque on $\frac{3}{8}$-24 NF bolts is 300 lb-in.

PIPE SIZES

Tube or pipe outside radius r (in.)	Bolt circle radius R r + 0.5 (in.)	No. bolts	Bolt separation (in.)	F_b(lb)	d (in.)	d^2 (in.²)	R/d	R/d^2	σ_{max} (psi)	θ (calculated) (deg.)	θ (actual) (deg.)
0.6575	1.1575	4	1.82	2,450	0.50	0.25	2.32	4.67	34,200	0.325	½° − ¾°
1.1875	1.6875	6	1.768	2,520	0.563	0.316	3.0	5.33	40,300	0.49	¾°, − 1
1.75	2.25	8	1.77	2,520	0.688	0.474	3.27	4.75	35,900	0.48	¾° − 1°
2.25	2.75	10	1.73	2,580	0.75	0.563	3.675	4.89	37,800	0.567	1° + 10' −0'
2.778	3.28	12	1.72	2,595	0.813	0.662	4.03	4.95	38,500	0.636	1½° ±10'
3.313	3.813	12	2.00	2,230	0.875	0.766	4.36	4.97	33,400	0.59	1½° ±10'
4.3125	4.813	16	1.89	2,360	0.938	0.88	5.13	5.47	38,800	0.81	2° ±10'
5.375	5.875	20	1.85	2,415	1.063	1.13	5.51	5.2	37,350	0.85	2° ±10'
6.375	6.875	24	1.80	2,480	1.125	1.268	6.11	5.42	40,300	1.01	2° ±10'
12.00	12.50	40	1.962	2,275	1.5	2.25	8.34	5.56	38,000	1.29	2° ±10'
18.00	18.50	60	1.398	2,300	1.75	3.062	10.57	6.03	41,600	1.80	2½° ±10'

TUBE SIZES

Tube or pipe outside radius r (in.)	Bolt circle radius R r + 0.5 (in.)	No. bolts	Bolt separation (in.)	F_b(lb)	d (in.)	d^2 (in.²)	R/d	R/d^2	σ_{max} (psi)	θ (calculated) (deg.)	θ (actual) (deg.)
.50	1.00	4	1.57	2,840	0.5	0.25	2.0	4.00	34,000	0.278	½° − ¾°
1.00	1.50	6	1.57	2,840	0.6	0.36	2.5	4.17	35,500	0.363	½° − ¾°
1.50	2.00	8	1.57	2,840	0.7	0.49	2.86	4.09	34,800	0.406	¾° − 1°
2.00	2.50	10	1.57	2,840	0.8	0.64	3.13	3.91	33,300	0.425	¾° − 1°

APPENDIX M: O-Ring Flange Table

Table M.1 gives O-ring and flange dimensions for joining sections (using tubing). To use the table, find your tubing size in column A. Column G gives the O-ring number for that tubing size and columns B and C give the flange diameter and thickness. Columns D, E, and F give data for the bolt circle, bolt size, and number of holes. Columns W, X, Y, and Z give data on the O-ring groove dimensions.

Only the O-ring flange is shown in the Figs. M.1 and M.2; the mating flange has no O-ring groove, but otherwise it has identical dimensions.

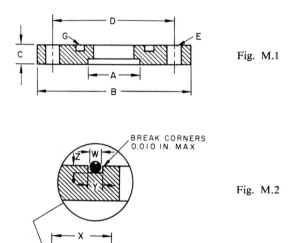

Fig. M.1

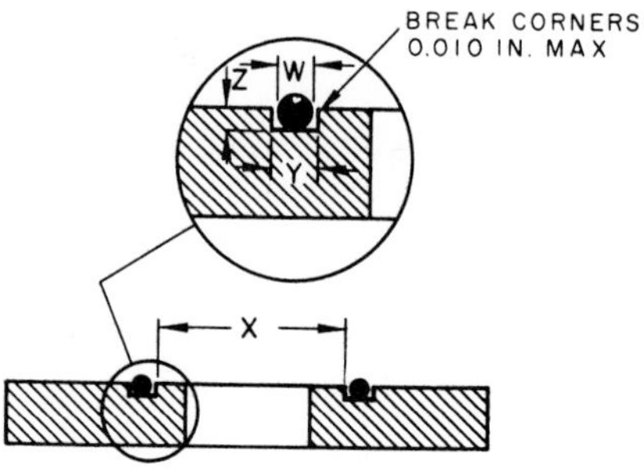

Fig. M.2

TABLE M.1. O-RING AND FLANGE DIMENSIONS FOR JOINING SECTIONS.

A Tubing o.d. (in.)	G O-ring No.	B Flange diam (in.)	C Flange thickness (in.)	D Bolt circle	E Bolt size	F No. of holes	W Actual size	O-ring groove diam (in.) X Diam	Y Groove width	Z Groove depth
1/4	AN 6227-6	1 1/8	1/4	7/8	10/32	3	0.070	0.317	0.113	0.044
3/8	AN 6227-6	1 1/8	1/4	7/8	10/32	3	0.070	0.317	0.113	0.044
1/2	AN 6227-11	1 3/8	1/4	1 1/8	10/32	3	0.103	0.510	0.151	0.064
5/8	AN 6227-11	1 3/8	1/4	1 1/8	10/32	3	0.103	0.510	0.151	0.064
3/4	AN 6227-17	1 3/4	1/4	1 13/32	10/32	3	0.139	0.887	0.205	0.086
7/8	AN 6227-17	1 3/4	1/4	1 12/32	10/32	3	0.139	0.887	0.205	0.086
1	AN 6227-21	2 1/4	1/4	1 3/4	10/32	3	0.139	1.140	0.205	0.086
1 1/8	AN 6227-21	2 1/4	3/8	1 3/4	10/32	3	0.139	1.140	0.205	0.086
1 1/2	AN 6227-27	3	3/8	2 9/16	1/4-20	4	0.139	1.518	0.205	0.086
1 5/8	AN 6227-29	3	3/8	2 9/16	1/4-20	4	0.210	1.639	0.297	0.134
2	AN 6227-33	3 1/2	3/8	3	1/4-20	4	0.210	2.134	0.297	0.134
2 1/8	AN 6227-33	3 1/2	3/8	3	1/4-20	4	0.210	2.134	0.297	0.134
2 1/2	AN 6230-8	4	3/8	3 1/2	1/4-20	4	0.139	2.532	0.205	0.086
2 5/8	AN 6227-37	4	3/8	3 1/2	1/4-20	4	0.210	2.600	0.297	0.134
3	AN 6230-12	5	3/8	4 1/2	3/8-16	6	0.139	3.042	0.205	0.086
3 1/8	AN 6227-41	5	1/2	4 1/4	3/8-16	6	0.210	3.159	0.297	0.134
4	AN 6230-20	6	1/2	5 1/4	3/8-16	6	0.139	4.051	0.205	0.086
4 1/8	AN 6227-49	6	1/2	5 1/4	3/8-16	6	0.210	4.168	0.297	0.134

"A" dimension counterbored 1/16 in.

Dimension tolerance

W ±0.004   X ±0.009   Y $+0.015 \atop -0.000$ Z $+0.008 \atop -0.000$

APPENDIX N: Ultrahigh Vacuum Welding

Tables N.1 and N.2 give a recommended method for welding thin (up to 0.125-in. wall thickness) cylindrical shells to relatively heavy flanges or plates. (Refer to Fig. N.1 for illustration of details.)

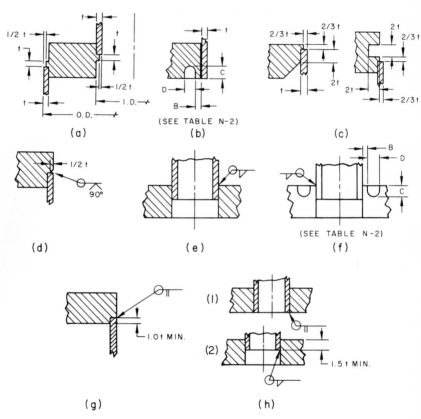

Fig. N.1

TABLE N.1. RECOMMENDED WELD DETAILS.

(Legend: G, good; F, fair; N, not recommended

Weld detail	Wall thickness t (in.)	Stainless steel OD[3]	Stainless steel ID[1,3]	Aluminum alloy OD	Aluminum alloy ID[2]	OFHC OD	copper ID[2]
a	0.030–0.040	F	G	N	F	N	N
	0.050–0.125	G	G	G	G	N	N
b[4]	0.005–0.025	F[5]	G[5]	N	N	N	N
	0.030–0.040	G	G	N	N	G[6]	G
	0.050–0.125	G	G	F[7]	F	G[8]	G
c	0.050–0.125	N	N	N	N	G[9]	G
d	0.050–0.125	N	N	G	G	N	N
e	0.060–0.125	N	G	N	G	N	F
f	0.030–0.050	N	G	N	N	N	N
	0.060–0.125	N	G	N	G	N	G
g	0.060–0.125	G[10]	G[10]	N	N	N	N
h	0.060–0.125	N	G[10]	N	N	N	N
	0.060–0.125	N	G[10]	N	G[10]	N	N

[1] No filler rod used — edges are fused together.
[2] Filler rod used, except on detail b.
[3] OD means that the tubing is outside the plate or flange; ID means the tubing is inside.
[4] This is the only practical, reliable way to weld tubing less than 0.30 inch thick to heavy plate.
[5] Copper clamping ring required.
[6] Steel clamping ring required over 2-in. diameter.
[7] Maximum OD 6 in.
[8] Steel clamping ring required over 3-in. diameter.
[9] Steel clamping ring required over 6-in. diameter.
[10] Cheapest to prepare and weld.

TABLE N.2. WELDING DETAILS FOR HIGH-VACUUM COMPONENTS.

t	B Dia.	B Tolerance	C (min.)	D (min.)
0.005	0.015		0.060	0.090
0.010	0.020		0.065	0.090
0.015	0.020	+0.003	0.065	0.090
0.020	0.025	−0.000	0.075	0.125
0.025	0.030		0.075	0.125
0.030	0.030		0.090	0.125
0.040	0.040		0.110	0.150
0.050	0.050		0.125	0.187
0.062	0.062	±0.10 t	0.125	0.187
0.090	0.090		0.187	0.250
0.125	0.125		0.200	0.250

Notes: Parts must fit tight, edges matching and square. The welder must be able to see the weld as well as reach it. Do not design the piece so the welder has to "reach in" more than $\frac{1}{4}$ in. for each inch of diameter, up to 3-in. diameter. From 3 in. to 12 in. do not reach in more than one diameter. Prefer welds out in the open. Use wall thicknesses under 0.060 in. only where really needed. On thinner material the welding cost goes up and the reliability goes down.

APPENDIX O: Vacuum References

Vacuum References

The following books and periodicals are all concerned with vacuum theory and/or applications.

1. Saul Dushman, "Scientific Foundations of Vacuum Technique," 1st ed., John Wiley & Sons, Inc., New York, 1949.

2. Saul Dushman; J. M. Lafferty (Ed.), "Scientific Foundations of Vacuum Technique," 2nd ed., John Wiley & Sons, Inc., New York, 1962.

3. A. Guthrie and R. K. Wakerling (Ed.), "Vacuum Equipment and Techniques," McGraw-Hill Book Company, Inc., New York, 1949.

4. L. H. Martin and R. D. Hill, "A Manual of Vacuum Practice," Melbourne University Press, 1946.

5. M. Pirani and V. Yarwood, "Principles of Vacuum Engineering," Reinhold Publishing Corporation, New York, 1961.

6. C. M. Van Atta, "The Design of High Vacuum Systems and the Application of Kinney High Vacuum Pumps," Kinney Manufacturing Division, The New York Air Brake Company, Boston, 1954.

7. E. Thomas (Ed.), "Advances in Vacuum Science and Technology," Pergamon Press, Inc., New York, 1960.

8. "Transactions of the American Vacuum Society," published yearly (from 1954) by Pergamon Press, Inc., New York.

9. J. W. Cable, "Vacuum Processes in Metalworking," Reinhold Publishing Corporation, New York, 1960.

10. "High Vacuum Data Manual," Lawrence Radiation Laboratory (Livermore) Rept. UCRL-5119 (1959).

11. J. R. Davy, "Industrial High Vacuum," Sir Isaac Pitman & Sons, Ltd., London, 1951.

12. L. H. Leck, "Pressure Measurement in Vacuum Systems," Chapman & Hall, Ltd., London, 1957.

13. W. H. Kohl, "Materials and Techniques for Electron Tubes," Reinhold Publishing Corp., New York, 3rd Edition in preparation.

14. *Vacuum* (a monthly journal), Pergamon Press, Inc., New York.

15. H. A. Steinherz, "Handbook of High Vacuum Engineering," Reinhold Publishing Corp., New York, 1963.

Index